Prin

JOHN WELLS taught at Eton before becoming joint editor
of the satirical magazine *Private Eye*, writing, with Richard
Ingrams, the long-running serials *Mrs Wilson's Diary* and
the *Dear Bill Letters*.

As well as playing the lead role of Mr Thatcher in his own
farce, *Anyone for Denis?*, he has appeared on stage in the
West End and at the National Theatre, for whom he
translated *Danton's Death* and *The Marriage of Figaro*. His
most recent work was a new version of *Cyrano de Bergerac*
at the Haymarket, with Robert Lindsay.

He has directed for D'Oyly Carte and Scottish Opera,
winning the Olivier Award with Jonathan Miller for their
production of Bernstein's *Candide*.

He was also the author of *The Projector*, an attack on jerry-
building in the East End of London, directed by Joan
Littlewood with music by Carl Davis, and announced, to
avoid libel damages, as 'an undiscovered eighteenth-
century opera by William Rufus Chetwode'.

His books include *A Melon for Ecstasy*, a novel written
with John Fortune, two collections of journalism, and a
history of the London Library, *Rude Words*.

John Wells, with Michael Austin, wrote the screenplay of
Princess Caraboo, and plays the Rector of Almondsbury in
the film.

Princess Caraboo

HER TRUE STORY

John Wells

PAN BOOKS
LONDON, SYDNEY AND AUCKLAND

First published 1994 by Pan Books Limited

a division of Pan Macmillan Publishers Limited
Cavaye Place London SW10 9PG
and Basingstoke

Associated companies throughout the world

ISBN 0 330 33630 4

Frontispiece portrait of Princess Caraboo by N. C. Branwhite
reproduced by courtesy of Bristol Museums and Art Gallery.

1 3 5 7 9 8 6 4 2

A CIP catalogue record for this book is available from
the British Library

Typeset by CentraCet Limited, Cambridge
Printed and bound in Great Britain
by Cox & Wyman Limited, Reading, Berkshire

For Teresa

Contents

'In this King Stephen's time also there appeared two children, a boy and a girl, clad in green, in a stuff unknown, of a strange language, and of strange diet, whereof the boy being baptised, dyed shortly after, but the girl lived to be very old; and being asked from whence they were, she answered, they were of the land of St Martyn, where there are Christian Churches erected: but that no sun did ever rise unto them; but where that land is, and how she came hither, she herself knew not . . .'

PART ONE

CHAPTER I

A CHINESE PINEAPPLE

ON A WARM Thursday evening in April 1817 a girl appeared in the village of Almondsbury – then pronounced Amesbury – near Bristol, speaking no known language. It had been a hard March, one of the coldest anyone could remember, and she seemed exhausted and half-starving.

She was wearing a loose black turban, a plain black dress with a high muslin collar and a red and black shawl draped over her shoulders, and had nothing with her but a little bundle wrapped in black cloth. She was small and delicate, had dark eyes, thick black hair, rather prominent lips and very white teeth.

It seemed likely that she had come down the steep hill into the village from the main Bristol to Gloucester road that runs along the crest. She knocked at the door of the first cottage she came to, the home of the village cobbler. The cobbler's wife could not understand her, and gave her a cup of milk and a piece of bread and butter, which she ate gratefully. Then she pressed her folded hands against one cheek, indicating that she was tired and wanted to sleep.

Thinking she was a foreign beggar, the cobbler's wife took her down the lane, through the village, with the white blossom on the cherry trees in the sheltered cottage gardens, to the Overseer of the Poor, Mr Hill.

It was not a good time to be arrested for vagrancy. England was emerging from twenty years of war with France. A largely aristocratic English government had set out to crush Napoleon's revolutionary ideas, and now it found itself threatened by revolution. Any mysterious traveller could be a political trouble-maker, or, in the case of a girl, a messenger for political trouble-makers.

Two years before, within weeks of his defeat at Waterloo, Napoleon had arrived briefly in England on his way to St Helena. On board the *Bellerophon*, at anchor in Tor Bay, he had drawn such crowds of adoring English admirers that rowing boats were jammed solid one against the other from the shore all the way out to the ship and beyond.

Far from being the defeated enemy, Napoleon Bonaparte represented to a great many Englishmen a kind of martyred saviour. Others dismissed him as the disturber of the peace of Europe, an impostor, a former corporal who claimed to be an emperor. But by opening every career to anyone who had the talent to succeed, Napoleon had shown the meaning of freedom.

Now, in 1817, directly inspired by his example, working men in England were arming for rebellion. The government, representing the old order, was becoming increasingly tough on dissidents. Anyone who broke the law was in danger of being transported in irons to Australia as part of a cold-blooded policy of ridding the country of trouble-makers.

The girl in the turban was making trouble: even if she was not begging, it was the Overseer's duty, according to the old law, to see that 'noe strangers came to settle'. Mr Hill, as Overseer of the Poor, was bound by law to arrest all 'common beggars, idle and disorderly persons, rogues and vagabonds', and to prevent them from 'infesting the Streets and Highways, to the great Terror and Annoyance of his Majesty's Subjects, and the Disturbance of the Public Peace'.

Anyone who brought a person suspected of begging to the Overseer was paid a reward. It was then the duty of the Overseer to bring the suspect before the Justice of the Peace, who in turn had the power to send a beggar or vagrant to prison for punishment. He could also return such a person by force to his or her own parish, to be set to work in the local workhouse.

But Overseer Hill was as baffled as the cobbler's wife. When he asked the girl in the black turban whether she was begging, she looked at him with blank incomprehension. He could hardly return her to her own parish when, for all he knew, she might have fallen from the moon; she was as strange in today's terms as if she had come from outer space.

But it was also in his power, as Overseer of the Poor, to help her, and wherever she came from she was extremely pretty.

The poor rates, paid by every householder in the

parish, also provided a fund that he could distribute at his own discretion in cases of genuine need to provide the hungry and homeless with food or even with a bed for the night.

In the towns, this charitable side of the system was beginning to collapse. Householders, hit by the post-war recession and unemployment, were refusing to pay the poor rate. In London that same week, according to the Bristol papers, over seven hundred impoverished householders in the parish of St Pancras had been taken to court for failing to pay. 'It is impossible', the report concluded, 'to relate the various complaints of distress submitted to the magistrate arising solely from the want of employment.'

But in a country parish like Almondsbury, six miles out of Bristol, things were still going on roughly as they always had, and Hill, moved either by charitable feelings or by the girl's shining eyes, offered her a shilling – two days' wages for a working girl – from parish funds to find herself a bed for the night.

To his amazement she refused it, repeating the gesture with her folded hands pressed against her cheek.

Even more puzzled, he decided to take her to the parson, under the old system regarded as the arbiter in matters of poor law charity. George Hunt, the minister in charge of the parish of Almondsbury, was forty-seven and had little money himself. Almondsbury was one of the best-endowed livings in the West of England, providing the rector with an income of fourteen hundred pounds a year, more than the annual salary of the Bishop of Bristol. This had come to the attention of the Bishop, who had immediately appointed himself Rector, taken the income, and paid George Hunt forty pounds a year to do the job.

But despite his poverty, Hunt was 'universally beloved for his benevolence, and admired for his erudition', having a large library of books. He would almost certainly understand what the foreigner was talking about.

George Hunt was not at home, and the door was opened by his wife. As Hill explained the problem, the girl pointed at a sofa she could see from the vicarage door, pressed her hands together against one cheek, and signified that she wanted to sleep. Mrs Hunt told Hill she did not like the look of her, and Hill decided to take her up to the big house above the village.

It was called Knole Park. It was the home of Samuel Worrall, Town Clerk of Bristol and local Justice of the Peace, and his American wife Elizabeth. Hill knew that they had a Greek manservant who spoke several European languages. He might be able to solve the mystery of where the girl came from.

As they approached the old rustic lodge and saw the high front of the mansion rising above the trees, the girl in the turban resisted violently and tried to get away. After a great deal of gentle reassurance and persuasion she agreed to go in.

Hill probably hoped to find Elizabeth Worrall

alone. She had a reputation for generosity and good works. She was an heiress with a great love of literature, wrote poetry, was thought of in Bristol as a 'bluestocking' fascinated by new ideas, and she was a member of various intellectual societies. But the girl's luck was out. It was Maundy Thursday, the beginning of the Easter weekend, and Elizabeth Worrall's husband was home. He was known in Bristol as 'Devil' Worrall for his violent drinking bouts and unpredictable temper. At first he was content to let the Greek manservant ask the questions, but he had no more success than Hill in making himself understood. The girl listened to his questions without a gleam of comprehension, and he gave it as his opinion that she was a foreign gypsy.

This could have influenced Elizabeth Worrall in her favour. After four hundred years of persecution in Europe, gypsies in this new Romantic age were suddenly becoming fashionable.

Throughout the eighteenth century, explorers had brought home Noble Savages, Tahitians and Mohicans, who were seen as specimens of natural man, unspoilt by western education, uncorrupted by material possessions.

Now, in intellectual circles like the Philosophical and Literary Societies in Bristol and Bath frequented by Elizabeth Worrall, the idea dawned: we had our own Noble Savages living among us all the time. The curl of woodsmoke from the clearing, the painted caravan with its grazing horses, the brown-skinned, bright-eyed children with their gold earrings squatting round a fire were suddenly exotic and beautiful.

Attempts were being made to record the Romany language, and a few years later one gypsy girl was entertained at a house not unlike the Worralls' for several weeks: she had the advantage of speaking English as well as Romany, but charming days were spent by the lady of the house and her family, all amateur linguists, trying to compile a comprehensive Romany-English dictionary.

What made the idea even more intriguing to a lady of Elizabeth Worrall's piety was the possibility of the gypsies being able to trace their descent to Biblical times. Some more advanced scholars were already establishing links between Romany and its true origins in the dialects of central India, but more romantic souls were convinced that gypsies were, as their name suggested, Ancient Egyptians, and the subject of Old Testament Prophecies.

One enthusiastic academic, examining the stones of the temple at Karnak, was convinced that the Ancient Egyptians had invented the steam engine. What if they had possessed more spectacular powers, and this knowledge had been lost? In the Book of Jeremiah, it was argued, God promised to drive the Egyptians out of Egypt and that they would live 'in the open fields'. What if the gypsies, who had indeed acquired their name by claiming to be pilgrims driven out of 'Little Egypt', still retained the mysterious lost knowledge of their forefathers? How else were they able to read a man's fortune in the palm of his hand?

Samuel Worrall belonged to another and earlier school of thought that put gypsies in the same category as beggars, rogues and vagabonds, and would no doubt have supported the Dutch, who at one stage organized hunting parties to shoot them down like animals. He represented the law, and the law was made to discourage people from wandering about making a nuisance of themselves. He now took over the interview, and began by asking to see her papers. She did not understand what he meant. He made signs, pointing to her bundle and the pocket in her dress, telling her to turn them out.

The girl delved into her pocket and put some coins on the table. There were a few halfpennies and a dud sixpence. Worrall examined the coin carefully. Thousands of pounds' worth of new silver currency had been brought to Bristol for distribution in February of that year, and a lot of the old coinage was still in circulation, officially worthless, but still in practice being accepted in the shops at roughly half its old value. Being found in possession of counterfeit money, on the other hand, could carry the death sentence. Elizabeth Worrall was anxious, but the strange girl seemed wholly unconcerned.

Worrall then ordered her to undo her bundle of black cloth. It contained a bar of soap pinned in a piece of linen, and what Elizabeth Worrall described afterwards as 'a very few necessaries'. He asked her if she had anything else. She shrugged and made signs that she had not.

Worrall made her show him her hands. They were soft and apparently unaccustomed to hard work, her fingernails clean and well kept. He then examined her ear-lobes, and found that they had once been pierced. He also measured her height. She was five foot two inches tall. He told her to lift up her black dress so that he could see her feet. She was wearing black worsted stockings and leather shoes.

Bit by bit Worrall's mood changed. Like Hill the Overseer he began to fall under her spell. He noted that her cheeks were 'faintly tinged with red', that her mouth was rather wide, her lips large and full, the lower lip 'a little projecting', and that her chin was small and round. He made her open her mouth, and was impressed by the whiteness and regularity of her teeth. Her hair, at the nape of her neck beneath her turban, was soft and glossy and black. 'Devil' Worrall conceded that she was very attractive.

When Elizabeth gave orders for the Greek man-servant and her own maid to take her down to the village inn and arrange for her to stay the night at their expense, Samuel Worrall made no objection.

Elizabeth Worrall sent a request to the landlady of the inn that the girl was to be given a private room – travellers in those days still being accustomed to double up with complete strangers – a good supper and a comfortable bed. She would come down herself in the morning to see how she was.

The girl was again reluctant to move, and seemed very footsore and weary as she walked the half-mile back to the inn, little more than a cottage on the unmade road beside the church. It was called the Bowl, and she brightened up when she was shown into the parlour. On the wall she saw an engraving of a pineapple. She pointed at it, indicating that it came from her homeland, seemed very pleased, and repeated the word 'An-an-a'.

The Worralls' servants reported this at Knole, and Hill, on his way home, told the vicar Mr Hunt. She had provided them with their first clue. 'Ananas' is the botanical name for a pineapple and is used in several European languages as the everyday word for the fruit. A glance at any book of reference would have told them that the pineapple grew originally in America, but had since been grown successfully in Africa and Asia. The word was all the more fascinating pronounced by those full lips and perfect white teeth.

Hunt was intrigued by the mystery. The vicarage was less than a hundred yards from the Bowl, and he walked over to see her for himself. Whether or not he actually witnessed what happened in the parlour at the Bowl, he was certainly told about it later that night.

Seeing that the landlady was about to cook her supper as Mrs Worrall had instructed, the girl made it understood that she would prefer a cup of tea. This was brought. Before she drank it the girl laid one hand across her eyes, bowed her head, and repeated what appeared to be a prayer.

The landlady offered her a second cup, but the girl shook her head, insisting on washing the cup herself before she would allow it to be refilled. Then she went through the same ritual with the hand across her eyes, the prayer, the bowing of the head, and drank it. The landlady's little daughter was delighted.

When she had finished her tea she was shown upstairs to her room, followed by the landlady and her daughter, both wondering what she would do next. She seemed never to have seen a bed. She repeated the gesture with her hands folded against her cheek, and curled up on the floor.

The landlady's daughter laughed, took her hand, and jumped on to the bed. She demonstrated how to sleep on it, showed her how comfortable it was, and the girl began to undress. Then she knelt down in her shift, seemed to be saying her prayers, and lay on the bed, still refusing to get between the bed-clothes, and was left to sleep.

The talk in the Bowl that night was of nothing else, everyone in the village having their own theory as to where she came from. The next morning Elizabeth Worrall was up at seven and walked down alone to the Bowl to see how she was, bringing her a clean shift and stockings. She was sitting by the fire in the parlour, looking very miserable, and seemed to have been crying.

When she saw Elizabeth Worrall her face was transformed. She became radiant, accepted the clean linen with great gratitude, and sat smiling at her across the hearth while the landlady made breakfast.

Elizabeth Worrall was not the only one who was excited that morning. The vicar arrived a few moments later. Good Friday is one of the major events of the Church's year, but Hunt had found the time to ransack his library and had brought with him a bundle of books he hoped might provide more clues.

Having thought about her turban, he decided she might have come from Asia, and brought with him coloured prints and engravings of far-off countries, hoping that she might respond to one of them as she had responded to the picture of the pineapple.

The experiment was partially successful. He turned the pages, watching her face for a reaction. At first there was none. Then she began to show clear signs of interest in pictures of China. She also pointed to a picture of a rowing boat. Then, cupping her hands, she indicated a larger boat, with masts and rigging and sails. She had come to England in a ship.

George Hunt left them, captivated. Elizabeth Worrall decided to take the girl back to stay with her at Knole. Surprisingly, she seemed alarmed at the idea, and was only very reluctantly persuaded to leave the Bowl and follow Mrs Worrall home.

The path to Knole took them past Almondsbury church, then whitewashed on the outside and with a tall spire of patterned lead. As they were passing it the girl turned in at the gate of the churchyard and went up the path to the church door. She turned the handle, found it locked, and seemed disappointed. Elizabeth Worrall was even more intrigued.

At Knole she was taken through the vast hall with its wide oak staircase, through the dark, panelled drawing room to the servants' hall, where the Worralls' servants were having their traditional Good Friday breakfast with hot cross buns. In the silence that followed her arrival, she very gravely reached for one of the buns, took a knife from the table, cut the cross off the top, and held it against her heart. She had large, firm breasts, and big, dark, appealing eyes, and it made an affecting picture.

Now the servants were intrigued; except for the Greek, who was convinced she was a fraud. When Elizabeth Worrall reported the vicar's theory that she came from China, he conceded that she was extremely pretty – but her skin was white, her features entirely European.

Samuel and Elizabeth Worrall left the girl with the servants and went to church. But like the vicar himself, Elizabeth Worrall remained preoccupied with a mystery more immediately compelling than that of God Incarnate dying to redeem mankind. Who was she, and where had she come from?

It was the kind of riddle, Elizabeth Worrall must have thought, that any clever woman could solve, and she was in a better position to solve it than her intellectual friends. The girl was also clearly very attached to her.

Elizabeth longed increasingly to discover her name. Back at Knole, she asked her again and again, but there was still no flicker of understanding. Finally Elizabeth Worrall sat down at her writing table with the girl beside her. She repeated her own name several times – 'Worrall, Worrall, Worrall' – pointing to herself, and wrote the name on a sheet of paper. Then she dipped the pen in the ink again and handed it to the girl in the black turban. She refused to take it, shaking her head and shrinking back. Then, for the first time, she said who she was. Pointing to herself, and speaking very gravely, she repeated a single strange-sounding word.

'Caraboo. Caraboo. Caraboo.'

CHAPTER 2

IN THE HOUSE OF
THE ALCHEMIST

THRILLED THAT she had at least discovered the stranger's name, Elizabeth Worrall showed her round the house.

Knole had been built three hundred years earlier by Thomas Chester, the third generation of Chesters in direct succession to be Sheriff and Mayor of Bristol, and his initials were carved over the stone arches in the cellar. The last Miss Chester had died in 1792, and the Worralls rented it from her heirs, the Chester-Masters.

It had been a fortified place since Roman times, taking its name from the knoll or low hill on which it stood, commanding long views in every direction over the fifteen hundred acres of the Knole Estate, including eighty-five acres of deer park and wood-land, seven dairy farms and twenty or thirty cottages.

The house was high and old-fashioned, and looked from the lodge like three houses built side by side. There were six gabled roofs and more beyond, rows of Elizabethan stone chimney pots and narrow leaded windows, and one wing jutted forward to make a triangular courtyard by the front door, beside which there was a tall, octagonal stone tower.

Inside there were high rooms with elaborate plaster ceilings, old oak staircases, and more dark wooden panelling between heavy iron-studded doors, with deep window recesses in the thick stone walls.

The stone tower, which stood beside the front door, was even older, with a winding mediaeval wooden stair that led up to a battlemented platform. From the top there were wonderful views to the west over the roofs and across the lake, fountains and gardens, the long avenue of yew trees and the green deer park to the long silver stretch of the Severn Estuary, where the sailing ships dipped past on their way to America, with the blue of the Welsh hills beyond.

Most of the house had been left as it had always been, but the Worralls' bedroom had been redecorated in the Chinese style in the eighteenth century, and one big room at the back, looking out over the park, had been remade with a floor of polished elm, two elegant alcoves decorated in summer with bowls of flowers on tall pedestals, and an elegant marble fireplace. This was the Worralls' drawing room.

Caraboo particularly admired the Chinese panelling in the bedroom, added by the last Miss Chester, and an oriental table in the drawing room. Chinoiserie had been very popular in the previous century, a vogue that had grown initially from travellers' tales of the orient, of a remote and mysterious civilization in China even more ancient than that of the Romans.

As she had with the picture of the pineapple, Caraboo pointed to the Chinese panelling, then to herself, suggesting they came from her homeland. Elizabeth Worrall noted this, confirming as it did the girl's response to Hunt's pictures of the Far East.

For the rest of Good Friday Caraboo remained under the close scrutiny of the servants, including the sceptical Greek. Eating in the servants' hall, she continued to behave as she had at the Bowl, insisting she be allowed to wash her own cup every time it was refilled. At supper that night she 'showed much disgust' when she was offered meat, sniffed the beer and cider the other servants were drinking and shuddered with apparent horror. She accepted only vegetables and drank plain water. That night she shared a bedroom in the attic with one of the maids.

What followed is open to speculation. It may be that the Greek manservant confided his suspicions to Samuel Worrall. As a Justice of the Peace, he had every reason to be alarmed. His judgement could be called into question, and sheltering a beggar, if she was a beggar, was a punishable offence.

But he had another reason to protect his reputation as a man of integrity and sure judgement. Samuel Worrall was the proprietor of a relatively new and not altogether stable private bank in Bristol that required absolute public confidence to survive.

By the morning, Worrall had made up his mind, and if Elizabeth Worrall protested, her protests had no effect. He bundled the girl into a carriage and took her into Bristol, to the Council House, to be tried before the Mayor.

Bristol on a spring morning in 1817, huddled round a curve in the river in the green bowl of the hills, as Samuel Worrall's carriage rumbled down the road from Gloucester, must have looked very beautiful. William Cobbett, who visited Bristol ten years later, described it as 'a great commercial city in the midst of cornfields, meadows and woods'.

High on the right there were the elegant Georgian terraces and crescents and green public gardens of Clifton, straight ahead the spires and towers of twenty churches rising above the jumble of sloping roofs and narrow streets that made up the old walled mediaeval city, and on the left, at the eastern edges of the town, three or four brick pyramids – the chimneys of the glass factories making bottles for imported wine, or for the beer and cider that were exported to the New World – smoking into the clear sky. Further away, on the other side of the river, the coalmines and slums of Bedminster made a sombre background, but even there, to the south, were more green hills beyond.

Their objective, the Council House, where Worrall had the offices of his bank, stood out clearly as a small core of newer buildings in pale grey stone grouped round the Exchange at the centre of the old city, an island of Georgian elegance in the surrounding maze of narrow winding streets and half-timbered houses.

Later, as they turned past the imposing eighteenth-century façade of the Infirmary and down Lower Maudlin Street, they would have seen the old docks, a sight that had so impressed Alexander Pope when he had visited the city a century before. 'It is the oddest and most surprising sight imaginable, a long street full of ships in the middle, and houses on both sides.' When they began to move down river on the tide he said it looked 'like a dream'.

In the streets, as they rolled across the bridge and the horses strained to draw the Town Clerk's carriage up into the old town, clattering under the stone gateway in the old city walls at the bottom of Small Street, there was a new colour and elegance after the years of war.

A few miles to the north, in the more industrialized Midlands, and in the Fens round Cambridge, there was rioting, but Bristol so far that year was peaceful. In Clifton, in particular, and at the Hotwells down in the Gorge, there was a sense of competition with Bath as a centre of elegance, and the bright, placid water-colours painted at the time in and around the old city show a world of girls in straw bonnets and loose, low-cut dresses and men in bold blue coats and wide trousers strolling in the sunshine.

The carriage came to a stop outside the Exchange, by the famous 'Bristol Nails'. They are still there today: high brass round-topped tables in the street, used by merchants for counting out deals, and the origin of the expression 'paid on the nail'. The old Council House stood next to it, also in pale grey stone. Worrall's offices were down a little alley to one side, between the Exchange and the ancient church of All Saints. It was the centre of power in Bristol.

Whoever she was, the unknown girl was now in very great danger. Her examination in front of the Mayor, John Haythorne, was a relatively informal affair, but if she failed to convince him of her innocence, Caraboo would be tried at the Assizes. Samuel Worrall himself, the month before, had accused a man of stealing a pair of his breeches: the thief had appeared at the Assizes and had been transported to Australia for seven years. A girl called Catherine Burgess had stolen a shirt and been sent to prison for twelve months.

When it came to passing counterfeit money – and Caraboo was on record as having been in possession of a dud sixpence – the prospects were even more terrifying: the other sentences handed down that month at the Assizes, reported in a local newspaper, speak for themselves.

> William Jones, for forging a promissory note with intent to defraud John Alvis, guilty, *Death*, Jeremiah Dunn for uttering a forged £5 Bank of England note, guilty, *14 Years Transportation*, William Carter, for uttering a forged £1 Bank of England note, guilty, *Death*.

The same local newspaper, *Felix Farley's Bristol Journal*, urged the authorities to carry out public hangings early in the morning to avoid the 'usual disgraceful thronging and levity', as the victim, often attended in Bristol by a Methodist minister and protesting his or her innocence, was 'launched into eternity' on the end of a rope.

Transportation, the fate of any 'trouble-maker' for as little as stealing a mutton pie, with the prospect of a three-month journey in irons and below decks, and brutal floggings on the iron triangle for any imagined offence during the years of hard labour in New South Wales, was a fate almost worse than death. Any term in prison for a girl of Caraboo's age and looks was the end to any hopes she might have had of leading a decent life.

John Haythorne, a man in his forties, was as baffled by the girl as anyone in Almondsbury. He heard the story of her arrival in the village, of her behaviour at the inn, of her description of being brought to England in a sailing ship, of her appearing to recognize things from the Far East. He noted her white skin, the fullness of her lips, and her dark European eyes.

She continued to use the name 'Caraboo', seemed to be speaking rationally and deliberately in her own language as she tried to make herself understood, and used her hands very beautifully in illustration of what she was saying. Haythorne examined her as the Worralls had done, looking at the traces of where the earrings had been in the lobes of her ears, verifying the softness of her hands and the perfect regularity of her white teeth, and gave it as his judgement that 'her language and manners were unlike anything he had ever heard or seen in his life'.

The girl seemed to draw reassurance from his attitude. Elizabeth Worrall, who had watched the proceedings with anxiety, was all for taking her back to Knole. Samuel Worrall preferred to suppress any feelings of romantic curiosity, and agreed with Haythorne that the law should take its course: she might be an innocent foreigner without any visible means of support, but cases like that were lodged at St Peter's Hospital. While she was there, further enquiries could be made, and as soon as her nationality was established she would be handed over to the embassy of her own country for repatriation.

Despite the current severity of the law, a strong charitable tradition existed in Bristol, from the early Quakers to the more recent Methodists, and a hundred years earlier St Peter's had been a model of enlightened civic responsibility, the first home for the poor of its kind in England. Until the Second World War it still stood down by the river, the most fantastic of buildings: a row of ornate Jacobean merchants' houses in white plaster and old oak beams, with overhanging eaves and jutting timbers, some decorated with carved devils, others with strange sea-serpents, others with grotesque comic heads.

The man who built the original house in 1453 was Thomas Norton, an alchemist who claimed he could transform base metals into pure gold, but who died a pauper. The whole row of houses was remodelled, with all the elaborate ornamentation, in 1612. They were occupied at first by wealthy Bristol merchants. Then, as their architectural style went out of fashion, they became derelict and were used as a sugar refinery. John Evelyn, the famous diarist, went there and saw the sugar being made into loaves. Then, for two years, Sugar House became the Bristol Mint, where all the coins were made.

By the time Caraboo was sent there it had been extensively restored. It was, like many charitable institutions of that date, a place of sharp contrasts. The old Court Room, where she was taken when she first arrived, and where the Guardians of the Poor held their regular committee meetings, was panelled in polished wood, with wooden gryphons and heraldic shields carved in a frieze beneath a heavily decorated plaster ceiling of intricate squares and circles, flowers and plumes. Over the stone fireplace were more elaborately carved and painted reliefs, with the city arms in the centre, and to either side the figures of saints engaged in acts of charity. There were highly coloured paintings of Ashak, Meshak and Abednigo in the burning fiery furnace, of Jonah in the belly of the whale, and of Eve covering her nakedness with an apron of fig-leaves. Dragons reared from the brass fender.

In January 1940 one German bomb destroyed every shred of the carved wood, painting and plasterwork. Other mediaeval buildings leaned drunkenly after the raids, spilling broken glass and tiles into the street. St Peter's Hospital was blown away as if it had never been, leaving one bare brick chimney stack and a row of iron railings at the end of the herb garden by the river.

If Caraboo's hopes were raised by the polished wood, the old furniture and the brass dragons guarding the fireplace in the Court Room, they were soon

dashed. The wards given over to accommodation of
the poor were plain plaster with worm-eaten oak
beams, low ceilings and narrow leaded windows.
The air was thick, and there was no hope of any
privacy. At the time of the cholera epidemic ten
years later there were as many as eight girls in one
bed, and in the boys' wards as many as eighty
inmates with eighteen beds between them. When
Caraboo arrived the numbers were roughly half that,
but it was still a hopelessly overcrowded doss-house.

A large proportion of the 'family' of three
hundred consisted of unemployed Irish labourers,
waiting for the next ship to take them home, but
many others were sick or mentally disturbed and the
atmosphere was noisy, smelly and violent.

In a room downstairs there were stocks and a
whipping post, with fixed shackles through which
the offender's wrists were pinioned while he or she
was whipped. It was officially known as 'Purgatory'.
To Caraboo, coming directly from Knole, with its
high rooms and flowers and distant views of the
Bristol Channel, the whole place must have seemed
like hell. She immediately went on hunger strike.

As in Almondsbury, Caraboo succeeded in having
herself treated differently. She was helped by the
authorities' awareness that the Town Clerk's wife
was particularly interested in her welfare, and the
Mayor himself showed his gratitude for the care
they took of the girl by agreeing, a few days later,
to become a governor of the Hospital.

The hospital staff tried to tempt her with 'eggs

and other delicacies'. She still refused. Given a bed to share, she declined even to lie down, let alone sleep on top of it. She was clearly a girl accustomed to having her own way.

She must, too, have been accustomed to having a great many gentlemen admirers. Hill, Hunt, Worrall himself and even Haythorne the Mayor had all been enchanted by her, and at every stage of her story there are always 'gentlemen' in evidence concerned for her well-being.

It was Easter Sunday, a day for parties. News of the beautiful stranger had spread rapidly through fashionable Bristol society, and several of these gentlemen appeared at St Peter's Hospital to call on her. They brought with them various foreigners of their acquaintance in the hope of discovering what country she came from, what she was doing in England, and who she was.

One of the gentlemen who arrived first thing on Easter Monday was a talkative and pedantic Scot with a flowery turn of phrase, identified only by the initials 'JS'. Writing to Mrs Worrall from Leith in Scotland, he tried to justify his enthusiasm to gain admission to the poor house. Caraboo was, he wrote, 'a peculiar case' and 'must naturally excite in the breast of every feeling creature emotions of interest and sympathy'.

He was stumped, like the Worralls' Greek man-servant, by her apparently European features, but unlike the Greek he was determined to discover an explanation for it.

I think her *name* is not *Caraboo*, but rather that that is her *country*. I consider that she comes from the Bay of *Karabouh*, on the eastern coast of the Caspian Sea, and situated in Independent Tartary. She may easily have come from thence by the Persian Gulf, or still more easily by the Black Sea. The latter I consider by far the more likely, as many vessels (many hundreds) have come from the Black Sea to the European ports in the Mediterranean since the commencement of the present year.

He suggested that the girl might recognize her home if she were shown a map of the Caspian Sea, and perhaps be able to identify the names of places nearby.

Elizabeth Worrall, who had thought of nothing else all through Saturday evening and the whole of Sunday, drove into Bristol on Monday morning to find out how she was. The Scotsman said he would never forget the poor girl's distress, or 'the gratitude she so eloquently expressed on recognizing you, Madam, in the Hospital at Bristol'.

After a weekend of sleepless nights in a crowded women's ward, interspersed by intense visits from 'feeling creatures' enthralled by her beauty, each one producing more and more outlandish foreigners to quiz her in twenty different languages, Caraboo's relief was understandable.

Having been told by this time of her refusal to eat or sleep at St Peter's, Elizabeth Worrall took matters into her own hands. She had Caraboo discharged from the hospital and took her to her husband's flat above the Tolzey Bank in the elegant Georgian alley beside the Exchange.

There she put the girl in the care of her husband's cook and housekeeper and gave permission for her to be visited by anyone who might be able to establish her identity. During the following week gentleman after gentleman clumped up the stairs, each bringing with him some new theory and some new foreigner to question her.

Whatever Caraboo's own feelings, and it seemed impossible ever to discover what they were, it was an arrangement that can hardly have delighted 'Devil' Worrall.

To be seen to be sharing his respectable sash-windowed lodgings, looking down on the quiet passage that ran between the Exchange and the old church, with an exotic young foreigner was not something he would have welcomed at the best of times, and certainly not now.

He was sixty-three, he was under attack on two fronts, and his whole world seemed about to crumble.

CHAPTER 3

THE DEVIL, THE POPE AND THE PRETENDER

T HE MOST famous story told about Samuel Worrall when he was Town Clerk of Bristol was of how he had come back to his lodgings in the Exchange drunk after a party, fallen down the steps of the carriage and landed on his back in the gutter. A crowd gathered, among them a mild-mannered and rather nervous shopkeeper called Camplin who sold silk to ladies. Worrall, still on his back, focused his eyes blearily, pointed at Camplin, and shouted, 'That's the man that knocked me down!'

It is a tribute to Worrall's popularity as Town Clerk and Magistrate that the crowd immediately turned on Camplin and chased him off down the street, still bleating his innocence.

Samuel Worrall had trained as a barrister, having chambers as a young man in Orchard Street in Bristol and at Lincoln's Inn in London. In May 1794, when he was forty, he had married the twenty-seven-year-old Elizabeth Lechmere, daughter of a rich businessman from Boston, Massachusetts, by

whom in the course of the next four years he had
two sons.

He was a bluff, self-confident man, and a letter he
wrote to Nelson, preserved in the Manuscript Room
at the British Museum, offering him the freedom of
the city of Bristol, shows a plain, looping, large and
rather simple hand, with 'Townclerk' written as one
word. By the time Caraboo arrived he had been
Town Clerk of Bristol for more than thirty years.
Like Thomas Chester, he had inherited the position
from his father and his grandfather. His father had
also been Distributor of Stamps. This meant a great
deal more than running a post office. Every newspaper carried a stamp duty, which amounted in 1817
to fourpence of the purchase price of sevenpence,
and the official collector of such a sales tax was in a
very powerful and lucrative position. That job, too,
Samuel Worrall had inherited from his father.

Bristol had always been run by a very few families, with the power automatically passing down
from father to son. To wield such power required a
quiet ruthlessness that was in direct conflict with the
Christian-liberal tradition that had founded St
Peter's Hospital. Daniel Defoe, when he visited the
city, called it 'corporation tyranny'.

Bristol had been a proud and independent city
since soon after the Norman Conquest, the first to
demand its own municipal rights five years before
Magna Carta. That demand followed a century of
astonishing economic expansion, during which Bristolians in the Middle Ages had dug out a new bed

for the Severn, creating a wider loop of land at the north-western corner of the old walled city to extend the city boundaries.

Until the middle of the nineteenth century it even had its own local time, setting its clocks ten and a half minutes behind London.

Bristol was a central market for farm produce from the surrounding counties, but it was also a major port, bringing in wine from France, Spain and Portugal, and tobacco from Virginia. Even more important for its economy, it handled the bulk of trade with the West Indies, and the city's Society of Merchant Venturers was happy to boast that the real wealth of the city was founded on the slave trade.

For a century Bristolians had seemed content to be judged and taxed and governed by the same comfortable, prosperous men whom they could see every day about their business at the Exchange, acknowledging each other's greetings, sharing snuff, talking about trade and the weather. Even when they fell out of their carriages drunk and blamed innocent passers-by they were assumed to be in the right.

But times were changing. When Nelson wrote to Samuel Worrall in 1797, thanking him for the freedom of the city, he talked about the 'stimulus it would be to his future exertions', and said he would always be proud 'in having my name enrolled among the Freemen of the second city in England'. By 1817, with the slave trade coming to an end, Bristol was losing its old dominance. Liverpool was now the second city in England, and Bristol's future as an international port was in serious doubt.

Ever since the turn of the century there had been sporadic riots, sometimes for food, usually at election time, but the old governing class seemed oblivious to danger. Haythorne's dinner parties as Mayor at the Mansion House were notorious, with sixty-six bottles of wine for twenty-two guests, and when he entertained the Prince of Wales and the Duke of Sussex in 1807 the bill came to over twelve hundred pounds. It was calculated that he spent about a quarter of the city's income on 'display and feasting'. Haythorne had recently increased his own salary from two thousand to three thousand three hundred a year, and had submitted a bill for over a hundred pounds for 'breakage of crockery'.

The administration was becoming so unpopular that several more conscientious citizens, elected to the Corporation, paid a five-hundred-pound fine rather than serve on it.

Every kind of corruption flourished, the most extreme case being Bristol Grammar School, a well-endowed municipal charity where the headmaster, Dr Lee, collared all the funds and reduced the school to one pupil, who became known as 'Lee's chick'. In the city gaol it was possible to lie in irons in 'the Pit' for a year waiting trial, conditions were appalling and the warders kept cats to stop the rats eating the prisoners' feet.

To preserve themselves in power, the old regime handed out colossal bribes: the local Member of

Parliament reckoned to spend a thousand pounds a day on beer and other inducements before an election. There were dinners, drink and more money for the Army and those who kept the peace, with the Tory candidate handing out fifteen hundred blue bludgeons to his supporters to hammer home their arguments. At the 1812 election the same Tory candidate spent ten thousand pounds of his own money to get elected, and his overall expenses came to nearly thirty thousand.

So far, only a few radicals were in open rebellion. When the so-called 'Orator Hunt' stood for election, not having the Tory candidate's means of persuasion, he polled only a few hundred votes. But he drew passionate support at his public meetings from large crowds who four years earlier had torn down a statue of George the Third. Henry Hunt had since been in prison, but was out again and campaigning for public office. Now, with the noticeable decline in the city's fortunes, even the middle classes were beginning to turn against the Corporation.

In a desperate effort to reverse the decline, Bristol had followed the example of their ancestors and changed the course of the Severn. Even as far from the sea as Bristol, the river is still tidal, and wooden-hulled ships creaked as they settled on the mud, left leaning high and dry every time the tide went out. Beginning in 1804, huge works were undertaken, involving hundreds of Irish workmen, French prisoners and local labourers with shovels, horses and carts, to dig out a huge ditch half a mile long, the slippery mud slopes of which are revealed at low tide even today, still known as the New Cut.

This canal had the effect of diverting the tidal river, leaving the old deep-water port between the wharves and warehouses with a steady level of water, maintained by a system of sluices and locks.

The original estimate for the work had been over three hundred thousand pounds, and the cost had doubled before it was completed. The work had been financed with a huge loan, saddling the Bristol Docks Company with an annual interest payment of eighteen thousand pounds. This left the Docks Company with no alternative but to raise harbour charges, which in turn defeated the whole purpose of the scheme by making Bristol Docks still less competitive with Liverpool.

Haythorne, Worrall and the old regime were now coming under open criticism. 'The ruling principle of the Bristol Corporation', one critic wrote, 'appears to have been at all times the desire of power, the watchful jealousy that nothing should be undertaken with the limits of the city over which they cannot, at pleasure, exercise control.'

As Town Clerk Sam Worrall was not only becoming increasingly unpopular with the respectable citizens of Bristol for what seemed like a story of massive civic incompetence: he was also open to charges of personal corruption. Through his own private banks he had invested in the New Cut – he owned some of the land involved in the excavations – and by maintaining the high harbour charges he was feathering his own nest.

One bank he had inherited from his father. In his father's time it had been called Worrall, Hale and Newman, 'up one pair of stairs in the Exchange', Samuel Worrall's present flat and offices. Under Samuel Worrall's management it was still surviving, but shakily, first as Worrall, Hale and Blakely, then as Worrall and Oldham, and finally as Worrall and Gold. He had also started a bank of his own, the Tolzey Bank, from the same address.

Worrall and his three partners all had their nicknames. He was 'the Devil'. Andrew Pope, twenty years younger, a mild-faced inoffensive man who came from another old Bristol family of sugar refiners and had been Master of the Society of Merchant Venturers, was known as 'the Pope'. His other partner, John Edmonds, whom he had brought in from outside Bristol, was known as 'the Pretender'.

Small private banks like Tolzey's no longer exist today, but in the early nineteenth century they were familiar in many country towns, offering what was often a false sense of security to middle-class depositors. Each issued its own banknotes, which, as today, 'promised to pay the bearer' the amount printed on the notes and were accepted as legal tender all over the country – so long as the bank remained solvent.

Though it was then not enforced by law, every bank was supposed to hold sufficient funds in gold, whatever investments it might be making on its own initiative, to cover the value of all the banknotes issued. This rule was frequently broken, and in the unsettled period that followed the Napoleonic wars, several such banks failed, blighting the lives of their investors.

There is a heart-rending scene in Mrs Gaskell's *Cranford* where a shy old lady of slender means waits for weeks before buying a shawl, proudly selects it in front of a shopful of people, pays for it with a banknote, and is told that the note is worthless. The bank has failed, and all her savings have gone with it. There is a picture, too, by the Bristol painter, Rolinda Sharples, called *The Bank Failure*, with a whole street full of people standing stunned by the news.

In founding the Tolzey Bank in 1808, Sam Worrall had done his best to banish any such anxieties from the minds of his depositors. Tolzey was a good, reliable, old-fashioned sounding Bristol name, originally meaning a tollbooth: the mediaeval bridge over the river had been called the Tolzey Bridge. Worrall also printed on his banknotes an engraving of the Bristol High Cross in College Green, another image of old Bristolian stability.

It was unfortunate that Tolzey Bridge had been pulled down fifty years before, and that the old High Cross was no longer there – it had been sold off some years earlier to the designer of the gardens at Stour Head, where it still stands today as part of the Gothic garden ornaments.

In any event, the proprietor of such a private bank needed to be a figure entirely above reproach, utterly reliable in his judgement and backed by vast securities.

Worrall could not make any such claims. He had married a rich woman, but his own resources were increasingly slender. Knole was rented, and he was now, at his wife's insistence, sharing the only property that belonged to them with a pretty girl young enough to be his granddaughter, who didn't speak a word of English and whom he suspected of being an illegal immigrant.

Samuel Worrall had been patient for days, watching a cavalcade of besotted gentlemen trooping up the stairs, bringing with them foreign 'experts' to talk their gibberish to Caraboo, each one more absurd than the last. It must have been a kind of relief to him when a Portuguese traveller was brought in who had visited the East Indies and was familiar with the Malay language. His name was Manuel Enes or Eynesso.

He spoke to the girl for some time. Then, to Samuel Worrall's amazement, she talked back. After what seemed like a long and dramatic narrative in her odd sing-song language, emphasized by hand gestures, the Portuguese turned to Samuel Worrall and translated.

She was a princess. She came from an island called Javasu. She had been kidnapped by pirates who had sailed into northern waters, she had managed to escape by jumping overboard in the Bristol Channel and had swum ashore.

CHAPTER 4

LAMPOON

CONGRATULATING HIS WIFE on her perceptive-
ness, Samuel Worrall brought the girl back to
Knole in triumph. To have a foreign princess staying
in the house was a very different thing from har-
bouring a vagrant, and made an agreeable change
from the grim political realities of financing the New
Cut, harbour charges and troubles at the bank.

He still only had the word of the Portuguese
traveller, but if her story was true she could be of
untold value to him. Royalty, even foreign royalty,
represented prestige and security, exactly what he
needed to carry him through the present
uncertainties.

For Elizabeth Worrall it was a dream come true:
her sons were grown up, she had no daughter, and
she could devote herself singlemindedly to a study
of things oriental. All her bluestocking friends began
to flock to Knole, and for the next few days they
displayed all they knew from their reading, from
their own travels abroad, from stories of other
travellers they had heard and vaguely remembered.

One of them was curious about the form of
greeting observed in the Princess' native country and
demonstrated the Indian *salaam*, with the hands
pressed together, thumbs against the forehead.

Mostly they brought books, and odd objects that might be of interest to the Princess: peppers, semi-precious stones, fans, and pieces of coral.

The single object that excited Caraboo most was a Chinese chain purse. She also seemed to recognize a Chinese puzzle, and a canister of green tea. But she responded with almost equal enthusiasm to a bottle of Indian ink, an Eskimo carving in soapstone, and some white and brown sugar candy.

Caraboo was given the run of the house, garden and park, and as the days became warmer and sunnier at the end of April she began, like an exotic animal in captivity, to repay her captors by displaying more and more extraordinary facets of behaviour.

Whenever she walked beside the lake she would kneel and perform some sort of ritual, anointing her forehead with water and praying. Another time she made a kind of arbour in the bushes for her devotions, splashing it with water and covering her head with a shawl before she knelt to pray.

Archery was then very much in fashion, part of the Romantic interest in the Middle Ages. Caraboo showed remarkable skill with a bow and arrow, the quiver over her left shoulder, running and turning with the bow held parallel to the ground, and releasing arrows with great accuracy as she ran.

She also performed a kind of war-dance, putting flowers and feathers in her hair, taking a gong from the house and making a solemn progress through the garden, striking the gong on her back and banging a tambourine. She also showed herself perfectly at home in a rowing boat and, as Mrs Worrall sat under her sunshade in the stern, would skim across the lake, 'using the oars very dexterously' to turn and steer.

On several occasions she seemed to be pleading with the Greek manservant to let her take him boating on the lake, perhaps to humour him, as he was the only one of the servants who still treated her with reserve and scepticism.

She climbed trees, and as the summer weather came in May, began, when she was assured she was alone, to swim naked in the lake.

What seems to have impressed eye-witnesses, and particularly men, was her theatricality. Every word she spoke was accompanied 'in a very striking manner by gestures and animation of countenance which it is impossible to describe', and the eager intensity in her dark eyes as she listened to those who spoke to her was hard to resist.

Sometimes she danced, apparently for her own pleasure, but to the delight of onlookers. 'She assumed an infinite variety of attitudes, far from destitute of elegance, bent her body in numberless shapes, but never offensive to delicacy or propriety, occasionally dropping on one knee, and then rising with uncommon agility, holding up one foot in a sling, and performing a species of waltz with the most singular twists and contortions.'

One admirer was a retired naval officer, Captain Palmer, recently returned from the Far East, who shared Elizabeth Worrall's interest in anything new in philosophical and literary questions, as well as new discoveries in geography and science. He lived in a house in Bristol called Cathay, and brought a Malay dagger or *kriss* to show her. He explained how they were worn and used by the natives. The Princess recognized it at once and begged to keep it. Afraid that she might cut herself, Elizabeth Worrall at first refused. Then the traveller drew her attention to the fact that she held it against her left side, in the traditional way, and persuaded Elizabeth Worrall that she was obviously familiar with its use. She was allowed to keep it.

Palmer also explained to Elizabeth Worrall and a fascinated audience of Bristol ladies that the Malays had the habit of smearing the tips of their daggers with vegetable poison, ensuring the death of any victim, however lightly grazed in a fight. Princess Caraboo shortly afterwards confirmed this by going to a pot of flowers on a pedestal in one of the alcoves in the drawing room, rubbing a leaf between her fingers and moistening the tip of her *kriss* with the juice. Then she laid it against her arm, pressing the point into her skin, and pretended to faint.

She also made herself a wooden sword that she hung on her right side, with bow and arrows over her left shoulder, and practised fighting. She held the sword in her right hand and a wooden dagger in the left, and even Samuel Worrall was persuaded to join in the game. He claimed to have been 'a tolerable fencer when young' and fought her with a foil. Looking into her dark, witty eyes, watching her full lips draw back from her white teeth as she fenced with him, he conceded defeat.

In exchange for the Worralls' hospitality, Caraboo was required to submit to more research into her origins, and an attempt to make a basic dictionary of her language. Initially, her responses had seemed to suggest that she came from China itself, but this again raised doubts about her appearance. She did not look Chinese. One visitor then produced a recently published book, Hager's *Elementary Characters of the Chinese*. Using simplified illustrations, it showed how Chinese numerals had been formed originally from representations of a knotted string, the first means of counting in Chinese, and the direct ancestor of the abacus. It also gave examples of Chinese characters. The Princess examined them gravely, but made no sign of comprehension.

One of the most successful recent books on the Far East had been Stamford Raffles' book on Java. This too was laid before her, and they watched her face for signs of recognition as she turned over the pages. It was enormous and elaborately illustrated with colour plates: *Antiquarian, Architectural and Landscape Illustrations of the History of Java, by the late Sir Thomas Stamford Raffles F.R.S., formerly Lieutenant Governor of Java and its Dependencies etc etc. With a Large Map of Java and its Dependencies and several interesting plates now first published*.

Caraboo responded with great interest to the picture of the Rajah of Bali, wearing a headdress very similar to the one she had worn herself. She smiled as if pleased at the drawing of Radan Rama Depura, a native of Java who accompanied Mr

Raffles to England. Everything about Java seemed to delight her.

Java was already tantalizing to Romantic intellectuals as one of the last places of mystery left on earth. The Malays who lived there were described as being of a 'wild, ferocious and sanguinary character, filled with ungovernable passions'. They believed in strange spirits, that took the form of birds covered with long black hair who could turn at will into animals or men. They sucked the blood of their victims by moonlight.

There was also the Tuju Jindang, a tiny fiend in the form of a silkworm, that could be sent out by witchcraft. It entered its victim through the back of the hand or between the shoulder blades, leaving only a blue spot, and gnawed out the heart and entrails. Other blood-sucking spirits, the Polong and the Panangham, were invisible, and kept by certain witches in a jar. Released, they would attack young girls, entering through the thumb, sucking out blood and beauty, which they then brought back to their mistress.

There were also witches who would poison the tips of daggers, or burn them in a fire of plantains, after which they could destroy an enemy merely by pointing the dagger at them, however far away. When they began to die, blood formed on the blade of the dagger.

Raffles' book made Java even more spellbinding by producing evidence, as in Ancient Egypt, of lost civilizations. It plotted the foundations of the Temple of Lora Jongram at Brambanan and of the nearby Temple of Boro Bodor with the care only previously given to the ruins of Greece and Ancient Rome. There were sketches of stone reliefs resembling Greek friezes, metal casts of Indian Elephant Gods and Shiva, as well as far earlier figures more closely resembling the ancient civilizations of South America, together with exact drawings of weapons and agricultural instruments.

Raffles also included several pages of mysterious primitive writing found on tombs and pyramids, one 'supposed to date from the Javan year 700'. All these illustrations the Princess examined with interest, and seemed keen, if only her listeners could understand her, to speak about them in great detail. As she pointed happily at the illustrations of Java there was growing excitement: it became clear that this was Caraboo's homeland.

Proof, it seemed, finally came from a third book, Fry's *Pantographia*, which could roughly be translated as *Writing Everywhere*. It gave examples of every kind of written or printed script from all over the world: Greek and Arabic, Russian, Chinese and Japanese, arranged for easy reference with a sample of each language – a translation of the Lord's Prayer – and a short specimen vocabulary of perhaps twenty or thirty words.

Again, Caraboo turned the pages without any trace of recognition: then, almost at the end of the book, she came to examples of two dialects, Lampoon and Rejang, spoken in Sumatra. She pointed to it eagerly, and Captain Palmer, by comparing her spoken words with those printed on the page, was finally able to interpret exactly what she was saying. She was saying that her father had black teeth.

Elizabeth Worrall was confused. It seemed an odd thing to say. On the contrary, Captain Palmer assured her, it was perfectly explicable. He had been to that part of the world and had seen the natives chewing betel-nut. This, of course, discoloured their teeth.

Although they only knew a few words of it and had no dictionary, they had discovered her language.

CHAPTER 5

AKE BRASIDOO

S AMUEL WORRALL, though charmed by their colourful guest and tolerant of the progress made by his wife and her intellectual friends in solving the mystery of Princess Caraboo, still refrained from making her arrival public. Like his Greek servant, he was still not entirely convinced.

Various attempts had been made to test her authenticity. The Worralls' second son, Frederick, in his last year at Westminster and about to join the Army, was home for the holidays and was convinced his mother was being made a fool of. He confronted the Princess and told her she was a fraud.

She responded with great dignity but clearly stung, answering in the nearest approach she ever made to speaking English by saying, 'Caraboo no fraud!'

Elizabeth Worrall's housekeeper, with whom she shared a bedroom, defended her: if she was English she would give herself away by talking in her sleep, but she never did. Shortly after the housekeeper first mentioned it she had admittedly shouted in her sleep, but again it was in her own language. Probably at the instigation of the Greek manservant, two of the maids ran into the room shouting 'Fire!', but the Princess looked at them blankly, showing no sign of alarm.

It was after one such episode, when the Princess had been left alone in the house with the male servants, that Elizabeth Worrall returned to find her gone. She looked everywhere for her, calling, and eventually found her in the upper branches of the cedar tree.

The weather was now settled, hot and sunny, and for three idyllic weeks, through the driest April on record and the beginning of May, Caraboo continued to play in the garden, fulfilling Elizabeth Worrall's wildest Romantic dreams: a savage princess among the yew hedges and the roses, performing on the newly mown lawns the rituals and dances of her home among the jungles of Javasu.

Almost every day more gentlemen visitors and bluestocking ladies would come to examine her. They watched the way she turned her head, her manner of greeting them, with one hand flat against her right temple if she was acknowledging what she called a *Manjitoo* or gentleman, or with a hand to her left temple if it was a *Lazor*, a lady.

Caraboo now agreed to write symbols and characters in her own language. In her country, Elizabeth Worrall explained to visitors, she would have used a camel-hair brush, but here she drew the characters in ink. Some looked like Arabic, with extravagant loops and odd dots and dashes, some Hebrew, some not unlike Greek, and some more oriental, like Chinese or Japanese. It did not tally exactly with the specimens of Rejang and Lampoon in Fry's *Pantographia*, but it was assumed that she was writing in some kind of regional dialect. The Princess herself read them fluently aloud, and with her usual charm.

It was one of Elizabeth Worrall's intellectual friends who suggested sending a page of these characters to Oxford to see if any scholar there could identify their exact country of origin, and a copy was sent to Stamford Raffles himself at the offices of the East India Company in London.

Caraboo seemed conversant with other even more obscure eastern languages, hitherto untranslated, and read confidently from manuscripts that were put before her, chanting out loud in her peculiar sing-song tone, and provoking fierce arguments among the gentlemen callers as to whether she was reading from top to bottom, like the Japanese, from right to left, like the Arabs, or from left to right, like the Europeans.

But most of all the gentlemen examined her hands, the lobes of her ears, her bright eyes and her white teeth, and said how 'interesting' she was. In the first years of the nineteenth century the word was charged with a great deal more sexual meaning than it is now. A pretty girl passing in the street was 'interesting', and Princess Caraboo was more interesting than any girl they had seen for a long time. Elizabeth Worrall, in her early forties and nearly twenty years younger than her husband, basked in the girl's reflected glory. Samuel Worrall found her increasingly alarming.

On one occasion she was standing in the sun by the kitchen door and saw a pigeon. She immediately took up a knife, stalked the bird, caught it with one hand, cut its head off, slit it open, and performed some strange ceremony over it, burying the head and entrails. Then she plucked it, cooked it herself with curry powder, and ate it. She called it *Rampoo*.

She was, it seemed, not strictly vegetarian.

Woken one morning by unearthly chanting, Worrall searched the house, climbing the stairs to the servants' bedrooms under the roof, to find where the sound was coming from. Then, from an attic window, he saw her. She was standing on the roof of the old stone tower, looking out across the chimney pots and roofs over the vast panorama of warm summer green in the morning light towards the Bristol Channel and the ships bound for the New World, chanting and calling on Alla Tallah. He eventually climbed the old oak stairs to the top of the tower and brought her down, afraid she would fall. But there seemed no harm in it. She was apparently worshipping the sun.

An examination of Fry's *Pantographia* showed that Alla Tallah was the Sumatran name for God. From then on, every day Caraboo was at Knole, she prayed to Alla Tallah night and morning, climbing the spiral staircase to the top of the tower every Thursday, which was apparently her Sabbath, and fasting on Tuesdays.

Whatever Samuel Worrall's reservations, Caraboo was also becoming increasingly popular in the farm cottages on the estate, where she would arrive unannounced, usually accepting a cup of tea, though she always insisted, according to her custom, on washing the cup herself. It seemed to the country people very gracious of a princess. She was a particular favourite of the farmers' daughters, who would sit or kneel at her feet, staring up at her, listening to her language and imitating her movements.

One day she seemed in particularly high spirits, and told them, using a knotted string to count the years, that it was her father's birthday, and that he was forty-seven.

For Elizabeth Worrall, with her love of poetry, Princess Caraboo was everything she had ever dreamed of: Coleridge's Damsel with a Dulcimer, the Abyssinian Maid he had seen in a vision. In her adoring presence the Princess flowered.

Bit by bit they began to understand and record her language. Most often, out in the garden, she talked about the natural elements. When she looked at the sky, she used the word *samen*, or Heaven, when she touched the earth she called it *tarsa*. A stone she called *toree*. The sun was *sanatoo*.

On the first night in May, as she sat with the Worralls in the garden, they watched a full moon rising over the park. The apple-blossom glowed white in the moonlight, there was distant music from the village as the young men and women danced round the maypole, and as the moon rose high in the sky it was mysteriously shadowed by the curve of the earth. Looking up at the eclipse the Princess pronounced the word *arra*.

Fire was *apa*, the water in the lake *ana*. When she wanted to swim in it she said *toose*. Touching her own bare feet after swimming, she called them *nease*, and her arms *nater*. A bracelet of mother-of-pearl she called *sirrea*.

When it came to mealtimes – much of her own food she insisted on preparing herself, preferring rice to bread, and often making her own curries – she would call them in to eat. *Ake brasidoo* meant 'Come to breakfast', *ake dosi* meant 'Come to dinner', and *ake sacco* 'Come to supper'.

She was also happy to tell them her words for things on the table. Milk was *mo*, an egg was *nee*, a potato was *archee*, an onion *oree*, salt *oser*, pepper *makey*, sugar *suso*, tea *zee*, a knife *savoo*, a fork *foso*. By the time she had been there a month, she had also taught them to count to fifteen in her language. *Eze, duce, trua, tan, zennee, sendee, tam, nunta, berteen, tashman, limmenee, judgbennee, artinne, ferney, fissmen*.

Money seemed to be of no interest to her, but when she was shown English coins she had oddly familiar-sounding names for them. A shilling she called a *bob*, a sixpence a *tanner*, a penny a *win* and a halfpenny a *tanee*. Elizabeth Worrall found this peculiar, but Captain Palmer suggested that she must have learned these words after she was cast ashore: she could hardly have known the coins in her own country.

But it was when she spoke of that more exotic world of Javasu, her homeland, that her listeners became really enthralled. She called it Puloponnaung, literally translated from Lampoon 'the Betel-Nut Island'. It was in the Straits of Malacca. Making use of signs and gestures, of pictures, of maps and odd objects, the Princess began to tell her story.

As she told it her eyes became very sad and she often wept. She used the word *alkader* or destiny. She had clearly suffered a great deal.

Her father, she said, was Chinese, her mother Malay. She identified the Chinese chain purse as coming from her father's homeland, a piece of coral and a red pepper from her mother's country. This at once explained the mystery of her physical appearance: she was of mixed race.

She grew up, she said, on the island of Puloponnaung, or Javasu, and recognized cinnamon, white pepper, mother-of-pearl, and the dried remains of a flying fish as being familiar to her from her life on that island.

In one of the earliest periods of interrogation, when she was being questioned by old Captain Palmer, she appeared to contradict herself, saying that her name was Sissu Mandu. This produced consternation, but she explained very patiently that she had been renamed Caraboo in celebration of a great victory won by her father.

He was called Jessee Mandu, a man of high rank and distinction. Captain Palmer asked her about his colouring, and she said it was pale. It was his birthday she talked about to the farmers on the estate, and when she spoke of him alone with Elizabeth Worrall it was clear that she was very fond of him.

Her father's family came from Congee or China. He had four wives, and was carried everywhere on a kind of palanquin, borne on the shoulders of three *macratoos* or serving men. He wore a kind of cap decorated with three *paza*, peacock feathers, attached to a headdress, fixed with a gold button on the right side of his *prabha* or head. He also wore a twisted gold chain round his neck, with a golden locket on it set with an amber-coloured stone.

Caraboo demonstrated the etiquette observed among the Maudins, the Malay people, the gestures of respect made to their ladies and gentlemen, by the simple *mosha* and *raglish*, working men and women. It was customary, she said, when approaching her father, to kneel on both knees and to make a *salaam* by raising the right hand to the right temple. When greeting her mother, the servants raised a hand to their left temple. When their servants brought food to her father they also knelt on both knees, kneeling only on one knee when they served him, holding the dish, as she charmingly demonstrated, with their fingers spread and on their fingertips. At their great feasts, musicians played, sometimes on pipes made from reeds, sometimes on a small harp held between their knees.

Her mother was a Maudin or Malay, with yellow or brownish skin. Her arms were painted or tattooed, and she wore a jewel in her nose with a gold chain from it to her left temple. Her mother, she said, wanted her to have her nose pierced too so that she could wear the same kind of gold chain, but her father had forbidden it. Her parents also disagreed about religion. When Caraboo was shown a drawing of a Sumatran stone idol she expressed great horror. Her father, she said, prayed to a graven image like that, but her mother told her that if she did the same she would be burned in the fire and that she should worship only Alla Tallah.

Her mother was subsequently killed in a war between the Maudins and the Bugaboos, or Cannibals. The Cannibals were black, and when they took white prisoners they cut off their heads and arms, roasted them on a fire, and danced round it before eating them.

This would have struck a chord of sympathetic horror in the heart of Elizabeth Worrall. A few years before, a Cornish girl, Mary Bryant, had escaped with her husband, two children and a handful of other convicts from Botany Bay. They had made their way in an open boat across the Timor Sea, where they had been pursued by the same kind of terrifying cannibals.

They reached Kupan in Sumatra, where Bryant's husband got drunk and confessed to the Dutch governor, who sent them in chains to Batavia in Java. Mary Bryant eventually reached England, her husband and children having died on the voyage; James Boswell successfully campaigned for her to be pardoned, and her story received wide publicity.

Princess Caraboo's own adventures after her mother's death had been equally remarkable. Walking in her garden on the island of Javasu, attended by three *sammens* or serving-women, she had watched as a single-masted ship had moored down by the shore. She was surprised at the size of the ship, because the water there was very shallow. It was of an unfamiliar design, with a sail made of matting or rushes, sewn vertically and of a different shape from those of her own island, which were stretched on bamboo poles.

This sent the travellers hurrying to their books. They asked her if the ship had carried guns, and she said it had not. They asked her if she could remember what colours it flew, and opened a coloured chart before her, showing every flag and ensign flown on the seven seas. Running her finger over each one, she eventually seemed to settle on a flag almost at the bottom of the page. It was the Venetian Battle Ensign.

But the men she had seen running towards her up the beach and into the garden were certainly not Venetians. They were, she said, oriental pirates, and they had seized her. She had with her only her *kriss*, but she had struggled free, killed one of her attackers and wounded another. But there were too many of them, they had overpowered her, tied her wrists and ankles with rope, and gagged her.

Then they dragged her out of the garden, carried her across the beach and into the ship, making her three serving-women prisoners at the same time. Her father saw what was happening and came running after her. Standing in the shallows he shot an arrow which hit one of her serving-women and killed her. Then the ship swung out to sea and her last sight was of her father, screaming after them in the shallows.

Elizabeth Worrall found the story horrifying but intensely romantic. It reminded her of Byron's *Don Juan*.

On board ship the pirate Caraboo had wounded

was treated by a *Justee* or surgeon and recovered.
The pirate captain who carried out the kidnap was
called Chee-Min. He had copper-coloured skin and
wore a turban, short breeches and a kind of scarf
over his shoulders. She would say nothing of how
she was treated on board, but seemed distressed at
the memory of it.

After eleven days at sea they came alongside
another ship. Again, her listeners pressed her for
more details in an attempt to identify it. They
showed her pictures of various battleships and merchant vessels, and she indicated that it had been a
brig. This ship, she said, did carry guns and had a
crew of about forty.

An extraordinary shouted exchange then took
place as the two ships ploughed along side by side,
the captain of the brig hailing Chee-Min and offering
to buy his prisoner for a bag of *doteau* or gold dust.
Without slackening their speed the two captains
haggled over her, and Chee-Min finally agreed a
price. She had been sold to the captain of the brig,
and a boat had ferried her from one ship to the other
as they continued to move through the water.

What became of her serving-women she never
said. The captain of the brig, she remembered, was
called Tappa Boo and had a darker complexion,
with long black whiskers and thick black hair plaited
down his back, tied at the end with a bow. He wore
a kind of sealskin cap, and an earring in his right ear.
Asked by the experts to try to identify his nationality, the Princess pointed to a flag on the chart which
turned out to be Spanish.

She remembered little of the voyage with Tappa Boo, except that she had been very ill. Her head was shaved, the *Justee* on board had taken blood from the back of her neck, her arm and wrist, and she was confined to her hammock for a long time.

Questioned about the cause of her illness or what it might have been, she became upset. Elizabeth Worrall did her best to understand what she was saying, and came to the conclusion her illness had been brought on by 'her crying and her great unhappiness in consequence of her miserable and forlorn situation'.

Caraboo estimated that she was ill for something over a month, at the end of which they arrived at a port, which she thought might have been Batavia on the north-east coast of Java, though she could not be certain. The experts again showed her the page of flags, wondering if she had noticed a flag flying in the harbour, but she pressed her fingers against her eyelids and shook her head. She was confined below decks and could see nothing.

The next stage of her journey was more difficult to plot. With an atlas open in front of her, she was able to trace what she believed had been their course from Javasu, first northwards towards the coast of China and then back to Java. They spent, she thought, three days in the harbour in Batavia. Four women had come on board, not prisoners like herself, but educated passengers who wrote and talked in a language she did not understand.

From Sumatra she then traced a line south-east-wards, saying that they had travelled to the Cape of

Good Hope, a journey she estimated to have taken, if they understood her correctly, five weeks.

This presented Elizabeth Worrall and her gentlemen visitors with the second real challenge to her story since the mystery of her white skin. A child would have known that the Cape of Good Hope was not south-east of Sumatra but due west. The mistake was so basic that it seemed to cast doubt on everything else she had told them.

There were other inconsistencies, too. If they were pirates, why had they not attacked any other ships? Why had they carried passengers? Why had they put in at ordinary trading ports?

On the question of the length of the voyage, it was possible they had misunderstood her calculations. She measured the length of her journey with knots tied in a piece of cord, and this particularly impressed one of the orientalists present at this stage of her narration by confirming that she still used the primitive Chinese method of counting on a knotted string.

Elizabeth Worrall was also prepared to be tolerant. The girl was still often tearful and withdrawn as she had been at the Bowl and in St Peter's Hospital. Had she been raped by the pirates? Had they tortured her? In any case, Elizabeth Worrall decided, correctly as it transpired, she had suffered some kind of severe psychological damage.

If she refused to talk about the pirates or what they had done to her, if she seemed dazed and confused about her nightmare journey, it was because there was more to understand than could be conveyed by signs, occasional words and images in books. She urged the Princess to go on.

When they reached the Cape of Good Hope, she said, she was again kept a prisoner in her cabin. The four women passengers were put ashore, and after three days in port Tappa Boo sailed due west out into the South Atlantic, the route followed by the China Fleet. She believed they called at St Helena before heading north towards Europe and into the North Atlantic. This leg of the journey, she estimated, took nearly three months.

It seemed to Elizabeth Worrall and the experts that the girl's mental health might have been improving as she became accustomed to her imprisonment on board.

Determined to escape, the Princess waited until they were close in under the English coast, jumped overboard, and managed to swim ashore. When she landed she was wearing the gown in which she was captured, embroidered with gold thread, and a turban of the same material. She remembered a house with a green front door, and a woman living there who gave her dry clothes, a black dress and a cotton shawl, in exchange for those she had on.

These were the clothes she was wearing when she arrived in Almondsbury. She estimated that she was on the road six weeks, wandering, and said that during that time she was very hospitably treated. Elizabeth Worrall wrote down every detail of the story.

Then, at the end of the first week in May, when the Princess had been with them for three weeks, the Greek manservant came early one morning to Elizabeth Worrall's bedroom to tell her that the Princess had gone.

Everything she had been given during her stay – the Malay *kriss*, the pieces of coral and mother-of-pearl, a gold necklace and a bracelet – was still there. They searched the house, but could not find her. Mrs Worrall called in all the gardeners, had the garden searched, and the park. Servants ran through the village asking at cottage doors. No one had seen her.

Caraboo seemed to have vanished into thin air.

CHAPTER 6

THE COMING
OF COSMO

IF THERE WAS one person Samuel Worrall thought about with real fear as he sat considering the figures in his office at the Tolzey Bank, or as he listened, when he got home, to his wife's distraught account of Princess Caraboo's disappearance, it was a man who was to become notorious throughout Bristol and far beyond as 'Cosmo'.

Cosmo was the pen-name of John Matthew Gutch, editor and proprietor of a weekly newspaper *Felix Farley's Bristol Journal*, and when the time came he was to show himself capable of destroying not only the Tolzey Bank, but the whole arrogant, easy-going old regime in Bristol, the Docks Company and the hereditary rule of three generations of Worralls.

He was also obsessed throughout his long life with the question of fraud. If the girl playing in the park at Knole was not who she claimed to be, Cosmo was an expert in detecting impostors and would never rest until he had discovered the truth.

Both his background and his politics made John Matthew Gutch a most unlikely trouble-maker. His father was a Fellow and Chaplain of All Souls, Oxford, for sixty-two years, a fox-hunting, bee-keeping don, 'of small stature, courteous and suave in manner and of a gentle disposition, somewhat negligent in looking after his own money matters, and ever ready to help antiquaries'. John Matthew Gutch took after him. He was gentle and polite, never made any money, and the great love of his life was his collection of very old and very expensive books.

His handwriting is the opposite of Samuel Worrall's: small, scholarly and neat. His letters, some of which are preserved in the manuscript collection of the British Library, are sealed in red wax with a gold signet ring bearing the family emblem of a boar's head in flames.

One of the more radical weekly newspapers, the *Bristol Mercury*, condemned *Felix Farley's Bristol Journal* under Gutch's ownership as plain reactionary. It was known for 'the rabid bigotry of its ultra' – extreme right-wing – 'political instincts, and the favour which corruption and abuses found in its columns'. Gutch did not always print the truth, according to the *Mercury*, and the paper was satirized as 'Felix Far-Lie'.

This kind of abuse was to some extent deserved. Gutch's editorials in April 1817, when he wasn't pouring scorn on the idea of Catholics having the vote, let alone occupying public office, were largely devoted to the iniquity of spending money on the undeserving poor. Public money should never be handed out automatically 'except to the infant, the diseased or aged who cannot help themselves'. Funds should never be 'squandered on idleness'.

In another editorial, on the 'intended insurrection' in Manchester, he raged against the 'blind violence of the lawless mob' that would 'embrace the overthrow of everything that is good and valuable in the State'. Distresses, he conceded, were great, but there must be no mercy for those 'malevolent spirits, these fomentors of civil strife, these abetters of rebellion', and 'popular excesses should be met with the greatest fierceness and vigilance by the magistrates'.

Elsewhere he wrote that as editor he considered it his duty to exercise his pen in support of 'that Constitution, which ensures to us blessings and advantages enjoyed by no other part of the habitable globe'.

Gutch was outraged when the radical Henry Hunt styled himself 'Hunt of Bristol'. Hunt only came to Bristol once a year, Gutch jeered in an editorial in November 1816, and then only to celebrate the occasion when he had managed to win his 456 votes from an electorate of 10,000 Bristolians. Gutch made no mention of the thousands of pounds he would have had to pay in bribes if he had hoped to win more.

Hunt replied by accusing *Felix Farley's Bristol Journal* of being 'in the pay of the Government'. This produced an explosion of rage from Gutch, who denied 'by everything that is most sacred in the estimation of an Englishman' that any British newspaper received 'directly or indirectly a single shilling from Government for its services'.

The word 'services' was unfortunate. Gutch and the rest of the Tory press may not have been literally in the pay of the Government, but the whole way of life the Tory press represented and commented on – solid, reliable working people, enterprising trades-men, secure landowners and the elegant dukes and marchionesses, even princes and princesses – depended on that Government for its very existence. Whether Gutch admitted it or not, he was unques-tionably in the service of a very repressive regime.

The big political story at the beginning of April 1817 was the Government's banning political pam-phlets critical of the present regime, and its suspen-sion, after a fierce debate, of the *habeas corpus*, allowing the arrest and imprisonment of anyone thought to be likely to disturb the peace, indefinitely and without trial.

The Prime Minister, Lord Liverpool, had announced that the stock market had responded wonderfully, and the more liberal *Bristol Gazette* printed a satirical poem in celebration.

> A noble minister of state
> Informs us in a late debate
> The Gagging Bills have sent
> Such comfort to the good and wise
> The stocks, and not the people rise,
> At least an eighth per cent.
> And thus the noble Lord avails

> To raise the hope he mocks
> For surely that which fills the gaols
> May elevate the stocks.

The radical William Cobbett had made his protest by emigrating to America, and the *Gazette* had printed his farewell address before embarking in Liverpool virtually in full. Cobbett said he was going for one reason only, the personal danger to which he was exposed 'by the passing of the late acts'.

England, he said, was never destined to be inhabited by slaves. He urged his fellow countrymen to fight for their ancient freedoms, their parliamentary rights, and warned them 'not to be humbugged by any of the publications of corruption'. Gutch's newspaper would certainly have fallen into that category.

Gutch barely reported the speech, and resorted to one of his 'far-lies', suggesting that Cobbett had only gone abroad because he couldn't afford to pay his printers' bills.

But Gutch had another side. In private he was superficially very cynical. He dismissed his rival editors as 'tradesmen, mere tradesmen, without an idea beyond their printing offices', and shrugged off his tub-thumping Tory editorials as being designed to appeal to his readership, who were 'of the old school'. He had enough of a newspaperman's instinct to know what they wanted, and for the moment his readers of the old school wanted to support the Government, the Docks Company and the Bristol Corporation.

Deeper down he was also a Romantic. He was a close friend and loyal public supporter of the poet Coleridge, and neither role was easy.

They had been at school together at Christ's Hospital with Charles Lamb – as a young man Gutch had shared his lodgings in Southampton Row with Lamb and his poor mad sister – and he had consistently defended Coleridge in the face of a great deal of ridicule from his readers of 'the old school'.

In 1813, at the height of his opium addiction, Coleridge had come to Bristol to deliver a series of bewildering philosophical lectures on poetry, painting and sculpture. Gutch gave them enthusiastic reviews and even reprinted them in *Felix Farley*, weathering the storm of protest from his readers that followed. Gutch and Coleridge were now, in the spring of 1817, in the middle of a very embarrassing business transaction.

The year before, Coleridge wrote to Byron saying that 'a few friends in Bristol were undertaking the risk of printing two volumes for me', and he later mentions Gutch more specifically as 'an old schoolfriend' who had agreed to print his literary autobiography, the *Biographia Literaria*. It took a great deal of goading from Gutch to write it, but he finally delivered the manuscript in the autumn of 1816.

In a letter written in September, Coleridge reports that he has 'delivered compleat to my printer (Mr Gutch of Bristol) the manuscripts of two volumes octavo – the first Biographical Sketches of my *literary* life; and of my opinions on Religion, Philosophy, Politics, and Poetry.'

Gutch began printing, but stopped after page one hundred and forty-four when he realized that the manuscript was not long enough to make the two volumes that Coleridge had promised him. He remained patient and polite as always, urged Coleridge to write more, and sent him a copy of another book he had printed, *The Gull's Horn Book* – roughly 'The Mug's Guide' – as an encouragement.

Coleridge agreed to complete the material for the second volume, but began negotiations behind Gutch's back with another firm of printers in London called Gale and Fenner. Gutch was therefore left with over a thousand copies of the printed sheets as far as page one hundred and forty-four while Coleridge wrangled with another publisher for a higher advance. The sheets were eventually bought by the London printers, who published the book, but it was a blow to Gutch's pride. He had, not for the first time, been too gullible.

It was perhaps because he recognized his own vulnerability to deception that John Matthew Gutch was so fascinated by fraud: by far the most expensive things that he had bought for his library were original documents to do with famous hoaxes.

He had bought, for example, the Thomas Chatterton papers. They included a transcript of the coroner's report on Chatterton's suicide, which he submitted many years later to be published in the Victorian journal *Notes and Queries*. The manuscript itself, much to Gutch's embarrassment, turned out to be a forgery.

Chatterton was the greatest of Bristol hoaxers. By an odd coincidence it was *Felix Farley's Bristol Journal* in the seventeen-sixties, when the old Tolzey Bridge was demolished to make way for the New Bridge, which had published a collection of long-lost poems 'taken from an ancient manuscript', one of them about monks crossing the old mediaeval bridge, which had been built over, like the old London Bridge, with houses and shops on either side. Thomas Chatterton, then sixteen, claimed he had discovered them in a chest of old papers in a loft in St Mary Redcliff. They were immediately hailed as works of genius. Then Chatterton admitted that he had written them himself.

Gutch also bought all the original manuscripts of the Great Shakespeare Hoax of the seventeen-nineties. In 1790 William Henry Ireland claimed he had found a collection of papers left to one of his ancestors who, he said, had saved Shakespeare from drowning. It included a letter from Queen Elizabeth addressed to Shakespeare at the Globe Theatre six years before it was built, and an unpublished play by the Bard called *Vortigern*, which was subsequently performed at Drury Lane and booed off.

A great many people were taken in. James Boswell himself fell on his knees in front of the manuscripts, 'and in a tone of enthusiasm and exultation thanked God that he had lived to witness their discovery and that he could now die in peace'.

Gutch also collected old ballads and broadsheets,

and all the earliest accounts of Robin Hood and his Merry Men, defending him for being an outlaw: far worse crimes, Gutch wrote, were committed by those who hunted him down. Somewhere inside him there was a dreamer and a rebel. He had, as a very young man, turned his back on everything his father believed in and gone to the Midlands to make carriages.

He bought a partnership in a firm in Birmingham, owned suitably enough for a carriage-works by a Mr Wheeley, and married his daughter. Then, perhaps because he saw his chance of running a newspaper that had once printed Chatterton's poems, he moved to Bristol and bought a share in *Felix Farley's Bristol Journal* and set up his own printing works. Gutch was then twenty-nine, and determined to establish *Felix Farley* as a newspaper to be reckoned with.

He succeeded to a degree unheard of at the time. Except for the more sensational news stories that were 'networked' nationally from other local weeklies, newspapers in the provinces depended for almost all their copy on news and editorials from the London press, reprinting their material from the last batch of papers that had arrived on the post wagon. When Gutch became sole proprietor he managed to reverse that. During the later stages of the Napoleonic wars his editorials in *Felix Farley's Bristol Journal* were actually reprinted in the London press, and quoted, as he himself was happy to boast, 'by some of our most distinguished statesmen'. It is no coincidence that later in life he founded and became the first president of the Provincial Newspapers' Association.

Felix Farley's Bristol Journal, when Gutch took it over, was an old and distinguished newspaper that had fallen on hard times. Like a lot else in the West Country, the press for nearly a hundred years had been in the hands of one family, in this case the Farleys. It had never been a comfortable trade. One member of the family had died in prison in Exeter for writing an editorial in support of the Old Pretender, and Sam Farley in Bristol had a running battle with Samuel Worrall's grandfather for refusing to pay stamp duty on his *Bristol Post Man*.

Old Samuel Worrall had closed it, and it had started up again almost immediately as *Farley's Bristol Newspaper*, now paying less stamp duty by being printed in a smaller format, and making most of its income out of selling Samuel Farley's own range of patent medicines.

The last issue of the *Farley's Bristol Newspaper*, before that too succumbed, contains an interesting apology after a libel case, where Joseph Robbins withdraws his allegation that the landlord of the Ship and Dove has been putting live toads in his beer to improve the flavour.

Felix Farley, Samuel's son, who gave his name to the new paper, was a Methodist and a close friend of both John and Charles Wesley. In 1752 he announced that he intended to make the paper more morally uplifting. It would be 'a kind of library of arts and sciences', and readers were advised to keep the back numbers for future study. This literary tradition survived to Gutch's day.

Felix Farley's paper had regular correspondents in Boston and in Philadelphia, although foreign news in general was not the paper's strong point. A rival newspaper, *The Intelligencer*, poked a good deal of fun at Farley for 'setting the Russian Fleet a-sailing on dry land, among Rocks and Mountains in Transylvania in Quest of the Swedish Fleet in the Finnish Gulf, and at the same time representing them to be near one another as shortly to expect a battle'.

Felix died and the paper was run for many years by his widow Elizabeth. She was not the only woman editor of a paper in Bristol: her sister-in-law, Sarah Farley, ran the *Bristol Journal*, and later handed it on to a cousin, Hester Farley.

Under Elizabeth Farley the paper became a great deal more critical of local politics. It was she who fought off a libel action brought by Joritt Smith, a local MP. She had printed a story accusing him of the traditional practice of bribing the electors to vote for him with free drink – 'the tap at the Nagg's Head has been running since yesterday morning'. When she was acquitted she ran the nearest thing possible in those days of close print and narrow columns to a banner headline: 'Not Guilty – A Triumph'.

But the Worralls were still bleeding the Farleys of their profits at a rate of a shilling stamp duty for every small advertisement for patent medicine. Elizabeth Farley retired, the paper passed into the hands of John Rudhall, and was inherited by his son, who died young. By the time Gutch bought it in 1805 the paper had lost circulation and was being beaten by rivals, particularly the *Bristol Gazette*.

But *Felix Farley's Bristol Journal* retained its readers of 'the old school', the rich, settled élite, and it still raised more money than any other local paper in an appeal for comforts for the Army in Flanders during the early stages of the Napoleonic wars.

From the moment he arrived in Bristol, Gutch proved that he knew how to sell newspapers. He immediately scooped every other paper in the country with the first news of Nelson's victory at Trafalgar. He made, he said, 'a bold request' to borrow a report from a naval officer at dinner, ostensibly to read it himself in the next room, and printed every word of it in the paper the next day. It produced, as he himself admitted, 'a phenomenal circulation'.

The following year, in 1806, he revived the newspaper's old line in patent medicines, circulating lists to country subscribers, and bought the rights to publish the equivalent of *Yellow Pages*, the *Bristol Commercial Almanac*. In May 1809 he extended the old printing works in Small Street to include a book shop, which he advertised as having over seven thousand volumes. The same year his son was born, and was christened John Wheeley Gutch.

Gutch's wife, Mary, died in 1816, and he found himself alone in his early forties with a son to bring up. Like many other gentlemen of Bristol, he was soon to fall in love with Princess Caraboo, and to write the story of her life, for which he would be remembered long after his collection of rare books, *Felix Farley's Bristol Journal* and his friendship with Coleridge were forgotten.

But now, in the month of May, when Princess Caraboo had been rescued from St Peter's Hospital, fêted for three weeks at Knole by the Bristol intelligentsia, and had mysteriously disappeared, he made no mention of her in his paper.

Leafing through the old rag-paper editions of *Felix Farley* for the months of April and May 1817, it is still possible to catch the day-to-day flavour of life in Bristol. The most noticeable feature are the advertisements.

> The Change of Climate, Study, Anxiety, Fevers, and Accouchements frequently occasion the human hair to fall off and turn grey – to prevent which use ROWLAND'S MACASSAR OIL, the first production in the world for eradicating all disease of the hair, and producing luxuriant growth on the baldest places, makes the hair curl and prevents the curl falling in damp weather, produces whiskers, eyebrows & etc. This oil is patronised by their Royal Highnesses the Princess of Wales, Duchess of York, the Duke of Sussex, his Imperial Majesty the Emperor of Russia, by their especial authority.

Foreign news is limited to the war trials still going on in Paris, and Jerome Bonaparte, the Emperor's brother, being sued for divorce by his American wife, Mrs Patterson. She was a girl from Baltimore whom he'd married when he was still a very young man. Napoleon had ordered him to abandon her when he crowned him King of Westphalia in 1807 and the girl lived for a time in Camberwell. She then returned to America when she was paid an annual pension of 60,000 francs. With Napoleon's defeat at Waterloo this pension had stopped and she was now asking for money.

On St Helena, Napoleon himself is reported to be 'growing more sullen in his demeanour', but 'still affects the Majesty of a Sovereign'. There are also many rumours about him: one that he is to be brought back to Europe, to a prison on the island of Malta, another that he has been circulating gold among the Malay slaves on St Helena to induce them to rise in his favour. There is also a report of him having been shot at by a British soldier on sentry duty. The paper makes no mention of the fact that the soldier was drunk.

There are recurrent rumours of corsairs and pirates: ships returning from the West Indies have been attacked by 'armed piratical vessels, chiefly under what they call the Independent Spanish flag, though they use the flags of all nations, as occasion may require', and a Royal Naval party cutting wood in the East Indies has been attacked by Malays, one officer losing an arm, another killed.

At home, there is some excitement about the wedding of the Prince Regent's daughter, Princess Charlotte, and Prince Leopold of Coburg, and Mr Bish's forthcoming Lottery. On the political front Gutch avoids wherever possible any news of the widening political unrest, and announces 'the death of an excellent gentleman, Mr Bastard, who departed this life on the 4th inst at Leghorn. He was 30 years Member for the County of Devon. It is reported his nephew E.P. Bastard Esq.re will offer for the county'.

At the Theatre Royal, in April, Gutch favourably reviews a performance by a visiting American actor, Howard Payne, in Miller's *Mahomet, the Impostor.* He is less sympathetic to a play called *The Iron Chest,* and is particularly hard on the leading actor. 'In Mr Young's acting there is so striking a resemblance to the conception and expression of Mr Kemble – the sudden look, the hoarse whisper – that we wonder if it be accidental or the subject of study.'

One retired actor has had a concert given for his benefit, and 'thanks the brilliant and numerous Assemblage who on Friday evening so liberally patronised this tribute to unassuming merit, labouring under the complicated evils of loss of health'.

There is a gleam of a more philanthropic future in a letter discussing the 'very original and striking suggestion respecting the formation of National Circulating Libraries, for the use of the lower orders . . . Having given them the capacity for reading, it seems but right that we should now furnish them with the most useful and amusing books.'

The Bath Philosophical and Literary Society has been addressed by the Reverend Mr Cockin, exhibiting to the society the bones of an alligator and a shark found as fossils near Keynsham.

There are, too, various horror stories, one about the driver of a West Country cheese wagon found dead 'in consequence of the wheel going over his face'. A boy apprentice has been brought into court in Bath with a wagon chain twisted round his leg secured with two padlocks, severely beaten, his flesh 'variegated by his bruises like a leopard skin'. A labourer has fallen asleep by a lime kiln, and woken to find himself terribly burned. 'He had drunk only half a pint of beer but no spirits all day. The foot was a perfect *cinder*.'

The paper's silence about Princess Caraboo is as significant as Sherlock Holmes' dog that did not bark in the night.

For other Bristol newspapers to have been kept in the dark is understandable: their editors, as Gutch said, were 'mere tradesmen', excluded by the social divide from the intimacy of those who governed Bristol. Gutch himself might appear to be a tradesman, working among the type-cases and hand-presses, the damp sheets of rag-paper and the smell of the oil and lamp-black in his office in Small Street, but he was within a few yards' walk of the Exchange, and saw Haythorne and Worrall every day of his life. In the evenings he met them several times a week at dinners and receptions in the houses of Bristol's ship-owners and wealthier merchants. He belonged to the same philosophical and literary societies as Elizabeth Worrall, they both contributed to the new library. Gutch was not a native Bristolian, but he was a gentleman.

Worrall relied on that. There might come a time when he was sure enough of Princess Caraboo's story to announce her arrival in the press, but at the moment he had persuaded his wife that it was better to keep her visit a secret and he relied on Gutch's admiration and affection for her to respect her wishes. When Gutch eventually came to write the story, Elizabeth Worrall was his heroine, a woman above criticism.

Gutch must have been very happy for her when he got the news that Princess Caraboo had returned.

CHAPTER 7

ELECTRICITY AND MAGNETISM

AT KNOLE, ESTATE workers had searched the park and the woods, servants had ridden to nearby villages to ask for news of the Princess, but no one had seen her. Had Tappa Boo and the pirates somehow found out where she was and recaptured her? Elizabeth Worrall had been inconsolable.

The Princess, everyone agreed, seemed unaccountably depressed at certain moments and subject to moods of great unhappiness, but for most of the time she had seemed content to be the centre of attention, demonstrating her archery or her swordfighting, her handwriting and her way of speaking to visitor after visitor, always looking at Elizabeth Worrall with absolute devotion in her dark eyes.

Now, after a day of grieving, Elizabeth Worrall was thrilled to hear that the Princess had returned. She was sitting in the servants' hall. She was obviously very tired, her clothes were torn, her shoes, hands and fingernails making it plain she had scrambled through hedges and across open country. She had with her a bundle of European clothes. She also had a high temperature.

Elizabeth Worrall examined the clothes and sent

them to be washed, questioning the Princess quite sharply as to where they came from: the Princess explained by mime and a few words of her own language that she had buried them before she had arrived in Almondsbury to prevent them being taken by what sounded like *macratoos*, either serving-men or robbers. She was by now very flushed, her teeth were chattering and she seemed delirious.

She was bathed and put to bed in a room of her own, attended by one of the younger maids, and the family doctor was called. William Mortimer was listed in the Bristol directory as a surgeon and apothecary rather than as a physician, but he was always referred to as Dr Mortimer. He now examined the Princess.

Mortimer confirmed that Caraboo had a high fever, felt her forehead, and prescribed medicine for a typhoid infection. Outside the bedroom he listened to Elizabeth Worrall's account of her story, and said he would like to bring a colleague to give them a second opinion. He had no doubts about her illness, which he did not consider to be serious, but like the Worralls' Greek servant he doubted her claim that she was a native of Java or Sumatra. He pointed out that her skin was white, that her features were entirely European. Apart from an inability or unwillingness to speak English and the evidence of the turban she had been wearing when she first appeared, there seemed nothing about her physically to suggest that she was not born and brought up in Europe. He strongly suspected that she spoke or at least understood English.

Elizabeth Worrall insisted that she had been in the house now for more than three weeks, she never at any time varied in her behaviour, that her own language and the words she used to describe familiar objects was always consistent, and that she had never once, despite considerable provocation from the servants and from the Worrall's younger son, given any sign of being able to speak or understand any other.

Mortimer remained unconvinced. To prove his point he asked Elizabeth Worrall's permission to make an experiment. Rather reluctantly, she agreed. He returned later the same day with another doctor from Bristol, and the two men examined her together. Then, with the maid and Elizabeth Worrall in the room and facing his colleague across Caraboo's bed, he asked him how he rated her chances of recovery. The other doctor said he thought it likely she would be dead within twelve hours.

Mortimer rose to his feet triumphant. The Princess had blushed. He had his proof. She could certainly understand English. Elizabeth Worrall thought it more likely she had sensed the meaning of the words from his tone and her own involuntary shock, but the maid had a different explanation: the Princess' face, she said, had flushed suddenly several times like that in the course of the day, it seemed to be a symptom of the fever.

Even the doubting Greek was now convinced, and treated her from then on with greater respect than any of the other servants, though he continued to decline her invitations to go rowing on the lake.

The Princess recovered, was extremely gracious to Mortimer, and one of her first pieces of writing when she was well again was a letter of thanks to him on her restoration to health.

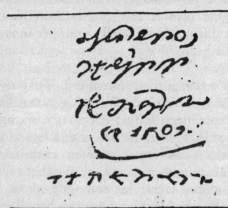

When she read it aloud to Elizabeth Worrall she made it clear that she was addressing Mortimer as *Justee*.

William Mortimer, like Samuel Worrall, remained suspicious. Worrall, though he still recognized her potential as a social asset, retained a lingering fear that the Princess might be trying to deceive his wife for some criminal purpose. All the evidence was against it: when she had disappeared she had stolen nothing from the house. She had even left behind her things of value that had been given to her as presents.

Mortimer also doubted her story, but tended more to the theory, put forward originally by Elizabeth Worrall, that she was in some way mentally disturbed. Again, there was not a great deal of evidence to support it. Anyone who had been taken by force from their home, carried halfway round the world to a strange country with a strange language and stranger customs might be expected to have occasional fits of weeping and moments of depression.

To encourage her recovery, Elizabeth Worrall now suggested that the Princess might like to wear her traditional costume: she brought her various materials, and the Princess chose calico, showing herself as proficient with a needle and thread as she had with a bow and arrow. She also made herself a more elaborate turban of white linen decorated as she had described with three peacock feathers.

The dress, even at a time when it was fashionable for girls to half-expose their nipples in loose summer shifts their mothers would have thought daring to wear in bed, was excitingly barbaric. The neck was square, and cut very low, showing her large white breasts, and had an embroidered border. The sleeves were long, like those worn by ladies in the Middle Ages, exposing the forearm but hanging down low from the elbow. These too were embroidered at the hem in a diamond pattern, as was the waist-band. What was shocking about it, at a time when dresses for as long as anyone could remember had reached the floor, was the skirt.

It was heavily embroidered above the hem and came to just below the knee, revealing bare legs. On her feet she wore wooden-soled open sandals, on her head the elaborate turban with its plume of peacock feathers. Round her neck, like her father, she had a gold chain. It was given to her by Elizabeth Worrall, with a gold locket in the shape of a heart.

Another of Elizabeth Worrall's circle, the artist Edward Bird, needed cheering up. He was the son of a carpenter in Wolverhampton, and had learned his craft first in a lacquer workshop decorating oriental trays. He had become the leading painter in Bristol in his day, famous for his brilliantly coloured landscapes, with girls in straw bonnets and young men in blue tailcoats strolling in dappled sunlight through green woods and beside sparkling rivers. Those who watched him painting in his studio described him putting on a kettle for tea and having all the main elements of the picture sketched in before it boiled. But recently he had become gloomy and worried about his health, and doctors had prescribed morphia. This kept him in a steady state of drugged resignation. Elizabeth Worrall thought it would entertain him to paint the Princess in her native costume.

This meant several journeys into Bristol to Edward Bird's studio. The Princess posed, Bird dipped his brush in the water-colours and remembered his days painting japanned trays, sketching in behind her an imagined shore in the East Indies, with a square-sailed junk, a pillared and turreted temple and a thatched hut standing among palm trees. The picture hangs today in the Bristol City Art Gallery.

The sky is cloudy, and she is holding a pale rose

between the finger and thumb of her right hand, laid across her left breast. Her left arm is lost in the folds of her sleeve, which trails like a train. The most striking thing about the portrait is her face. She has dark eyebrows and black hair hanging loose behind, below the turban, and her expression is strangely vacant: it may be the drugged eye of the painter, but she is smiling a dreamy half-smile, her eyes half-focused, as if she were in a trance. One foot is forward, and she seems to be walking.

On the way back from a sitting with Edward Bird one hot afternoon the Princess fell asleep in Elizabeth Worrall's carriage. Even Elizabeth Worrall could not resist waking her suddenly to see if she would in some way betray herself. But even drowsy from sleep, with no idea where she was, the Princess still spoke only in her own language.

In the middle of May an answer came from Oxford. It was not reassuring. The specimen of her hand-writing had been sent to Dr Whately, who had shown it to three dons: Dr Copleston, Provost of Oriel, another linguist at the same college called Hawkins, and Dr McBride, Principal of Magdalen Hall. Their judgement was unanimous. 'The language is not Chinese, it is not Circassian, it is *Humbug*.'

Both Samuel and Elizabeth Worrall must have been relieved, at that moment, to receive a visit from Dr Wilkinson of Bath. If there was one man in the West Country who could either prove or disprove the Princess' claim, it was Dr Charles Hummings Wilkinson.

Wilkinson was then fifty-four. As a younger man

he had worked in Leicester Square, specializing in what was called 'medical electricity', and had arrived in Bath about ten years earlier as plain Mr Wilkinson, mysteriously developing a Doctorate of Medicine soon after his arrival.

He had borrowed funds to buy the Kingston Hot Baths, and by 1811 had made enough money from the invalids, hypochondriacs and fashionable visitors who took the waters there to build a lecture hall. It was decorated with fossils arranged according to the strata at which they had been found, very much to the taste of an age in love with the mysterious past and ancient remains of every kind. In this hall he delivered lectures on a surprisingly wide range of subjects, including 'pneumatics, optics, hydrostatics, electricity and galvanism'.

On Easter Monday, when Elizabeth Worrall was rescuing Princess Caraboo from St Peter's Hospital and taking her up to her husband's apartment in the Exchange, Dr Charles Hummings Wilkinson was having dinner at the Egyptian Hall in Piccadilly with the Lord Mayor of London and the Duke of Sussex.

He described the evening in a letter to the *Bath Chronicle*: as the Duke of Sussex entered the hall, 'five hundred gaslights *at one instant* burst into a brilliant state of illumination'.

When he first read about the idea of gas lighting, he said, he decided it was entirely impractical, put forward by men in 'complete ignorance of the principles of chemistry and philosophy'. He himself had made experiments, pumping different amounts of water through pipes of the kind used to carry gas;

he had analysed the chemical elements in coal and in coal-gas, he had expressed his anxieties about waste being pumped into the Thames and the danger to fish or to animals drinking from the river.

Now, he was convinced, he had been mistaken. He had personally been shown round the new London gasworks beside the Thames 'in the most liberal manner' by the proprietor himself, who 'united great mechanical skill with considerable scientific information'.

There was no danger to fish, animals or human beings, the system was entirely practicable, and gas light was likely to be the greatest blessing to mankind. The only fact he omitted to mention in his long letter to the *Chronicle* was that he himself was Superintendent of the Works of the new Bath Gas Light Company in Abbey Street.

There was the same shrewd commercial instinct at work in almost everything Wilkinson did. When he revived the old Bath Philosophical Society, he charged its members a guinea for a course of nine lectures. He offered them the opportunity of witnessing real-life experiments, but also managed to work in demonstrations of new commercial products for which the manufacturers were all too ready to express their gratitude.

At the meeting of the Literary and Philosophical Society in April 1817 he discussed methods of detecting arsenic in a dead body, and demonstrated a new steel pen made by Mr Clarke, who had a shop near the York Hotel. There was also a display of glass-cutting with a diamond, and a proposal was made for a new method of dredging rivers. An interesting discussion was just beginning about the scientific advantages of glass in the manufacture of flutes when it was cut short by Dr Wilkinson who had to leave, and the Society 'adjourned at an early hour'.

Even such innocent gatherings of would-be intellectuals in a city as respectable as Bath were legally under threat that year from the newly passed Seditious Meetings Act, but Dr Wilkinson and his bluestocking band bravely soldiered on.

At their meeting on the evening of 19 May, members really got their money's worth. Dr Wilkinson began by demonstrating a new cutaway model of geological strata, a new 'patent elastic horse-shoe' made of nine metal parts sewn on to leather, a new cast-iron chain made by Spooner's of Birmingham, and then offered to show his listeners an experiment involving a shilling suspended on a piece of thread.

He rested his elbows on the table in front of him and dangled the shilling inside a glass tumbler. According to Booth's Theory, he said, the shilling would begin to vibrate, then to swing, and would eventually strike against the sides of the tumbler, 'and the vibrations terminate as soon as the number of times it strikes the glass corresponds to the hour of the day'.

Cynics attributed this to 'the fatigue of the muscles', and claimed that the motion was stopped 'by the will of the operator'. He asked them to watch closely. 'The experiment', according to the official report, 'upon being frequently tried before the Society, sometimes succeeded, but more frequently failed.'

He then read a letter from a doctor in Penzance, suggesting an alternative method for detecting the presence of arsenic in a dead body. Using nitrate and lunar caustic, arsenic would show first as a 'curdly yellowish colour': treated with phosphate of soda and angostura bark, it would show 'a uniform yellow colour', which would then go through all the shades of green and finally turn black.

After that he demonstrated a new brand of washable wallpaper. Then he produced a second letter, 'written by a female in the vicinity of Bristol, whose country had not been ascertained'. It was addressed to the medical gentleman who had attended her, a Mr Mortimer of Bristol. 'The letters and characters are well-formed, some resembling the Chinese, others the Greek; and although the writing has been submitted to the examination of the best Oriental scholars, no one had been able to read it.' He promised to exhibit a facsimile of the letter 'for the public inspection' at the Kingston Pump Rooms.

Wilkinson was used to being consulted as an expert: he received letters from all over the world, he said, asking him to analyse soil from Pennsylvania and tea from China.

'He *went into* everything,' one contemporary recorded, 'nothing was above or beneath his grasp. It was amazing to hear him theorise upon every new invention and dogmatise upon every conceivable topic.' It was perhaps inevitable, therefore, that he should have wanted to go into Princess Caraboo. Elizabeth Worrall could not have been more flattered.

Wilkinson's own account of his meeting with the Princess tells the story of what happened more vividly than it could have been told even by the most malicious observer.

He retells the story of her first appearance at the cottage door, mentions her 'appearance and graceful manners' that had so captivated Mrs Worrall, but gives himself away when he comes to a physical description of her. It almost becomes a love-poem. He talks of her finely arched eyebrows, the pleasing colour of her cheeks, her sweet smile, her rather large mouth, her prominent and full lips, her beautifully white and regular teeth. 'Her manners are extremely graceful, her countenance surprisingly fascinating. Such is the general effect on all who behold her, that if before suspected as an impostor, the sight of her removes all doubt.'

The Princess apparently found his enthusiasm excessive. 'She is', Wilkinson reports, 'very cautious in her conduct with respect to gentlemen, never allows them to take hold of her hand, and even if their clothes should casually come into contact with hers, she retires from them.'

Her mode of diet, he says, seems to be Hindoostanic, and he is particularly interested in her knotted string. It is, he reminds his readers, without crediting Joseph Hager's *Elementary Characters of the Chinese*, the origin of the system used in the Chinese abacus and had developed into the sliding beads, or *suon puon*.

He describes how she writes the characters 'with great facility, from left to right', saying that one or two characters bear some resemblance to the Chinese, 'particularly the Chinese *cho*, a reed'. Other characters seem to him more like the Greek, especially the *iota* and the *omega*. She has been shown publications in Greek, Malay, Chinese, Sanskrit, Arabic and Persic, 'with all of which she seems unacquainted'.

Everyone in Bristol and Bath with any knowledge of the Far East has been consulted, but without success. Copies of the characters she has drawn have been sent to East India House, and even to Stamford Raffles himself, but he has been 'unable to decypher it'. Those at Oxford who had been shown examples of her language, he concedes, 'have without a moment's hesitation, pronounced it to be *Humbug*', but, Wilkinson goes on, dismissing Oxford with scorn, 'serious scholars have judged it to be imperfect Javanese, or possibly Sumatran'.

'From my own observation', the infatuated Doctor concludes, 'I have deemed her more resembling a Circassian: her countenance, her complexion and her manners favour such a supposition, and probably her appearance here may be connected with the Corsairs who have been hovering about our coast.'

The most intimate and exciting moment in his examination came when Elizabeth Worrall allowed him to push his fingers into the thick black hair on the back of the Princess' head and examine her scalp.

'I examined the part. It had been scarified' – this meant that cuts had been made, and that blood had been drawn off using some form of suction – 'but not according to the English mode of cupping, or to any European manner with which I am acquainted: the incisions are extremely regular, and apparently employed with the caustic, a mode of cupping adopted in the East.'

This was a major new clue, and confirmed her story of the operation to the back of her neck on board Tappa Boo's ship *en route* to the Cape. Combined with Dr Wilkinson's assurance that anyone seeing her could tell at once that she was genuine, her authenticity was now beyond doubt.

Wilkinson's judgement was crucial, and Samuel Worrall finally agreed to some announcement being made in the press. It is not clear how many visits Wilkinson paid to Knole, but he wrote to the *Bath Chronicle*, enclosing the report of his findings, and it appeared on Tuesday 2 June. He asked that the report should be published in as many provincial papers as possible throughout the British Isles, in the hope that someone reading it might be able to throw more light on the Princess' origins. He advises readers, as he advised members of the Bath Literary and Philosophical Society, to examine the copy of her handwriting in the Kingston Pump Rooms. He does not mention any admission charge.

He adds a postscript describing her sudden absence, the illness that had followed her return, and, apparently abandoning his earlier Circassian theory, says that her father was Chinese 'of considerable consequence in his own country' and that her mother was a Malay.

John Matthew Gutch was more than happy to reprint Dr Wilkinson's letter in *Felix Farley's Bristol Journal*. The cat, after all, was now out of the bag.

CHAPTER 8

THE DAUGHTER
OF THE SUN

PRINCESS CARABOO WAS now, thanks to Dr Wilkinson, a national figure. Provincial newspapers printed his report as he had asked, and within a week Mrs Worrall was getting letters from all over the British Isles offering new theories.

Another Scottish gentleman wrote from Edinburgh. He had 'carefully read the description given of her in various Scottish publications', and was particularly anxious to know more about her. He himself had been brought up among Circassians, and everything he read about her diet, manners, prayers on the tower, and even her caution with gentlemen, convinced him that she was Circassian. He thought that she would prove, like most Circassians, to be a Muslim.

He had read that Caraboo climbed on the roof to worship the sun, but he found it more probable that she was turning towards Mecca, 'under the impression, on the Prophet Mahomet's account, that the Author of all things on earth makes that spot his chief abode'.

On the other hand, he said, he had never met a Circassian woman who could write, and if they did

93

they would write from right to left rather than left to right. Nor had he ever met a Circassian woman who wore the kind of dress that Caraboo was wearing when she first appeared, and certainly not worsted stockings.

Her language, too, puzzled him. He began with an analysis of the word *Javasu*. *Java* in Circassian meant either the surface of a thing, or the second person imperative of the verb 'to drink'. *Su* meant 'water'. *Malay* was more difficult. *Mal* meant a sheep, but *ay*, both in Tartar and Circassian, was no more than an interjection, like 'Ah!'

Jessee Mandu was even more baffling. *Jessee* in Tartar meant 'owner', but he had never come across the word *Mandu*. *Caraboo* itself he found easier. *Cara* in Tartar meant either 'black' or the second person imperative of the verb 'to look', and *boo* meant 'this' or 'that'.

He admitted that names were of little use in identifying a Circassian, because they were usually made up of words taken from two or three languages, and often had no meaning at all.

He enclosed a few simple questions, written phonetically in English characters, which 'carefully read to her' might enable Mrs Worrall to discover her true nationality.

Mrs Worrall, he instructed, should pronounce the vowel *a* as in 'fat', *u* as in 'full', and the *g* always hard, even before 'e' or 'i'. *Adigivzar uptshera?* he translated as 'Do you understand Circassian?', *Uadiga?*, rather surprisingly as 'Are you a Circassian?' *Set etsh ukyka?* 'What land do you come from?', *Ui yader adigit?* 'Was your father a Circassian?'

Etsar setit? meant 'What was his name?', *Ui yaner adigit?* 'Was your mother a Circassian?', *Ui tschema etsar set?* 'What is the name of your country?', *Adigivzer uptshama, ege unjessa pesselthabema juap kuzat,* 'If you understand the Circassian language, give an answer to the words now spoken.' (The *u* in *kuzat,* he explained, should be pronounced to rhyme with 'urn'.)

She could also try Tartar. The vowel *a* was again to be pronounced as in 'fat', *oi* as in 'oil', *e* either long as in 'me', or short as in 'Eden', suggesting that Eden in those days was pronounced differently even in English, or possibly Scottish. The *g,* as in Circassian, was pronounced hard.

Nogoi tillen hellasenma? meant 'Do you understand the Tartar language?', *Nogi senma?* 'Are you a Tartar?', *Nè jerden shuckhansen?* (the *shuck* pronounced to rhyme with luck) 'From what land are you?', *Atang nogoi edema?* 'Was your father a Tartar?', *Ata ne ede?* 'What was his name?', *Anang nogoi peshy edema?* 'Was your mother a Tartar woman?', *Senung jerungnung ata neder?* 'What is the name of your country?', *Eger nogoi tillda bellzung, sorrahan Humher jumb ber,* 'If you understand the Tartar language, answer the questions asked you.'

Elizabeth Worrall's Scottish correspondent hoped that these would afford some degree of satisfaction. He would be surprised if she did not understand the language, as 'Alla Tallah' was definitely a Circassian word and one he was familiar with. He asked Mrs

Worrall to transcribe any answers she got from
Caraboo, and to send them to him, together with a
description of everything she was wearing.

Dr Wilkinson's letter was published on a Tuesday.
On the following Saturday, whether or not it was
out of sheer exasperation with the new flood of like-
minded amateur academics who descended on Knole
as a result, Princess Caraboo again disappeared.
Once again everything she had been given, from the
Malay *kriss* to the golden heart-shaped locket, was
left behind.

That evening she was spotted in Bath by a man
called Carpenter, who had just read Dr Wilkinson's
letter to the *Bath Chronicle*, and who immediately
sent a message to Dr Wilkinson's home in Burling-
ton Street. The Princess, he said, had arrived at the
Pack Horse Inn, a noisy and popular establishment
where the coaches stopped on the way to London.

Wilkinson got the message too late to come to the
Pack Horse that night, but arrived first thing the
next morning, and found her having breakfast with
the landlady. She saw him, was clearly badly shaken,
burst into tears, and hid her face in her handkerchief.
Rather shamefaced at such a reaction, Wilkinson
crept out again, found a messenger, and sent off an
urgent letter to Elizabeth Worrall. When he returned
the Princess had gone, and he set to work with his
usual scientific thoroughness to discover what had
happened.

The man who had driven her into Bath was still
there, and ready to answer the Doctor's questions.
How she had got from Knole into Bristol he could

not tell him: he had found her walking on the road between Bristol and Bath, and she had made it clear to him by signs that she would like a lift on his cart.

Dr Wilkinson asked him very specifically how she had reacted to him physically. Had he noticed a reluctance on the Princess' part to allow his clothes to brush against hers? The driver said he certainly had: she had even refused his hand when he offered to pull her up on to the cart, preferring to climb up unassisted. Dr Wilkinson was reassured.

Unable to communicate with her, the driver had taken her with him to the Pack Horse, where he had handed her over to the landlady.

Wilkinson now questioned the landlady. It seems the Princess had wanted tea. At Knole she always asked for *zee*, which would probably have got her what she wanted. Instead, perhaps because she found herself among strangers, she had asked for paper, and drew a picture of a tree. After a great deal of puzzling the landlady and the rapidly growing crowd of onlookers in the Pack Horse decided it was a tea tree. Princess Caraboo nodded, there was general delight, and she was brought her tea. She seemed, as usual, to have gone through her ritual of cleansing the cup.

Wilkinson then went out, with no clear idea where he might find her, to look for her in Bath. He found her eventually among the regular morning promenade of fashionable spa guests in the Circus. Dodging behind buildings so as not to alarm her, and risking his dignity as Secretary of the Philosophical and Literary Society, he trailed her as she strolled aimlessly up and down, and eventually followed her back to the Pack Horse.

Wilkinson then plucked up courage to approach her. She seemed less alarmed by him this time, and agreed to accompany him into the dining room, where he left her under the supervision of a woman staying in the inn.

By twelve noon, the news had spread that the famous Princess Caraboo was in Bath. The Pack Horse was doing a splendid trade, filled with inquisitive visitors. The Princess was in danger of being mobbed. Afraid, on the evidence of their last meeting at Knole, that she would be 'annoyed by many visitors', Wilkinson urged two ladies who were sitting with her to take her home with them. They were, he said in his second letter to the *Chronicle*, motivated by pure generosity, by 'those feelings which show in the most inestimable point of view the human mind'.

They may also have realized that she was the biggest draw in Bath.

They called a sedan chair and had her taken to the house they had rented for the season from Mrs Ogle in the fashionable centre of Bath, behind the Assembly Rooms in Russell Street.

There, in the drawing room on the first floor, Wilkinson said, the Princess immediately became happier and more relaxed. She smiled, seemed very grateful, and 'tried to explain to the ladies the customs of her country, by actions the most graceful, and by manners highly fascinating'.

It was there, in the drawing room in Bath, that

the Princess had to submit to the most trying test of her authenticity. Still convinced she understood English, one old gentleman pushed his chair close to hers and, whispering in her ear, said, 'You are the most beautiful creature I ever beheld! You are an angel.' As before, her face remained entirely impassive.

By the time Mrs Worrall got to Bath on the evening of Sunday 7 June, Caraboo was the centre of attention, with ladies of fashion curtseying to her, stroking her cheek in wonder at her beauty. One gentleman had already been so moved by her plight in exile that he had pledged five hundred pounds to pay for her journey home to Javasu, and several others had followed suit, throwing ten- and twenty-pound Bank of England notes – of more reliable value than Samuel Worrall's Tolzey banknotes – on the table beside her chair as part of a collection for her benefit.

What particularly delighted the ladies watching was the way she let them slip through her fingers and float to the floor like leaves, having no idea what they were.

Elizabeth Worrall came into the crowded room unannounced, and the Princess' confidence collapsed. She seemed stricken with remorse, threw herself at Elizabeth Worrall's feet sobbing, clung to her skirts, and then ran, still weeping, through the crowd, out of the door and down the stairs. It was in the parlour below, according to Wilkinson's account, that Princess Caraboo, gesturing through her tears and using the few words Elizabeth Worrall had become familiar with during their weeks together at Knole, confessed to something she had never mentioned before. She was homesick, and longed to return home, not only to her Chinese father, Jessee Mandu, whom she had mentioned so often before, but also to her husband and child.

Elizabeth Worrall was very moved, forgave her entirely for the anxiety she had caused them, and on Sunday night they drove back to Knole together.

Wilkinson, like Mrs Worrall, was more deeply convinced than ever of Caraboo's good character: her honesty in leaving Knole 'without a farthing in her pocket' seemed final proof. If he had any doubt, it was about the exact geographical whereabouts of Javasu, which he was now tempted to believe was an island off Japan.

On Monday morning the Princess came into Elizabeth Worrall's bedroom. For the first time, she locked the door behind her and Elizabeth Worrall sensed that some further confession was on its way. If it was, the Princess suppressed it, and the day passed as usual.

That same evening, a woman named Mrs Neale called on William Mortimer at his consulting rooms in Bridge Street in Bristol and told him a story so remarkable that he immediately got in his carriage and drove over to Knole.

By an odd coincidence, as he was leaving Mrs Worrall's drawing room, the Greek manservant showed in a young man from Westbury, the son of a wheelwright. He, like Mrs Neale, had read the story in the newspapers and had an equally surprising story to tell.

That night at supper Elizabeth Worrall's face betrayed no sign of what she had heard. She said goodnight to the Princess as affectionately as ever, and went to bed.

The next day, Tuesday 9 June, Wilkinson's second letter appeared in the *Bath Chronicle*, and Wilkinson himself left for London to visit the East India Company to make further enquiries, promising to raise more money from the directors for Caraboo's fare home. Another newspaper, the *Bath Herald*, took up her story, also campaigning for a relief fund.

Princess Caraboo, meanwhile, was driving into Bristol. Elizabeth Worrall had woken her that morning, explaining that she should put on her costume as they were going to the studio of Edward Bird for a final sitting.

In Bristol Elizabeth Worrall called to the driver that she had changed her mind. They were going instead to Bridge Street.

The two women arrived at Dr Mortimer's house and the Princess was shown upstairs to wait in his consulting room on the first floor. Mortimer then took Elizabeth Worrall into the parlour downstairs to meet Mrs Neale and her daughter.

They repeated the story they had told Dr Mortimer the night before. They had read Dr Wilkinson's letter, which had been reprinted in *Felix Farley's Bristol Journal*. Mrs Neale and her daughter kept a lodging house in Lewin's Mead, a busy thoroughfare in the middle of Bristol. In March of that year a girl, in her mid-twenties and answering Wilkinson's description, had come to share a room there with one of their regular lodgers, Eleanor Joseph.

She was intelligent and entertaining, had become a friend of Mrs Neale's daughter, and even went to church with them on Sundays. The girl was English, but amused herself, and them, by sometimes talking a made-up language of her own. On the last occasion they had seen her, at the beginning of April, she was wearing a turban exactly like that described by Dr Wilkinson.

Elizabeth Worrall herself then told them what she had heard at Knole from the wheelwright's son. He too had read Wilkinson's letter in the newspaper, and swore he had met Caraboo two days before she appeared in Almondsbury. She was wearing the same turban, and he believed she was Spanish. Her diet was certainly not 'Hindoostanic': she had eaten a steak with him at a public house and drunk a glass of rum and water.

Leaving Mrs Neale and her daughter downstairs, Elizabeth Worrall and Dr Mortimer returned to the consulting room. The Princess was anxious. She had heard the sound of voices below and sensed trouble.

Mortimer watched her as Elizabeth Worrall asked her, in plain English, to account for the stories she had just heard.

The Princess' first response was extremely confusing. She burst into tears and sobbed the words 'Caraboo Toddy Moddy' – Romany for Father and Mother – 'Irish'.

Elizabeth Worrall, herself near to tears, remained very calm, and asked her again if she would like her to bring Mrs Neale and her daughter upstairs to confront her.

The Princess shook her head, sobbing, and slid to the floor, hugging Elizabeth Worrall's knees. Speaking English with a strong North Devon accent, she begged Elizabeth Worrall to forgive her and not to send for her parents. Then, clinging even more tightly to her, she whispered, 'Do not cast me off!'

Mortimer asked her who she really was. She said her name was Mary Baker, born Mary Willcocks, and she was the daughter of a cobbler from Witheridge in Devon.

It was a remarkable moment. It was as if the Princess of Wales, at the height of her popularity, had suddenly been revealed to be a Cockney shop assistant playing the part for a lark. The *Bristol Mirror* compared it to one of those transformations in classical literature where a beautiful woman turns within seconds into a rock or a tree.

By one of those beautiful and mind-bewildering metamorphoses, one of those transmigrations, which is not surpassed by Ovid, or in any novel, ancient or modern, this eldest Daughter of the Sun, this Moon of Moons, this inhabitant of Sirius was in an instant 'fallen from her high estate', and changed to Mary Baker, of Witheridge, in Devonshire. *Sic transit gloria mundi* – so passes the glory of this world.

PART TWO

LEUMAS LLARROW ERIUQSE

Elizabeth Worrall was dumbfounded. All her kindness in trying to understand and look after a princess in exile had been wasted on a fraud who had understood every word she had said from the moment she first entered the house.

She had loved the girl, and the girl had responded by playing like a much-loved and much-indulged child. She played Caraboo to her heart's content: Caraboo the hunter with bow and arrow, Caraboo fighting with a sword and dagger, Caraboo wailing her prayers at the top of the tower. And the more she played the more she was betraying the woman who loved her.

Now Elizabeth Worrall realized it. The betrayal was public, she would be laughed at all over Bristol, and thanks to Wilkinson's circulation of his letters to local newspapers elsewhere, all over the British Isles. Her husband, Samuel Worrall, would be discredited as a Justice of the Peace, as Town Clerk, as the shrewd trustee of other people's money at the Tolzey Bank.

But the emotion that was uppermost in everyone else's mind who heard the story was wonder at how she had done it. She appeared to be a rather simple-minded country girl, and entirely uneducated.

Mortimer immediately began questioning her. He asked her how she had learned about the East. When she got over her tears she said she had worked for four months as a children's nurse with a European family in Bombay. The same family had later taken her to 'the Isle of France', though whether she meant to Martinique or the part of France of that name was not clear.

It was Mary Baker's bad luck that William Mortimer happened to have lived in Bombay. He asked her two or three questions about the city. From her answers it was immediately clear that she had never been there.

If Elizabeth Worrall still felt any compassion for her at all, it must have been exhausted at that moment. Then a servant came upstairs and announced a visitor. It was John Matthew Gutch. Whether William Mortimer had alerted him, or whether rumours had reached him up the hill in Small Street, he was determined to hear the story.

The girl seemed to trust him. Like many authors before and since she was never entirely certain where fact ended and where fiction began, but she started to tell the nearest she knew to the truth. It was a story a great deal stranger than the tale of Princess Caraboo, and it often seemed more like a Romantic novel than documentary reality, but she had two powerful inducements to stop telling lies. The first was John Matthew Gutch's anxiety as a journalist to have accurate corroboration of every fact. The second was an astonishingly generous offer, once she had heard the general outline of the girl's story, from Elizabeth Worrall.

As she listened to her account, spoken in broad Devon, and lit with odd little comic observations and moments she remembered with great clarity, all Elizabeth Worrall's original instincts of love and concern for a lost daughter were rekindled. She could not bear to take her back to Knole, but if her past life was as blameless as she said it was and John Matthew Gutch could produce evidence to prove it, Elizabeth Worrall promised not only to spare her any severe punishment, but to pay her fare to the place she said she dreamed of going, which was not Javasu, but America.

Samuel and Elizabeth Worrall were both anxious to get out of the affair with whatever dignity remained to them, and Mary Baker in America would be less of an embarrassment to them than Mary Baker in Bristol. But it was still, after the massive practical joke she had played on them, very magnanimous.

How she had done it was one question: the other was why, and John Matthew Gutch set out to discover the answers to both.

Among the first hundred and forty-four pages of Coleridge's *Biographia Literaria* that Gutch had first proof-read with pride and more recently had turned over gloomily in the knowledge that Coleridge had double-crossed him and was taking the book to another printer, there is a particularly startling passage of literary criticism. Coleridge is talking about fantasy rather than imagination, about the sort of masturbatory day-dreams that then, as now, passed for romantic fiction.

> Nine-tenths of the reading of the reading public is a pass-time, or rather a *kill-time*. Call it rather a beggarly day-dreaming, during which the mind of the dreamer furnishes for himself nothing but laziness, and a little mawkish sensibility; while the whole *material* and imagery of the doze is supplied *ab extra* [from outside] by a sort of mental *camera obscura* manufactured at the printing office, which *pro tempora* [for the time being] fixes, reflects and transmits the moving phantasms of one man's delirium, so as to people the barrenness of an hundred other brains afflicted with the same trance or suspense of all common sense and all definite purpose.

The romantic novelist, Coleridge writes, has 'the power of reconciling the two contrary yet co-existing propensities of human nature; indulgence of sloth, and hatred of vacancy'. In the end, he says, reading novels can be put in the same category as

> gaming, swinging or swaying on a chair or gate; spitting over a bridge; smoking; snuff-taking; tête-à-tête quarrels at dinner between husband and wife; conning word by word all the advertisements of the daily advertiser in a public house on a rainy day and etc. etc.

In cross-questioning Mary Baker, and in checking her statements against evidence he collected from everyone he could find who had ever known her,

Gutch was constantly reining in her imagination. He was also himself resisting the temptation to which Elizabeth Worrall and so many of her gentlemen friends had yielded in the preceding weeks, of 'sharing the moving phantasms of her delirium'.

But he loved the Romantic poets, and it was inevitable that he would fall in love with her. For all his journalist's logic and the contempt he and Coleridge had for 'phantasy', he was ultimately to surrender altogether to the power of her imagination, born as it was of terrible suffering.

There is something very touching about Gutch's sudden infatuation with Mary Baker. Constantly in her company at Mortimer's house in Bridge Street, listening to her story, questioning her about names and details, sharing her jokes, he became intoxicated by her. He broke the rules of twenty years' experience as a printer, and the evidence is still there in the bound volumes of *Felix Farley's Bristol Journal*, printed in narrow grey columns on the thick hand-made paper, preserved in the Central Library in Bristol. He splashes Mary's Javasu handwriting and 'Oriental characters' in a great white window at the top of the page, spread across three columns. Except for advertisements no paper of that date carries illustrations of any kind: the boldest headline is one column wide. No newspaper had ever looked like that before.

The account underneath is printed in a single fat column, a space always previously occupied by three narrow ones. Gutch knew he had a good story, but he was also in the grip of an excitement he was unable to control.

CARABOO.

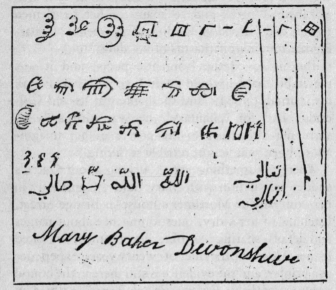

In the white window at the top of the page, readers could examine for the first time what Wilkinson and the Worralls and all the amateur academics had been poring over with such fascination for the last ten weeks.

'We present our readers', Gutch writes in *Felix Farley's Bristol Journal*, 'with a fac-simile of the characters which this young female writes with the greatest facility, and with which more than one of the *cognoscenti* was puzzled. Some of the more lettered readers may perceive, in the scrawl of this ingenious impostor, a few perfectly formed and conjoined Arabic characters.'

His readers, he said, would be hard put to decide which was more surprising: the ingenuity of the girl, or the credulity of the spectators. Gutch provided a brief sketch of her life, and promised a fuller account as soon as he collected more evidence. In the meantime, despite reports in other newspapers that she was being kept away from the public gaze somewhere outside Bristol, she stayed for the next two weeks with William Mortimer in Bridge Street, and seems to have become as attached to Mrs Mortimer as she was to Elizabeth Worrall.

As at Knole, she received in addition to Gutch a great many visitors: Elizabeth Worrall sent clergymen to speak to her about her soul, none of whom were able to produce any signs of repentance or regret for what she had done. But there were a great many others. 'Natives and foreigners, linguists, painters, craniologists and gypsies. Some pitied her, some condemned her, and others upheld her.' Most of them, like Gutch, were wild about her.

One other journalist, Harry Bonner of the *Bristol Mirror*, also succeeded in interviewing her, and even managed to scoop Gutch by getting hold of her original letter of thanks to Mortimer that had started all the trouble, and which Dr Wilkinson had pinned up in the Kingston Pump Rooms. He reprinted it in facsimile, together with her story, which later appeared as a single-page broadsheet. It is much slighter than Gutch's account, but more open and direct, suggesting that he brought out an irresponsible side of Mary that Gutch, working to clear her name for Elizabeth Worrall, may have chosen to overlook.

The ship in which Elizabeth Worrall promised Mary she could sail to America, a brig called the *Robert and Ann*, was already moored at the quay a few hundred yards from Bridge Street. It was due to sail on 25 June, and during that fortnight of waiting, whatever evidence John Matthew Gutch discovered, Mary Baker remained entirely confident and in very high spirits.

Thomas Lawrence painted her in crayon, chalk and pencil on grey paper: the portrait last appeared for sale in 1925, and is described as 'showing necklace, and feathers in headdress, face and lips heightened in colour'. Another of the painters who came was Nathan Branwhite. He drew her in the black turban and the black dress with the high muslin collar she was wearing when she first appeared in Almondsbury. Branwhite chose particularly to draw people who had tangled with authority, like Coleridge's friend John Thelwall, imprisoned for his republican views some years before, and James Acland, publisher of a radical paper called *The Bristolian* who went to prison for libellous attacks on the Corporation. He obviously admired Mary's daring.

Mary clearly responded to Branwhite's admiration. In his original drawing, in soft pencil on a small sheet of cartridge paper about six inches by four, the transformation is amazing. All the dreamy, vacant, trance-like mood of Edward Bird's watercolour portrait has gone. She is grinning like a mischievous schoolgirl, showing her beautiful white teeth, and looking the artist straight in the eye. Her own black eyes are sparkling in triumph.

Despite the threat of Gutch turning up evidence that would land her in gaol, Mary had every reason to grin. She was famous, and even at a time of rigid class distinctions, when the Government was exercising every effort to keep the lower orders in their place, nobody in Bristol criticized Mary Baker. Her escapade was seen as a wonderful joke, and every newspaper in Bristol joined in. It was celebrated largely in humorous verse, but behind the rhymes and the poetical tricks there is a clear pattern of public reaction to the story.

The *Bath Herald* produced a poem within hours of the story breaking. For them Princess Caraboo was a far-fetched Romantic fantasy, that came from the realm of fairies and witches or of early nineteenth-century science fiction.

> OH! aid me, ye spirits of wonder! who soar
> In realms of Romance where none ventur'd
>   before . . .
> Who ride upon broom-sticks, intent to deceive
> All those who appear *pre-disposed* to believe,
> And softly repeat from your home in the spheres
> *Incredible* stories to *credulous* ears;
> With everything marvellous, everything new,
> We'll trace a description of Miss CARABOO.

The writer then goes on to recall Joanna Southcott, also from Devonshire, who claimed to be a prophet directly inspired by God, and whose mysterious

Box, containing a few scraps of indecipherable gibberish, continued to be news for more than a century and a half after her death.

Southcott amazed her followers in 1814 by announcing, at the age of sixty-four, that she was pregnant and would give birth to a son who would be called the Shiloh. A certain Dr Richard Reece confirmed the old lady's pregnancy, and she lay in bed for some months with her disciples round her, eating a great deal, demanding fruit that was out of season, and on one occasion consuming a hundred and sixty heads of asparagus. She eventually admitted that the pregnancy appeared to have been a delusion, and died, but her followers' belief remained unshaken. Even when her body had begun to rot they insisted on a last examination, smoking pipes of strong tobacco to make their job less unpleasant. Eventually even they had to concede that there was no sign of any foetus.

> Though all hope of their virgin accouchement is o'er
> They shall meet with the smile of derision no more;
> *Their* wonders were weak, *their* credulity small –
> Caraboo was engendered from nothing at all!
> And where did she come from? And who can she be?
> Did she fall from the sky? Did she rise from the sea?

Attention then turns to Charles Hummings Wilkinson. The news broke on Tuesday 9 June, with Wilkinson still on his way to London to keep his appointment with the East India Company. He immediately became the lightning conductor, deflecting a lot of ridicule from the Worralls,

deservedly taking the several million volts of deri-
sion that crackled down, and was duly deafened by
the thunderous roar of laughter that followed.

No one could have served better as the victim
of the hoax. He had deliberately set himself up as
the universally respected expert on every subject
under the sun, was always anxious to show off his
knowledge in letters to the newspapers, advertising
gas or promoting new products at his lectures in
Bath, and of all Caraboo's gentlemen admirers he
was the one who had most transparently given way
to lust.

> Did she spring upon earth in a stream of *gas-light*?
> Did some philosophic analysis draw
> Her component degrees from some *hot-water spa*?
> Did some chemical process occasion her birth?
> Did *galvanic* experiments bring her on earth?

Less innocent hoaxers might themselves have
been ridiculed. In Mary Baker's case all the papers
agreed that it was the victims themselves who were
at fault for being so gullible.

> Astronomers sage may exhibit her soon
> As daughter-in-law to the man in the moon
> Or declare that her visits account for the rain
> Which happened last year and may happen again
> That she *may* be connected with corsairs; all these
> And as many more *possible things* as you please
> In what hand does she write? In what tongue does
>   she speak?
> Is it Arabic, Persian, Egyptian or Greek?

But even the *Bath Herald* sensed the excitement of those who first examined her:

> She then wore no ear-rings, tho' still may be seen
> The holes in her ears where her ear-rings have been;
> Leather shoes on her feet; a black shawl round her
>   hair
> And of black worsted stockings an elegant pair;
> Her gown was *black-stuff*, and my readers may
>   guess,
> If her *story* contains as much *stuff* as her *dress*.
> Of the fam'd Indian Jugglers we all must have
>   heard
> Who to gain a subsistence would swallow a sword;
> But men (without proof) who believe tales like
>   these,
> Would undoubtedly *swallow* whatever you please.

And they ended by conceding that if they had been in Wilkinson's shoes they might well have done the same.

> Even those, who have doubted the truth of her
>   tale . . .
> Have forgotten their doubts when they look's in
>   her face
> *I* never have seen her; but if when I see
> The truth of her tale is apparent to me,
> I will cancel these lines, and most gladly rehearse
> Her *swimming* and *fencing* in beautiful verse . . .

The *Bristol Mercury* printed a poem nearly ten days later, and during that time it was obvious other

more practical questions were being asked by gentlemen in Bristol. Was it possible that such a pretty girl
could be without a lover? And in any case, how
could she have carried it off without a man to
mastermind the hoax? It was dedicated to 'Molly'
Baker.

> O Molly, what a wag thou art –
> So *effectually* to play the part
> Of wandering, friendless Caraboo,
> Bespeaks a talent few could boast
> Ev'n from juggling India's coast –
> But prithee, tell me – can it ALL *be true*?
> Wert thou with ALL the men so shy,
> As ev'n thy beauteous hand deny
> In common salutation?
> Was there no tender *tête-à-tête*,
> Thy *admirers* thus to fascinate,
> Who puff'd thy beauty through the nation?
> Thy sloe-black eyes, and teeth so white,
> (By nature form'd to charm or bite)
> With lady-airs in plenty –
> Like opiates the senses lull'd
> Of reason and of vision *gull'd*
> Th'all-knowing *Cognoscenti*
> When to the house-top prone to stray,
> And would'st to ALLA–TALLAH pray,
> Hadst thou no HIGH PRIEST near thee?
> I mean not that imperious sun
> Of reckless Juggernaut, but one
> Well *pleas'd to assist* and hear thee?

It was a question that obviously occurred again and again to Gutch as he sat interrogating her in the house by the river in Bridge Street. It tantalized him, and he was never able to answer it. But the *Mercury*, like the rest of Bristol, was prepared to forget about the mysterious lover when they thought about her swimming naked in the lake at Knole.

> But where did'st learn (for Heaven's sake),
> To *swim* and *dive* like duck or drake,
> When water-dogs pursue?
> And when for *pure* ablution 'quipp'd
> *Lurk'd* there (as when Godiva stripp'd)
> No *Peeping Tom* – or *wanton Makratoo*?

The writer ends by cursing Mrs Neale for denouncing her, by imagining Wilkinson's rage at realizing he had been duped, and by prophesying a great future for her on the stage.

> Plague on that *meddling tell-tale* NEALE
> Eager thy *hist'ry to reveal*
> And *mar* the pleasing fable –
> Too sudden came the *denouement*
> Which proves thou art from *down-along*
> Where dumplings grace each table.
> 'Drat her *pug nose*, and *treacherous eyes*,
> *Deceitful wretch!*' the Doctor cries,
> (No more inclin'd to flattery)
> 'When next I meet her (spite of groans)
> I'll rive her muscles, split her bones
> With my *Galvanic Battery!*'

But heed him not – for (on my soul)
Whether at Bristol, Bath, or Knole,
I admir'd thy Caraboo.
Such *self-possession* at command
The *bye-play* great – th'*illusion* grand
In truth – *t'was everything but* TRUE.
Then Molly, take a friend's advice,
(To make thy fortune in a trice)
All wand'ring gypsy tricks resign –
Fly to *thy proper forte* – the STAGE:
Where thou in this half-mimic age
Princess of Actors, woulds't unrivalled shine!!!

It was a thought that Mary turned over in her
mind more than once as she waited in Bridge Street
for news of her future.

Samuel Worrall himself, slightly disguised since
he was still Town Clerk, figures largely in the *Bristol
Mirror*'s parody of its racing page, 'Sporting Intelligence Extra'.

Caraboo is entered to run for the Knole Plate. She
is thought by all who have seen her to be the
cleverest mare in this part of the country . . . She is
5 feet 2, and rising 26. Caraboo's pedigree is war-
ranted to be true *Circassian*; got by the *Chinese
Corsair*, JESSUE MANDUE, out of a Devonshire
Gypsey; own sister to FORTUNE TELLER. She has been
lately in famous training (about a mile from
Almondsbury) at the mews of LEUMAS LLARROW
Eriuqse, many years well known as a keen Glouces-
tershire *Sportsman*, and an excellent *Judge* – of horse-
flesh!

There are then a lot of complicated puns about her diet, her manner of greeting visitors, her swimming in the lake – 'to the astonishment of the stable-boys' – and a reference to the operation scars uncovered by Wilkinson on the back of her head: 'how Caraboo ever came to Submit to be *hogged* in the *mane* and *fired*, is most surprising'. Wilkinson is tipped as likely to be 'her rider' – 'one JUSTEE, a famous Jockey from Bath', and there is a final reference to a form book called *Wilkinson's Humbugiana*. Should there be disputes after the race they will be referred to the Town Clerk.

How she had carried off the hoax and why she had done it was still a mystery, though Gutch was already making some remarkable discoveries, but she liked the idea of becoming an actress: 'she more than once expressed the wish that the tale might be dramatised: and nothing, she said, would have given her greater pleasure than to have acted the part of CARABOO!!'

She was certainly treated like an actress, and a successful one. As well as Gutch and the 'natives and foreigners, linguists, painters, craniologists, and gypsies', various privileged visitors were allowed to see her, including the two Far Eastern experts, Sir Gore Ouseley and Sir George Thomas Staunton, and two aristocrats, the most distinguished guests listed by the newspapers to be staying in Bath at the time: the Earl of Cork, a would-be literary Irish peer ridiculed by Coleridge as the 'Earl of Bottle', and Lord Salisbury.

Salisbury christened her 'The Caraboo', as if she

was a great actress or opera singer, and all of them roared with laughter at the discomfiture of the Worralls and hooted at the thought of Dr Wilkinson.

Then a week before she was due to sail to America, with all the evidence collected by Gutch indicating that what she had told him was true, a story appeared in a newspaper in Exeter.

Exeter, 18 June – In the House List of Prisoners, Summer Sessions 1814, at the Castle of Exeter, a MARY ANN BAKER of the Parish of Witheridge, then aged twenty-one (whose black eyes, arched eyebrows, white teeth, sweet smile &c &c are recollected to bear a striking similitude with the bewitching features of CARRABOO, so *exquisitely* described by DR WILKINSON) was tried, convicted, and sentenced to six months imprisonment, for stealing a piece of cloth. A young man, (her sweetheart) the receiver of the stolen goods, was tried at the same time, and transported for 14 years.

It seemed that the *Robert and Ann* would sail without her. Elizabeth Worrall was again disillusioned. Mary had lied before. The habit of lying, as Dr Whately of Oxford who had examined the Caraboo handwriting wryly observed, was not something like measles that you could only catch once. Gutch questioned the staff of the *Bristol Mirror* who had reprinted the story, and enquiries were made in Exeter to confirm that the story was true.

The weather during the days of waiting was unbearably hot, with temperatures of over a hundred in the shade: the air was breathless and horses were falling down dead on the roads.

Then the news came from Exeter. It was the wrong Mary Baker. In *Flindell's Western Luminary* of July 1814, it was true, there was a report of a girl called Mary Ann Baker stealing 'a piece of linsey, some dowlas' – calico – 'and bombazeen' from her master, Elias Baker, a farmer near Axminster. The records of the Summer Quarter Sessions at the Devon County Court showed that the theft was actually of a pair of breeches belonging to Charles Baker, five yards of woollen cloth, a yard of black bombazeen, a quarter of a yard of silk, and five small pieces of calico belonging to Elias Baker.

Joan Baker, Elias Baker's wife, was also present in court, and with such a clan of Bakers involved, and no reference in the papers to the accused Mary Ann Baker coming from Witheridge, it seemed safe to say that it was a case of mistaken identity.

Mary was free to go to America. With that the clouds opened. Hailstones the size of golf balls smashed greenhouses all across the West Country, sewage rose from the flooded drains in Bath and burst through the back doors of terraced houses, cascading down the front doorsteps and into the street. On Sunday 28 June 1817, in pouring rain, the Mortimers took Mary down to the quay and put her on board the *Robert and Ann* bound for Philadelphia.

To avoid publicity, Mary's passage was booked in her mother's maiden name of Burgess. On Elizabeth Worrall's instructions she was put in the care of three maiden ladies, Jane Andrews, Ann Lamb and

Sarah Hinchcliff, on their way to teach at a new school for girls in Nazareth, Pennsylvania, recently started by a Revd. Mr Steinhauer who had spent three years in Bath and may, coincidentally, have been a friend of Dr Wilkinson. They were to find her work with a 'pious family' in Philadelphia, and if she behaved herself Elizabeth Worrall arranged that she should be given money there.

The women were Moravians, an austere Protestant sect, originally from Germany but now firmly established in Bristol, much admired by John Wesley and the early Methodists. They were best known for their great courage in the face of death. John Wesley crossed the Atlantic with some Moravians a hundred years earlier. Their ship had been struck by mountainous waves, the mast broke, they seemed about to drown, and the Moravians joined hands and sang. They told Wesley they believed they were already 'in God', and that death would only be a happy release into paradise.

Such passionate fundamentalists seemed to Elizabeth Worrall likely to succeed where the clergymen she sent to Bridge Street had failed: the girl, she was sure, would realize how wicked she had been and determine to lead a more sober life.

The *Robert and Ann* was relatively new, registered at North Shields in 1814, but it was primarily a merchant ship carrying nearly two hundred tons of cargo: pig-iron, Bristol glass bottles, clay pipes, tin plates, sixteen casks of pickled whiting, three kegs of tripe, and eleven baskets of cheese.

The three Moravian sisters had the best cabin. In

addition to eleven other cabin passengers, including two families, there were eight who had to travel steerage in the hold. Of those, Mary was the only woman. She told Gutch she intended to come back from America 'with her coach and four horses', but he dismissed it. She was a 'poor, visionary, deluded girl'.

The prospects, even for the voyage, were not promising. The weather showed no sign of improving, and a ship off the coast of North Devon carrying gunpowder had been struck by lightning.

Elizabeth Worrall did not go to the quay to see her off, but the Mortimers sent her a letter, or something resembling a letter, that Mary Baker had written the day before she sailed. It did not provide much comfort. Gutch copied it out, and added it to the growing collection of correspondence and transcriptions of interviews that would make up his story of Princess Caraboo.

The *Robert and Ann* sailed, and that seemed to be the end of the story. Except for a rumour, recorded by Gutch, that when the *Robert and Ann* reached the Bristol Channel, still in driving rain, Mary Baker looked back at Knole, standing in the distance on its green hill at the end of the long avenue of yew trees, and wept.

CHAPTER 10

A BRIDE FOR
BONAPARTE

Princess Caraboo had gone, but for weeks afterwards Bristol continued to celebrate her memory.

There were other distractions and excitements. Mr Bish's Lottery, which had been advertised all through the spring and early summer with prizes of £30,000, was finally drawn, with a winning payment of £13,057. It was so successful, according to Mr Bish, that he was asking permission to organize another.

At the end of May, Mr Bastard, after a dubious first count, had been elected as Member of Parliament for Devon with 679 votes to his opponent's 490, and had then 'come forward and made a most impressive speech, which was received with the warmest acclamation by several thousand persons, with torrents of applause'.

A report from Windsor signed by George the Third's doctors suggested that his mental health was no better, but there was a Grand Display of Chinese Fireworks in Bath to celebrate his birthday.

A Royal Salute of Maroons, A Boreal Wheel, a Grand Light of Grecian Fire, two snake wheels with a Grand Russian Cross, Gold and Silver Fire, concluding with TWO LARGE MOSAIC PIECES with the Crown and Initials and a WATERLOO BOMBSHELL, Chests of Artillery etc. Transparencies of Naval Columns, Exhibition of the Cascade, Vocal and Instrumental Music.

At the same time real artillery was being used in anger by British troops on British citizens. The Dragoons fired into barricaded farm cottages outside Ely, killing two men and taking over a hundred prisoners. In Norwich, according to Gutch in *Felix Farley*, 'the Dragoon Guards executed their duty with moderation, but with vigour, and, in dispersing the rioters, allowed no obstacle to stand in their way. They galloped up steep steps, rode over posts and rails and followed up the ill-disposed wherever they thought themselves most secure.'

Many Bristolians were more upset by news from the sugar plantations in Barbados. Rumours that the Government in London was considering the abolition of slavery had reached the slaves, but had been denied by their owners. The slaves rose, burning the sugar cane. 'About two thousand of the Negroes have been killed, but as they made little or no resistance to the troops, the loss of the latter has been 2 or 3 men. The Insurgents are not composed of Negroes only, a *white man* was executed yesterday. Happily they are now quieted, and tranquility is said to be quite restored.' One plantation owner, a native of Bristol, wrote to *Felix Farley* blaming the slaves' 'Philanthropic Friends in Parliament', and predicting the ruin of the West Indies.

Mary Baker might seem to have been lucky to get away when she did, but Bristol was turning her into a heroine. Nearly a fortnight after her departure the *Bristol Mirror* remembered Princess Caraboo with a long parody of Sir Walter Scott's *Lochinvar*, and a slightly different version of the story. The 'club of *Bas-Bleu*', Elizabeth Worrall and her would-be intellectual bluestocking friends, are blamed directly for imagining her to be a princess, and Knole, or 'Worralby Hall', becomes a wild hubbub of language experts and mad phrenologists, with Wilkinson fencing with her rather than Samuel Worrall, and taking most of the blame as ring-leader.

It looks as though Samuel Worrall, by the end of June, was trying to wriggle out of the limelight, telling his cronies at the Exchange that he had always been the cautious sceptic, insisting on more proof from the East India Company and finally bringing the hoax to an end single-handed. But the poem also reflects a growing lack of respect for him as Town Clerk.

O young Caraboo is come out of the West
In frenchified tatters the damsel is drest
But, save one pair of worsted, she stockings had
    none,
And she walk'd half unshod, and she walk'd all
    alone
But how to bamboozle the doxy well knew –

There never was gypsey like young Caraboo
She staid not for brake, and she stopp'd not for
   stone
She swam in the Avon where ford there was none
But when she alighted at Worralby gate
The Dame and the Doctor receiv'd her in state
No longer a gypsey, the club of *Bas-Bleu*
To a princess converted the young Caraboo.
So boldly she enter'd the Worralby Hall,
Amidst linguists, skull-feelers, blue-stockings and
   all;
Then spoke the sage doctor, profoundly absurd
(But the sly Caraboo utter'd never a word)
'Art thou sprung from the Moon, or from far
   Javasu,
Or a mermaid just landed, thou bright Caraboo?'
To these questions sagacious she answer denied –
Though hard was the struggle her laughter to
   hide –
'But, since they decree me these titles so fine
I'll be silent, eat curry, and touch not their wine;
With this imposition I've nothing to do
These are fools ready made' thought the young
   Caraboo.
She looked at a pigeon, the dame caught it up;
Caraboo had a mind on the pigeon to sup
She look'd down to titter, she look'd up to sigh
With the bird in her hand, and the spit in her eye
She dress'd it, she ate it, she call'd it Rampoo –
'This proves', swore the Doctor, 'she's Queen
   Caraboo.'

When she fenc'd with the Doctor, so queer her
  grimace,
Sure never a hall such a galliard did grace
But her Host seem'd to fret (tho' the Doctor did
  fume,
Should any to question her titles presume)
And 'twas currently whisper'd, the best they could
  do,
Was to send up to London the young Caraboo
The hint was enough; as it dropped on her ear
It ruin'd her hopes, it awaken'd her fear;
So light to the Quay the fair damsel she ran
'Oh take me, dear Captain, away if you can!'
She's aboard! She is gone! 'Farewell Doctor
  Rampoo
They'll have ships swift that follow', said young
  Caraboo.
There was bustling 'mong dames of the Worralby
  clan
The Blue-stocking Junto they rode and they ran
There was racing and chasing from Bath to the Sea
But the lost Queen of Javasu ne'er more did they
  see
What a hoax on the Doctor, and club of *Bas-bleu*!
Have ye e'er heard of gypsey like young Caraboo?

With the political climate changing so fast, the
idea was beginning to sink in that the joke was not
simply at the expense of Dr Wilkinson, Elizabeth
Worrall and the bluestockings, but of the entire
comfortable ruling class, and at the end of July a

satirical letter appeared in the *Bristol Journal*, 'found in our Box at the end of last week', written in a broad mock-Devon accent in the style of a comic straw-chewing rustic.

Mr Printer, Sir,

Heering so much about Scarrobo, who proves to be amary wilcox, of withridge, in Devon shire, I my self being a native Near withridge knows the name of wilcox well; and, the other Day, I meet with a Native of withridge, who gives a full account of Mary wilcox, and knows her from a Child, and her Carictor agrees very well with your Statement in your last weeks paper . . .

I must confess it diverts me to think that one Comming out of Devonshire, where is Record so many Dupes and Flatts [the current word for an idiot] should Make Dupes of so many of the larned and wise.

I think, Mr printer, you Might well Stile her the withridge tuff, as that being a Nick Name as the Neighbouring parishes Calls the withridge people; and I also think that the Devonshire people ought to Commend her verry much, for I think she has fully Redeemed thier Carictor, that one of thier Menest and Eletarate beings, brought up in the feilds in all kinds of Drugrey, Should be so art full as to Deceive the most Discreet, and amongst the quality of the first Rank should pass for a foreign princess; an how She must laugh within her Self to See what homage She had paid her.

If such Craftyness as this Springs up from the Dunghill, what will their pruned gardens yeild?

Pleas to tell them in futer to put no more tricks on the west Countrey and Devonshire, but let them put on their Cap of knowledge and there Spericles and Consider and Desirn there own weakness and folley; for we have seen of late many instancences of Craftyness and impostrey Carried on and maintaind in the greatest splender, and upholded by the quality, when a poor tradesman is, that has Stuided his artisem to Earn an honnest peny, is Neglected and thought Not good Enough to Come in thier presence or to Speak to them; but Mary wilcox was Crafty Enough to give them plenty of Chatt and save her own speech.

So, Mr printer, I shall Conclude this Epicle, and leave it to your consideration whither any part of this is worth your Notice; and I was liken to have forgot to tell you the mening of a withridge tuff; it arises from asort of Cakes as they youst to make there and sell at there Neighbouring fairs and Revels, which looks very well, but so tuff thy would almost Chucke [choke] one to Eat them; and further more the Jock Runs this, if thy went from home to astrange place, thy would make fast one of these Cakes to the Door post [the image seems to be a very gummy dough that could be pulled out like elastic] and lead them selves by it, like a string or a guide. So much for the withridge tuff.

Your Most obedant & etc. Z. W.

Gutch had by now collected all the material he needed and began printing his book in Small Street. At the beginning of August he announced it in *Felix Farley*. 'CARABOO An Authentic Narrative of the Adventures of this singular impostor. A whole length Portrait of Caraboo, in the costume she described herself to be dressed as Princess of Javasu, was taken by Mr Bird R.A. and is engraving by Meyer. An admirable likeness also, sketched by Mr Branwhite and engraved by the artist, will accompany the publication.'

Gutch was then held up by the same kind of publishing troubles he had had with Coleridge. The text was printed, but there were delays with the engravings. Nathan Branwhite was engraving his own drawing and delivered on time, but Edward Bird was notoriously touchy and appears to have been dissatisfied with Meyer's engraving of his water-colour. Gutch announced a postponement, promising the book 'as soon as the accompanying engravings can be completed'.

Finally, on 23 August, with the Bird engraving pasted in as a separate folding sheet in every copy, the book was published, and officially announced in *Felix Farley*: 'CARABOO – price 5s. A NARRATIVE of a SINGULAR IMPOSITION practised upon the Benevolence of a Lady residing in the vicinity of the city of Bristol, by a young woman of the name of Mary Willcocks, *alias* Baker, *alias* Bakerstehndt, *alias* Caraboo, Princess of Javasu. Illustrated with TWO PORTRAITS, engraved from Drawings by E. BIRD Esq. R.A. and MR BRANWHITE. *Qui vult decepi decipiatur*'

[He who wishes to be deceived will be deceived]
'Printed by J. M. Gutch, 15 Small-street, Bristol;
and published by Baldwin, Craddock and Joy, Pater-
noster Row, London, and sold by all Booksellers in
Bristol, Bath and Cheltenham.'

It sold extremely well: less than twenty copies
remained in Gutch's library when it was put up for
sale thirty years later, and the book can still be found
today in libraries all over the world.

But memories of Caraboo were beginning to fade.
Another impostor appeared, this time asking for free
accommodation at the Swan Inn at Tewkesbury, 'a
well-dressed man on horseback, representing himself as Sir U. Burgh, aid de camp to the Duke of
Wellington and announcing that it was the Duke's
intention to honour the Corporation of Tewkesbury
with a visit on Monday next'.

Like Princess Caraboo, he was undone by the
newspapers. The landlord of the Swan had read
about him: he had hired a horse in Bristol and tried
the same trick some days earlier at the White Lion in
Upton. His real name was Webster, and he finished
up in Worcester Gaol.

It certainly refreshed memories of Caraboo, when
a remarkable story appeared in *Felix Farley* in the
middle of September. Even with the knowledge that
Gutch's *Singular Imposition* had been published two
weeks before and that the story appears directly
under an advertisement for the book, few people can
have been taken in: not, at least, if they read the
introduction. It was always omitted by those who
later reprinted the story as gospel truth.

It is headed 'LATEST INTELLIGENCE – Felix Farley's Journal Office – Ten o'clock Friday Evening. Extracted from the London Papers, just received. BUONAPARTE and CARABOO. (State Paper and Original Intelligence Manufactory).'

There is then a long tongue-in-cheek preamble about the 'Manufacture' of State Papers in terms of manufacturing wallpapers or fly-papers, casting doubt on official documents released by Vienna and Paris, and, in particular, on a recently leaked letter from the Pope to the Emperor of Russia.

It goes on:

The Editor of this Journal is most truly happy in being enabled, through the medium of an Amanuensis employed in this State Paper Office, to communicate the following original Intelligence relative to no less a person than the celebrated Female Impostor CARABOO! By *Alla-Tallah* it is true, the girl has got an introduction to Buonaparte himself!!

A letter from Sir Hudson Lowe, lately received from St Helena, forms at present the leading topic of conversation in the higher circles. It states, that on the date of the last dispatches, a large ship was discovered in the offing. The wind was strong from the South South East. After several hours' tacking, with apparent intention to reach the Island, the vessel was observed to bear away for the North West, and in the course of an hour, a boat was seen entering the harbour.

It was rowed by a single person. Sir Hudson

went alone to the beach, and to his astonishment saw a female of interesting appearance drop the oars and spring to land. She stated that she had sailed from Bristol, under the care of some missionary ladies, in a vessel called the *Robert and Ann*, Capn. Robinson, destin'd for Philadelphia; that the vessel, being driv'n out of its course by a tempest, which continued for several successive days, the crew at length perceived land, which the Captain recognised to be St Helena: that she immediately conceived an ardent desire of seeing the man with whose future fortunes she was persuaded her own were mysteriously connected, and her breast swelled with the prospect of contemplating face to face an Impostor not equalled on earth since the days of Mohammed, but a change of wind to the South South East nearly overset her hopes.

Finding the Captain resolved to proceed according to his original destination, she watched her opportunity, and springing with a large clasp knife into a small boat, which was slung at the stern, she cut the ropes, dropt safely into the ocēan, and rowed away. The wind was too strong from the land to allow of the vessel being brought about to thwart her object.

Sir Hudson introduced her to Buonaparte under the name of CARABOO!! She described herself as Princess of Javasu, and related a tale of extraordinary interest, which seemed in a high degree to delight the captive chief. He embraced her with every demonstration of enthusiastic rapture, and besought

Sir Hudson Lowe that she might be allowed an apartment in his house, declaring that she alone was an adequate solace to his captivity.

Sir Hudson subjoins:

The familiar acquaintance with the Malay tongue possessed by this most extraordinary personage (and there are many on the island who understand that language) together with the knowledge she displays of Indian and Chinese politics, and the eagerness with which she speaks on those subjects, appear to convince everyone that she is no impostor. Her manner is noble and fascinating in a wonderful degree.

A private letter adds the following testimony to the above statement:

Since the arrival of this lady, the manner, and I may say the countenance and figure of Buonaparte appear to be wholly altered. From being reserved and dejected, he has become gay and communicative. No more complaints are heard about inconveniences at Longwood [Napoleon at the time was waging a long propaganda battle against Hudson Lowe, an unimaginative civil servant who had been imposing restrictions on his captive's already very limited activities]. He has intimated to Sir Hudson Lowe his determination to dissolve his marriage to Maria Louisa, and to sanction his indissoluble union with the enchanting Caraboo!!

Gutch may have felt slightly ashamed of himself, selling Caraboo's story like a serialization in a modern Sunday newspaper, shouting her name like a showman exhibiting a freak, but there is something inspired about his telling of the St Helena story, and it was Princess Caraboo who had inspired him.

CHAPTER 11

THE ROAD TO JAVASU

As Gutch walked up the hill from Bridge
Street, turned left past the Exchange and
returned to his printing offices in Small Street after
his long interviews with Mary Baker, he must have
been powerfully reminded of a story contained in
one of the unbound sheets of Coleridge's *Biographia
Literaria*. It concerned a girl of Mary Baker's age in
Germany, and could provide a key to the secret of
her astonishing performance.

A case occurred in a Catholic town in Germany a
year or two before my arrival at Göttingen, and had
not ceased to be a frequent subject of conversation.
A young woman of four or five and twenty, who
could neither read, nor write, was seized with a
nervous fever; during which, according to the asser-
vations of the priests and monks in the neighbourhood, she became *possessed*, and it appeared, by a
very learned devil.

She continued incessantly talking Latin, Greek
and Hebrew, in very pompous tones and with most
distinct enunciation. The case had attracted the
particular attention of a young physician, and by his
statement many eminent physiologists and psychol-
ogists visited the town, and cross-examined the case

on the spot. Sheets full of her ravings were taken down for a month, and were found to consist of sentences, coherent and intelligible each for itself, but with little or no connection with each other. Of the Hebrew, a small portion only could be traced to the Bible; the remainder seemed to be in the rabbinical dialect.

All trick or conspiracy was out of the question. Not only had the young woman ever been a harmless, simple creature; but she was evidently labouring under a nervous fever.

In the town, in which she had been resident for many years, as a servant in different families, no solution presented itself. The young physician however determined to take her past life step by step; for the patient herself was incapable of returning a rational answer. He at length succeeded in discovering the place where her parents had lived; travelled thither, found *them* dead, but an uncle surviving; and from him learnt, that the patient had been charitably taken by an old protestant pastor at nine years old, and had remained with him some years, even till the old man's death. Of this pastor the uncle knew nothing, but that he was a very good man.

With great difficulty, and after much search, our young medical philosopher discovered a niece of the pastor's, who had lived with him as his housekeeper, and had inherited his effects. She remembered the girl; related, that her venerable uncle had been too indulgent, and could not bear to hear the girl scolded; that she was willing to have kept her, but

that after her patron's death, the girl herself refused
to stay.

Anxious enquiries were then of course made
concerning the pastor's habits; and the solution to
the phenomenon at last obtained. For it appeared,
that it had been the old man's custom, for years, to
walk up and down a passage of his house into which
the kitchen door opened, and to read to himself in a
loud voice, out of his favourite books. A considerable number of these were still in the niece's possession. She added, that he was a very learned man
and a great Hebraist.

Among the books were found a collection of
rabbinical writings, together with several of the
Greek and Latin fathers; and the physician succeeded
in identifying so many passages with those taken
down at the young woman's bedside, that no doubt
could remain in any rational mind concerning the
true origin of the impressions made on her nervous
system.

This authenticated case furnishes both proof and
instance, that reliques of sensation may exist for an
indefinite time in a latent state, in the very same
order in which they were originally impressed; and
contributes to make it even probable, that all
thoughts are in themselves imperishable, and that
this, perchance, is the dread book of judgement, in
whose mysterious hieroglyphics every idle word is
recorded!

The cases at first sight seemed very similar. Mary
Baker was almost exactly the same age as the girl in

Germany, and suffered, as Gutch soon discovered, from recurrencies of rheumatic fever. She also appeared to be entirely uneducated and slightly simple-minded. In investigating her story, therefore, Gutch followed the same rational and painstaking approach adopted by Coleridge's young doctor in Germany.

He retraced every step of her earlier life, trying to determine what had turned her into Princess Caraboo. If he was constantly amazed at the credulity of those at Knole who had used her as a kind of screen on which to project their own fantasies, he was still more deeply intrigued by Mary Baker.

He treated her invention of Princess Caraboo and her sustained performance of the role not as an act of wilful fraud but as a case of spirit-possession, as if she had been inhabited by the soul of a long-dead princess of the Nile. He was looking, certainly, for psychological causes, but he accepted that for a great deal of the time Mary Baker, shaken awake in Elizabeth Worrall's carriage or shocked with shouts of 'Fire!', believed she *was* Princess Caraboo.

The first real information Mary gave Gutch, and she gave it with great reluctance, was her father's address. He was a cobbler in Witheridge, a little village about fifteen miles north of Exeter and ten miles west of Tiverton, high up on a spine of round-topped, wooded hills and open farmland between Exmoor and Dartmoor. He was called Thomas Willcocks. Gutch immediately wrote to the vicar of Witheridge, asking him to see her parents and confirm that she had been baptized in the church, as she said, twenty-five years before.

Then the girl began to talk about her childhood. She told Gutch that she had always been 'very wild', and had never been to school. This was not true, but it was what she chose to remember: a childhood different from other children. She also thought she had been wandering all her life. She told Harry Bonner of the *Mercury* that even as a little child 'she was accustomed to roaming about'.

Her mother taught her to spin wool – wool spinning and weaving was a standard cottage industry in that part of Devon – and when she was eight she set her to work regularly every day at the spinning wheel in her parents' cottage. Sometimes she was sent to work on local farms, driving horses or pulling up thistles in the cornfields.

What she remembered best was wanting to do better than the boys. She told Gutch about how she had played cricket, and fished and swum, but oddly he did not attach much importance to it. Harry Bonner was more interested, and wrote that 'she evinced a strong inclination to follow the occupations and amusements of a boy'.

When Bonner pressed her on what had by now become the sensational question of her swimming, she began to re-invent it in her memory in a way she rarely dared to when she was talking to Gutch. She imagined herself driving 'her father's horses' – as a shoemaker it is unlikely he had even one horse – and told Bonner that 'when she was fatigued she would go into the water and thus learned to swim and dive'.

Bonner himself may have decorated it: he knew that was what the gentlemen of Bristol wanted to read about, and having seen Mary it was understandable that many would want to picture her, hot and sweating, slipping off a horse's back, out of her clothes and into the water as the other horses pulled at the grass on the river bank.

Gutch discouraged her fantasies. His objective all the time was to establish real proof of her existence as Mary Baker, asking her how she had earned her living, how much she had been paid, where she had slept and eaten, how she had lived.

She therefore told him – something she never mentioned to Harry Bonner – about her first steady job. It was with a family who were to remain loyal to her for many years. Their name was Moon, and they had a farm called Bradford Barton half a mile or so to the north of Witheridge. It was an old low-built farmhouse on the side of a hill, with a little bedroom over the kitchen where Mary and the children slept, a cobbled yard and high barns that are still there today, with goose-pens and haylofts, surrounded by orchards.

It was in Bradford Pond that she learned to swim. Between Bradford and Witheridge the Little Dart broadens into a wide stretch of still water, covered in summer in Mary's day with water-lilies, before narrowing down to a fast-flowing stream by a bridge, until 1950 driving an old water-mill.

She went to Bradford in 1807 when she was sixteen as an 'indoor girl' to look after the Moons' children, and stayed two years. Gutch asked her how much they paid her, and she said tenpence a week, with board and lodging. She was still determined to be tougher than the men. She used to watch the farm-labourers working in the cobbled yard, boast that she could carry heavier sacks of apples or grain than they could, and then prove it.

At the end of two years Mary also showed the strength of her will. She demanded a pay rise from tenpence to a shilling a week; the Moons refused to give it to her, and she walked out.

In the interview she gave to Harry Bonner she never mentioned this. With Gutch it is possible that she sensed his interest in money and wages, and began to imagine herself as a workers' heroine bargaining hard with her bosses.

At another stage of her life she invented a story about having a lover who lived at Rackenford Rectory, a mile or so further north. All she told Bonner was that her mother was uneasy about her way of life at Bradford Barton and sent her to Exeter.

Exeter was the nearest town of any size, an old city on a hill, full of ancient churches, with elegant old houses looking out on the green lawns sloping down to the cathedral, quaint mediaeval alleys and busy streets. It was also on the main road from Cornwall to London.

Gutch asked her how she found a job there: in response she spun him the kind of day-dream she might have dreamed as she came down the narrow road from Witheridge in 1809, through wooded round-topped hills, past scattered farms set back from the road, and saw the vast smoking panorama of Exeter for the first time.

Mary said she arrived in Exeter knowing no one, and heard about the work from a fish-woman she happened to meet in the street. The job was with a shoemaker, like her father, called Brooke, in Fore Street, the continuation of Exeter High Street that runs steeply downhill to the south towards the bridge over the river Exe. Some of the houses survived the German bombing raids of the last war: substantial, elegant eighteenth-century façades directly on the road. They are shabby now, but they were occupied in Mary's day by the more successful businesses. Mr and Mrs Brooke were townsfolk, and they had money.

They wanted someone to do more general work than she had done at the Moons' in Bradford: they had other servants, but Mary was expected to clean the house, help with the cooking, and do the laundry.

The story Mary told Gutch was that Mrs Brooke 'liked the look of her because she was a country girl', offered her the job at three shillings a week – more than three times what she had been earning at the Moons' – but 'suspected she might be a runaway apprentice'. Mrs Brooke sent her home again for a fortnight while she made enquiries about her, and told her to come back with references. Gutch pressed her on who had provided them, and she said the Moons.

As usual, a great deal of Mary's invented narrative was based on real events and experiences, rearranged as they would be by any novelist to increase the interest of the story. There must have been a great many people in the years that followed who 'liked the look of her because she was a country girl', and many who believed she was a runaway apprentice. The Moons, too, did at one point provide her with a reference.

In fact her job at the Brookes' was found for her by her cousin William Burgess, a thirty-three-year-old carpenter, and she admitted as much to Harry Bonner when she told him her mother, as he put it, had 'procured her a job in Exeter'. But the version she told Gutch, typically, has greater dramatic tension: the girl on her own arriving in a strange town, people liking the look of her but secretly thinking she must be a rebel. It was also, she must have sensed, the sort of story Gutch wanted to hear, exciting but also respectable, making concessions to the world of his own experience, to the proper procedure in employing servants.

The next part of her story – however she re-wrote it for Gutch – must have shocked him. After eight weeks she found the job too much like hard work and walked out.

As an 'indoor girl' with the Moons she could entertain herself in her spare time during the day playing the tough heroine out in the farmyard, where she was not officially employed to work, and at night spin bedtime stories for the Moon children upstairs under the roof. At the Brookes' she was making beds, scouring pans and washing the family's dirty clothes. It was no job for a dreamer.

Before she left Exeter she did something on impulse that probably changed the course of her life. She should, by the accepted rules of the day, have gone back to Witheridge, handed over to her parents what remained of the twenty-four shillings she had earned, and begged for their forgiveness for walking out of a good job.

Instead, wandering among the shops in Exeter, flattered perhaps by an enterprising shop assistant, she spent every penny of it on a white dress.

There is always the temptation, in trying to disentangle the mystery of Mary's real life, to assume that sex was the major determining factor in what happened to her. She was then just eighteen, extremely attractive, and alone for the first time in a big town. Was it perhaps some kind of imaginary wedding dress, bought in a fit of mental instability after Mary had been seduced and let down by some man in Exeter, even perhaps by her employer?

On the other hand, given Mary's love of theatricality, it could have been entirely innocent. She had grown up in Witheridge, a tomboy, always wearing dull working clothes. Exeter was the big town, it was the first time she had ever had a lot of money, her first chance to buy anything pretty, and she simply bought it.

She told Gutch that she got home, wearing the dress, and her parents were furious with her. In one account, not by Gutch or Bonner, her father was quoted as saying, 'Twadden vitty for the likes o' she to be fettled up in such fal-lals and fantisheeny clothes!' Her mother told her to take it off at once, and she refused. Her father then thrashed her with his leather belt.

It was not simply that she had squandered money she should have saved and shared with them. They were convinced, Mary told Gutch, that she had 'dishonestly procured it', that she had either been given it by a man she had been to bed with, or had simply stolen it.

It was a desperately unhappy period of her life. Talking to Gutch, she mentioned a 'friend' – it was the only time she ever did so – though she did not specify whether it was a man or a woman: she said her friend, too, had been suspicious about the dress.

She even walked over to her old employers, the Moons, determined to show the dress off to them, and their reaction was the same.

At that point Mary couldn't stand it any longer: she found village life unbearable. She told Gutch she knew she was innocent, she hated the hostile gossip, she hated her family and all her relations. At the end of a week she ran away from home. She must have run away on impulse, in the middle of a very violent row, because she left all her clothes behind, including the white dress. She also went without any money.

From now on, for Mary, Witheridge barely existed, and reality took on the texture of a dream. As she continued to tell him what she remembered, or imagined she remembered, Gutch asked a friend to verify that she had really run away from home.

He began his search in Devon. Mary's family lived in a little thatched cottage, now demolished, in a row of three or four others, still standing today, on either side of a little lane just above Witheridge, and known as Stretchtown or Stretchdown. In earlier times it had the reputation for being the poorer and less respectable end of the village, and in living memory there was still a story going round that Nelson had a mistress who lived there, a foreign princess.

The overwhelming impression is one of isolation: long views out across the moors, high banks under the hedges as a shield against the wind, a few small fields and windblown trees.

Thomas Willcocks and his wife Mary were summoned, some time early in June, to go to the vicarage, a little house built beside the old Norman church, then shielded from the main road and the village square by a row of alms-houses. Waiting for them, as they arrived in their best clothes, were the vicar's wife, Mrs Pery Dicken, and Gutch's reporter, 'a respectable tradesman of Bristol', travelling in Devon on business.

Thomas Willcocks, a small, swarthy man with bright, intelligent brown eyes, was fifty-seven, and had walked with a limp all his life. His wife was fifty-three. Gutch's reporter began by asking them how many children they had: they said they had a son, Henry, in his early thirties, a farm-labourer in the village, and a daughter called Mary, who was twenty-six. There was a younger son, Thomas, fifteen, and Susan, who was nine, both of whom lived at home.

He asked them where their daughter Mary lived, and they seemed embarrassed. They said she had left the village eight years before.

Gutch's reporter told them the story of Princess Caraboo and they were horrified. Although Gutch never realized it, the whole story, from Mary's running away from home to her great hoax at Knole, was as humiliating for Mary's parents as it was for the Worralls. The Willcockses were one of the oldest families in the village, related by marriage to everyone of any consequence. Her grandfather had been the blacksmith in Witheridge for years, and so had her great-grandfather. Other members of the family with more money owned large farms in the area. Mary's mother had been born a Burgess, and the Burgesses, too, had been there for over a century as bakers and stone-masons.

Gutch's reporter promised them there was no danger of her being prosecuted, and explained that if their daughter was now telling the truth Elizabeth Worrall was still prepared to help her.

They said their daughter's name was Mary Ann Willcocks, and the vicar was able to confirm from the parish register in the vestry that she had been baptized on 23 November 1791. She had spent a certain amount of time at school, but had never learned to read or write properly. The Willcockses also confirmed all the salient points of her story as far as the episode of the white dress.

Her father admitted that he had taken his strap to her more than once, and could never really understand her. She had never been able to settle down at school, and every spring and autumn seemed to grow restless. He thought she was a good girl at heart, but he believed that all the trouble started when she was fifteen and had rheumatic fever. 'Since then', he said, 'I believe she had not been right in her mind.' This was very probably true. The condition, known nowadays as SBE or sub-acute bacterial endocarditis, produces recurrent fevers associated with bouts of delirium.

Mary was not alone in wanting to get away from Witheridge: the population today is roughly half what it was in 1817, and the two younger Willcocks children later moved away to marry and produce large stable families. But Mary shared with her older brother Henry an inability to settle down in a conventional marriage. He is listed in the village census of 1851, still unmarried and a pauper, though a girl who may have been his daughter appears in the parish records some years before. There may also have been tensions in the family that Gutch only hints at. Four of Mary's brothers and sisters survived, but six died. Mothers in those days were used to babies dying, but two of the Willcocks children had died, more terribly, when they were much older: one boy when he was seven, and a girl when she was fifteen. Thomas Willcocks mentions more than once his wife being 'sick with worry', or 'ill with fretting'. It is more than possible that her mother, with a new baby daughter, had become neurotic, and could no longer marry Mary off. Her father's relationship with Mary was obviously more direct and passionate.

When she told the farm-workers at Knole that it was her father Jessee Mandu's birthday, it was almost certainly Thomas Willcocks' birthday. His exact date of birth is not preserved in the family records, only the day he was christened. But watching her marking off numbers on her knotted string, the farm-workers at Knole believed she was saying he was forty-seven: the fact that he was actually fifty-seven makes it seem very probable that they misread one digit.

In any event the Jessee Mandu in her story, always treated with respect by the people of her homeland, who killed one of her serving-women as he tried to save her from the pirates, and who was her last memory of home, shouting after her in the shallows as she was carried away, remained a powerful image.

Mary told Gutch that she got as far as Exeter – due south of Witheridge down a winding lane – and that she then went north-east to Taunton. This lends credence to the idea that there was someone in Exeter she wanted to see, and it wasn't her cousin the carpenter. Her parents said there was another girl who ran away with her, but who later lost her nerve and came home. Dreaming her own dream of the journey, Mary never mentioned her.

She told Gutch that she wandered about, 'not

knowing where to go', and begging from anyone she met. She eventually arrived in Taunton, and as she could have got there by way of Witheridge it seems likely that she considered returning home with the other girl and then decided against it.

Gutch tried very hard to determine exactly where she had been, but she told him 'she was very young then, and did not recollect the names of the places'. She was probably just nineteen.

Gutch wanted to know how people treated her. She remembered some who gave her money, some who said it was a shame that 'such a young creature should be wandering about the country'. Others threatened to have her arrested or to horsewhip her. She said she spent a lot of time crying, and wanted to kill herself.

Gutch asked her where she slept. She said that when she was given money she spent it on lodgings, when she had none she slept in barns or sometimes in haystacks. Her only memory of the road between Exeter and Taunton was so melodramatic that it could well have come out of a religious tract, though there may have been elements of truth in it. It was, in any case, the kind of story calculated to touch the heart of Elizabeth Worrall.

She said that she left the main road, walked some way along a lane, undid her apron and tied her apron-strings to the branch of a tree, meaning to hang herself. Then she heard a voice: 'Cursed are they that do murder, and sin against the Lord.'

Gutch, taking his line from Coleridge's rationalist friend in Germany, asked her if she was sure she had really heard a voice, and Mary, to do her credit, said she might have imagined it. In any case she untied her apron from the branch.

She walked back towards the main road, still crying a lot, and after a while she met an old gentleman coming the other way. She remembered his words exactly. He said, 'My pretty girl, what is the matter with you, crying so? Where are you going?'

She said she didn't know, and he asked her what her name was. She admitted to Gutch that she 'did not tell him her real name', for fear of being sent back to her father. But she did tell the old gentleman why she had run away from home, and told him the story about trying to hang herself from the branch of the tree and hearing the voice.

He was very stern with her, and said it would have been very wicked of her to take her own life. Then he gave her five shillings – nearly two weeks' wages at Mrs Brooke's – and Mary again remembered his exact words, 'Go away in peace: put your trust in the Lord, and He will never forsake you!'

Bonner, who was a great deal less scientific in his approach to Mary's story, was fascinated by her ability to remember words and phrases, and saw how relevant it was to her sustaining the hoax. Gutch at this stage was more concerned with separating truth from invention, but even her inventions depended on a very retentive memory. He did not press her any further on the possible source of the story, but he remained sceptical.

He asked her how she had spent the old gentleman's five shillings. She said on three nights' board and lodging in Taunton. Then she set off on the main road, still begging, and arrived for the first time in Bristol, starving.

Whether she walked or was given a lift on a cart, she found herself in Lewin's Mead, where she was approached by a man called Freeman, who was a member of the Stranger's Friend Society. This part of her story was never verified by Gutch; nor can it be verified now as the records of the Society were destroyed in the bombing of Bristol. But it sounds true.

The Stranger's Friend Society was founded by the Methodists 'to administer comfort to the most abject and neglected of our fellow-creatures, by alleviating their sufferings, both in body and mind, whether occasioned by penury or disease'. Most of its work was with the poor in Bristol, distributing bedding and food, but food and lodging was sometimes provided for vagrants who could make a good case, and, more important, seemed inclined to repent their evil ways.

Members of the Society were required 'zealously to exhort the unconverted to flee from the wrath to come' and met regularly for prayer-meetings. They were brutally fined for arriving late at their meetings, and fined a great deal more if they failed to turn up at all. They were also penalized if they were late in bringing in their case-books. The high point of their year was a 'social meal' every Boxing Day, culminating in a Methodist 'Love Feast', when members spoke of their Christian experience and 'related some peculiar cases of distress'.

Mary, tired and hungry and wanting only money to get food and a bed, found herself being cross-questioned by Freeman not only about her spiritual life but also about her father and why she left home. It was the Society's policy wherever possible, as with similar organizations today, to get the runaway back to his or her family. Mary refused to answer.

Like many other gentlemen, however, Freeman was predisposed in her favour. He gave her four shillings – more than enough to find food and a bed for the night – and told her to come back and see him again in the morning. Imagining this would mean an official letter to her father, Mary left Bristol before dawn and took to the road to London.

The next thing she remembered clearly was arriv-ing in Calne in Wiltshire. Her story about what happened there sounds a little too much like a standard joke told in a gypsy encampment or at a gathering of the homeless round a fire, but Gutch appears to have believed it. She said she was begging from door to door. Being in a strange town she knocked on the door of the house belonging to the local constable. He arrested her, shut her up in his front room and told her he would take her down to the Magistrate first thing next morning, and she would then be forcibly returned to her own parish. Mary said she waited till he had to go out into the yard to relieve himself, then she opened a window and ran off down the road.

There were facts about Mary's life that Gutch was to discover after she had left for America that might well have persuaded Elizabeth Worrall to change her mind about helping her, but on the question of her begging both Gutch, Elizabeth Worrall and contemporary readers of his book seem to have been lenient. Mary argued at one stage that she had never actually asked for money, only for food or shelter, and that her definition of begging was not criminal.

What may have influenced those who heard her to be merciful was the vulnerability of a young girl from a country village travelling alone on a main road. Whatever adventures she may have had with men, the very fact that she was still starving and still on the road is evidence, if not of her absolute innocence, at least of her desire to be independent. But the strain was telling, and the combination of anxiety, sleeping rough, and living off scraps finally made her too ill to walk any further. Somewhere near Windsor, still thirty miles from London, she collapsed.

She told Gutch she remembered sitting by the side of the road under a hedge and a wagoner offering a ride on his cart. She saw that he had two women with him, and accepted. The wagoner was an older man, and kind. He told her he had seven children of his own, and often wondered what would become of them. The women had some food and drink with them, and offered to share it with Mary, but she was too sick to eat anything.

They drove through Hammersmith and Kensington, and stopped some time late in the afternoon at

Hyde Park Corner, where the wagoner said he would lose his job if he took them any further.

The two women realized that Mary was very ill and could not be left alone, and asked her where she was going. She said, as usual, that she didn't know. They asked her if she had any friends. She said she knew nobody, she'd never been to London before. According to one of her stories, she was following the lover who had been staying in the Rectory at Rackenford, but this time it seems likely that she really knew no one.

What she could not tell them was the real reason for being there: it was not because she wanted to be in London, but because she didn't want to be in Witheridge. It had begun as an act of bravado, a violent act of rebellion against her father and mother, and now she was alone, without money, without friends, in a vast and terrifying city. In that loneliness she was to discover Javasu.

She remembered very clearly them both taking her by the arm, one on each side, and going to a house – she couldn't remember where it was – and waiting there until it got dark. Then they took her to St Giles' Workhouse Hospital in Kennington. It was now dark. She sat down on the doorstep, and they left her there.

Harry Bonner was convinced it was the Middlesex Hospital, and Mary herself was hazy about names when Gutch questioned her more closely, saying the doctor who had treated her was called Burgess. It was her mother's name, and she used it more than once when Gutch was pressing for details.

It could have been St Giles' Workhouse near Seven Dials, off Drury Lane, but the evidence suggests that it was the other St Giles, four miles to the south-east, and it remains a mystery how the two women got her there. It is possible that they got a lift on another cart, and that Mary in the meantime lost consciousness: she was already suffering from a severe recurrence of her rheumatic fever, brought on by poor food and exhaustion.

Mary remembered her admission to the hospital very clearly. Gutch asked her how long she was left sitting on the step, and she thought it had been about a quarter of an hour. Then the watchman had found her.

Drunks and derelicts who wanted to spend the night at the St Giles' Workhouse assembled from nine o'clock in the evening onwards on the steps at the other end of the building. The sexes were segregated in two dormitories. New arrivals surrendered their clothes in exchange for a numbered tag, and were given a bath described by one visitor as 'the colour of mutton broth'. The women were issued with a shift, the men a shirt for the night, then queued for a piece of bread, three-quarters of a pint of watery soup, a blanket and a bag half-filled with straw to sleep on.

The only surviving record by a journalist who got into the men's hostel some years later describes a night continually disturbed by drunks and male prostitutes arriving until one in the morning, raucous singing, villains stealing bed-clothes from those too weak to protect themselves, men getting up at all hours of the night to drink from a tin cup in a pail of water or to urinate noisily in the yard. The visitor was also appalled by the loud bragging about sex and semi-public homosexual activities among the inmates.

In exchange for the night's shelter, the men were expected to do five hours' work the next morning, turning a huge capstan to grind corn, the women needlework or cleaning. Mary was to experience a great deal more of this later, though she never at any point in her story to Gutch complained of the conditions. On this first visit, however, she escaped the system.

She was taken to the watch-house and asked questions, but was considered to be too ill and exhausted to answer. She remembered them fetching a doctor, who shook his head, said her condition was very serious, and ordered her to be admitted to the fever ward.

Gutch asked her how long her illness lasted, and she said she thought it was for several months. For much of the time she was unconscious, and the nurses told her afterwards that she used to ask them every morning whether she was dead.

It was there that she underwent the terrible operation Princess Caraboo described on Tappa Boo's boat going to the Cape. She remembered being given scalding hot baths, but had only a limited recollection of the operation itself. It would have been performed without any anaesthetic, and must have been excruciatingly painful.

Her head was shaved, the back of her skull was

'cupped'. Cupping, as a means of letting blood, survived in France into the twentieth century, but in 1817 it was still standard practice. It had a long medical history, going back to the Greeks, and was widely used among primitive peoples. It was prescribed for a great many conditions, from excessive menstruation to flatulence, lumbago and various kinds of fever, and was sometimes called 'the artificial leech'.

Cupping the back of the head was the regular treatment for any kind of 'brain fever', which would have been diagnosed in a case like Mary's where a high temperature appeared to be making the patient delirious. In some primitive societies it was done simply by sucking at the skin through a hollow tube, but in Europe it got its name from the use of heating and applying cups to create a vacuum. 'Dry' cupping consisted of pressing a heated glass or horn to the patient's skin, and sucking the blood to the surface to form what looked like a heavy bruise. In 'wet' cupping, the treatment given to Mary, the skin was first cut or scarified in a series of slits. It was the scars of these cuts that Dr Wilkinson, spreading the black hair on the back of Mary's head, had excitedly identified as having been made by no European doctor.

It is probable, given the regularity of the pattern noted by Wilkinson, that the cuts in Mary's case were made with a machine called Heister's Apparatus. It consisted of a box with a single handle. The front of the box was pressed against the part of the body to be treated, and sixteen blades cut into the skin simultaneously, the depth of the incision controlled by a central screw. By the time of Mary's operation the machines were made so that they could be dismantled and the blades kept free of rust. Dr Bayfield, the leading authority of the day, recommended oiling the blades before the operation, and wiping them afterwards on a piece of new bread.

Hot glasses were then applied in sequence to the cuts, and replaced as each filled with blood. There was always the danger of the glasses being too hot and the patient being burned, and in the case of 'wet' cupping there was the risk of infection. It would have been as a precaution against this that the doctors at St Giles' used the caustic noticed by Wilkinson.

Mary was in an upstairs ward, and there was a fire burning there in winter, but she clearly remembered it as a place of horror. She told Gutch that as soon as she was strong enough to get out of bed she begged 'Dr Burgess' to let her go downstairs to the yard to get some fresh air.

According to Mary, the doctor told her she wasn't strong enough. She kept on pestering him, and he finally agreed that if she could carry a heavy kettle from the fire to the other end of the ward he would let her go downstairs to walk in the yard. The doctor, Mary said, did not realize the kettle was full of boiling water. Her legs gave way, the doctor caught her, but the boiling water scalded her and she had to stay in the fever ward for another four weeks.

Gutch did not question the truth of this story, but it sounds very much like one of Mary's gruesome tales, a story told as a warning to children. Anyone, and a doctor more than most, would have recognized that walking in the yard was less taxing than carrying a heavy iron kettle, quite apart from the danger of the boiling water. Mary almost certainly scalded her leg and had to stay in hospital for another month, but it may well have been the result of some prank of hers that went wrong, or a brawl in a public ward full of very alarming women.

At the end of the month she was moved to another ward, occupied by tubercular patients, and stayed there till she was well enough to leave.

What followed varied slightly in Mary's account to Gutch and what she told Harry Bonner. She told Gutch she owed her deliverance to a woman: she told Bonner she owed it to a man.

In the version she told Gutch, the matron at St Giles', discovering that she had no friends or any prospects of work in London, recommended her to the care of a Presbyterian clergyman, the workhouse chaplain Mr Pattenden. In the version she told Bonner, Pattenden himself had been visiting another patient, liked the look of her, and came over to her bed to talk to her.

In either case, Mary succeeded in charming those in authority exactly as she was to charm Elizabeth Worrall, and again succeeded in beating the system: by law, the matron and the hospital chaplain should have sent her back to her own parish, to Witheridge. Instead she was allowed to say in London.

CHAPTER 12

AN IMAGINARY
CHRISTENING

Lᴵᴷᴇ Gᴜᴛᴄʜ, Pᴀᴛᴛᴇɴᴅᴇɴ was a man Mary decided she could trust. He promised to find her a job if she could produce references, and Mary took the risk of giving him the address of the Moons at Bradford Barton. Exhausted and weakened by her illness, though still in no mind to go home, she also, very reluctantly, gave him her father's name and address in Witheridge.

Pattenden wrote to him, and it is an indication of her father's respect for authority and general level of sophistication, even after a lifetime spent behind his cobbler's bench in Witheridge, that he immediately wrote two letters.

The first was to the Reverend Mr Pattenden, saying how relieved he and his wife were to get news of Mary, and thanking him for looking after her. The second, sent by the same post, was to his friend Horsewell, a linen-draper in Exeter, who made regular journeys to London on business. He asked him, on his next trip, to find out whether Pattenden was as respectable as he sounded.

Horsewell reported back almost immediately, reassuring Thomas Willcocks that his daughter had nothing to fear from Pattenden's protection except possibly the tedium of being preached to.

Pattenden was an earnest, slightly pompous Presbyterian clergyman with daughters of his own, living in Islington. He took a keen interest in Mary, but his interest seems to have remained entirely paternal. He had her to stay with him and his family in Cold Bath Fields, off what is now Rosebery Avenue.

He first met Mary in the workhouse hospital in the spring of 1811, and when Gutch wrote to him six years later with news of the Great Caraboo Hoax at Knole, Pattenden remained very fond of her, though he still couldn't resist the chance to preach.

'I sincerely pray, notwithstanding her past conduct, which displays such great wickedness,' he wrote to Gutch, 'that the Lord may give her grace to repent; and that at some future day we may hear of her being a bright and shining character, one that truly fears God and departs from all iniquity.

'I don't think there's any harm in her, but she was always so odd and eccentric that it would fill a volume if I were to transcribe everything I knew of her.' It would be nice to think, when he was older and had more time, that he did, but so far I have been unable to trace any of his direct descendants who might have kept his papers.

The Moons, despite her having walked out the year before over money, sent her a good reference, and Pattenden found Mary a job with a Mr and Mrs Matthews, looking after children in Kennington, not far from the workhouse, at 1 Clapham Road Place, now Clapham Road. She was to stay there for three years, until she was twenty-two.

The name of the road has changed, and the house in which Mary worked was demolished in the middle of the last century to make way for a school, but houses further down the street survive, and number one, like them, was an imposing double-fronted town-house. It had large sash windows, a flight of steps up to the front door, an elegant late eighteenth-century staircase, a drawing room and dining room on the ground floor above the kitchens, big bedrooms on the first floor for the Matthews family, and smaller bedrooms for Mary and the other servants high up under a shallow slate roof. There was a large garden at the back, and within a few minutes' walk, past the Grecian portico of the nearby church, there was the public park and gardens.

After the workhouse hospital, it must have seemed to Mary like a dream of comfort. The neighbours on one side were a prosperous orthodox Jewish family, and Mary immediately became fascinated by Judaic ritual, the Hebrew alphabet, the sound of their prayers and their diet.

Like Coleridge's German doctor, Gutch was quick to identify this as the first discernible source of the character who appeared at Knole. The sound of the chanting, the strange shapes of the Hebrew letters, the ritual and diet were romantic and exotic and magical, and moved Mary in a way she was unable to explain. It released her imagination, it was the very opposite of the bare everyday reality she hated in Witheridge.

She became a great friend of the Jewish family's cook, and Mrs Matthews remembered her pegging out laundry in the garden and talking to her over the fence. Mrs Matthews also taught Mary to read and write, and one of her daughters, whom Mary called 'her young Miss', helped her with her lessons. Her parents were grateful, and sent Mrs Matthews a present of three fat ducks and a pint of Devon cream.

Talking to Gutch's reporter at Witheridge, Mrs Willcocks said that Mary could read a little when she left school, and always read books when she was out of work, but the evidence of Mary's own letters home makes this very debatable. It is possible she read more later. Some of Caraboo's story may have come out of books, but those available to her at Clapham Road Place were of a very limited kind, and more likely to have inspired the hanging scene on the road to Taunton. Certainly the evangelical tracts she was given to read at Mrs Matthews' house coloured the letters she wrote home, some of which her mother had kept and handed over to Gutch.

Despite some words that are hard to understand and which may have been misread by Gutch's type-setter in June 1817, these letters also allow us to hear for the first time her North Devon accent.

The first is dated 24 November 1811.

My dear father and
Mother and my Love and duty to my dear brothers and

sister I hop i shall find you all in good helth Ples give my Love to grandmother and ant burgess and all friends Im in most delightful place and my mistress Treats me with all imaginable kindness.

She says that *my youn miss*, Mrs Matthews' daughter, *is Larnd me to write* and hopes that by the time she sends her *nax Letter* she will be able to write without help.

The next sentence seems to be in answer to a question from her parents about whether she knows anyone of her own age in London. She writes *i hve ver good friends*, but goes on immediately to talk about her appearance, suggesting that no 'friend' would want her: *but my dear Mother i m got so fat that you wel not lard now me* – will not hardly know me.

Mrs Matthews told Gutch that Mary would sometimes 'not eat for several days together to show how long she could go without food'. Modern psychiatrists might diagnose some eating disorder, but if the kosher food they cooked next door influenced her invented 'Hindoostanic' diet at Knole, her Tuesday fasts there, like the hunger strike at St Peter's Hospital, seem now to have been part of a familiar pattern, even when there was good food available, of starving herself to stay thin.

Mary's letter then turns to thoughts about her home in Witheridge, suggesting that her parents' life, whether from the deaths of their other children or from poverty, had been very hard. *I wnt to now the situation that you Live in with it is beter now and it nas* – that it was – *when i Live ther it was bad Enough then with I hop it is beter now*.

Mary asks them to write to her – *and i hop you will send me letter to Let me now how all of you are* – and then takes on Mrs Matthews' tone of moral concern about the dangers of what she calls *ple* – play – suggesting that she had herself been given some very stern lectures about the perils of play-acting. *but my dear father i hop hoo will kip my dear sister from ple for it will be the raun of her for i* – the ruin of her for ever.

Never did my time pas mor agreeably, she goes on, catching Mrs Matthews' conversational style, *for i do my work wil paleasure*. She talks about her enjoyment of reading – *wen i hav dond reading* – and says she never goes out except to church – *i never go yout ont is to church*. Then, as if to reassure her parents that she is not keeping bad company, she writes *i naver so happy when im bmy salf*.

This was probably true: hours of walking the road alone, sleeping rough, resisting gentlemen who wanted to look after her, delirious in the workhouse hospital, Mary learned the habit of withdrawing into her own imaginary world. The children she looked after were prepared to share it in her bedtime stories, but it was not until she reached Knole that she found grown-ups who were ready to believe in it.

The next part of the letter could be interpreted as getting at her mother for being over-anxious, or simply as concern for her mother's well-being as she tries to make up for the white dress episode by sending them a pound note – *wan pond not* – from her wages. *but my dear mother I whe you wer so happy as im I hop my dear brothers will never let you want for ant thin I wich it was in my por to mker you comfortable but my dear mother I have send you wan pond not and I hop it wall be acceptable presents wen my dear father I have got wan vever* – good strong Devonian for favour – *to beg of you that is to send my aged for i wich to now how hold im* – my age for I wish to know how old I am.

She ends *yous most humbly dutyf Loving daughter Mary Willcocks Mr Mathews clapham rod place kennington No 1 November 24.*

Written across the bottom of the letter, in what Gutch notes to be another hand, is the postscript, dated nearly a month later, 22 December 1811. *Mrs Baker would thank Mrs Wilcock to call at Mr Horsewell's Linen Draper No. 81 Fore-street Exeter to let her know if this arrive safe.*

The name Baker is one of the most puzzling pieces in the jigsaw puzzle of Mary's life, and this first mention of it, four years before she adopted it as her own, remains a mystery. There were at least five Baker families living in Witheridge at this time, all of them probably related to Mary by marriage, and from the sense of the postscript this Mrs Baker had some hand in bringing Mary's letter from London.

As she had with the Moons, Mary invented games and stories for the children, but in April 1812 she finally found Clapham Road Place too much like real life to bear. It was, as her father had noticed, spring, and she ran away, just as she would run away from Knole.

Whatever day-dream she was pursuing, and whether or not there was a man involved, she again settled for poverty as the price of independence. Mrs Matthews, like Elizabeth Worrall, forgave her and took her back, and never mentioned the incident to Gutch. But according to the records of St Mary's Workhouse, Lambeth, which Gutch never saw, she was 'admitted by the Committee' on 9 April and was discharged four days later. She used her real name, and gave her age as twenty-two.

As before on the road to London, the anxiety brought back her fever. Mrs Matthews admitted to Gutch that 'she had the illness in my house', and she seems to have been ill for nearly two months. Mary herself writes about it in her next surviving letter, dated 19 August 1812.

The style suggests that she has had more lessons in reading and writing from her young Miss.

My Dear Father and My Mother i hop you are wall as iam tho the blesed of god I have ben vary hill but Iam Much bater thenk The Lord for it Pleace to give My Duty and Love to My dear brothers and sester and i hop they Are wall and i hop you will be so kind as to remember Me to ant Burgess and all Friends I want to Bed a favory – begging a favour was still obviously difficult to spell *– of you if you pleace to sen me Word weere sally dinner live as I wich to see her.*

Sally Dinner was another Willcocks-Burgess-Baker cousin, apparently working in London.

Mary then begins to take on another voice, and

the lines that follow are clear evidence of her extraordinary mynah bird ability as a mimic. *I have very good friends so you see i have got thee 3 Fathers ther is Mr Pattenden you Mu Dear and i hope i have got a heavenly Father I hope you will tell me of any good that may Attend you give my opportunity to rejoice hide Not from me any evil that may befal you That i may mingle My tears with yours.*

i Bend me down with gratitude for the Last Paternal gift you made me which has Proved My salvation. Whether this was simply money or some intervention by Thomas Willcocks in the row that followed her running away is not clear, but she now takes her Pious Presbyterian impersonation into overdrive, based on Pattenden himself or on some tract of Mrs Matthews, possibly the last speech of a converted felon: *. . . and it will add Batterness to my Years force to my groans and sharpness to the stripe if the virtues and sufferings of this life are Not sufficient to atone for the last act of disobedience May every happiness and comfort attend you My Last Prayers in this world will be for those that have loved me wich I am your most obliged affestionate.*

This letter, perhaps from the strain of sustaining the parody at such a high level, is not signed.

Mrs Matthews, like Pattenden, was apparently still very fond of Mary five years later. 'Her conduct', she writes, suppressing the story of her running away, 'was always correct, except that she told terrible stories; yet after all they were such as did no injury to others, or good to herself. Always strange and eccentric in her behaviour, and her ways were so mysterious no one who didn't know the girl would believe them if I told what occurred . . . She would sometimes say she would like to go and live in the woods.'

Mary claimed that she later really did live in the woods, but the place she chose to stay next was a great deal stranger. The story of how she came to leave Clapham Road Place is relatively well documented in letters from Pattenden and Mrs Matthews herself, but it provides more questions than answers.

Some time in the autumn of 1813, according to Mary, a member of the Jewish family next door was getting married, and their cook invited Mary to go to the wedding. It was to be held at the Horns, a picturesque old coaching inn pulled down in the nineteen-sixties and replaced by a grim concrete office block.

Mrs Matthews would not allow her to go, saying she was 'too young and inexperienced'. Mary, whether from affection for the Jewish family or her own fascination with the sound of their chanting, was determined to be there, and persuaded a local shopkeeper, Mrs Baynes, to provide her with an alibi.

Mrs Baynes had just had a baby, and wrote a letter to Mrs Matthews asking if Mary could come to the christening. Mary described to Gutch how exciting it was to go with Mrs Baynes to post it, and to be there when it was delivered next morning at Clapham Road Place. Mary took it up to Mrs

Matthews, who agreed that she could go. The only condition she made was that Mary should be home by eight o'clock in the evening.

Mary went, as she had wanted, to the wedding at the Horns, and was home by eight as she had promised, but for some reason Mrs Matthews was suspicious. To test Mary, she asked her what name the child had been christened. Mary immediately, and without hesitating, said, 'Edward Francis.' This, it has to be remembered, was in her own account of the story told to Gutch four years later, but the names were to be significant.

Still not convinced, Mrs Matthews asked her if there had been a large party. Mary said yes, and blushed. Now certain that she was lying, Mrs Matthews went out, made enquiries, and discovered the truth. She returned and sent for Pattenden.

Mary said that Mrs Matthews 'scolded very much', that she was afraid of having to face Pattenden, and ran out of the house 'without her bonnet'. She said she 'waited about, thinking he would be gone in half an hour, but he stopped all night'.

Mary told Gutch she spent the night in the back lane behind the house, and was still walking up and down in the morning when Mrs Matthews saw her, had her called in, and scolded her again. Staying out all night, she said, was an additional offence.

When Gutch asked Mrs Matthews and Pattenden about it, they had no very clear recollection of the event, remembering only that they had to reprimand her 'for playing some unaccountable prank, or telling some unaccountable story'. Mrs Matthews may, of course, have been covering up for Mary, as she did about her running away.

Mrs Matthews told Gutch she was always very fond of Mary, that everyone who came into the house and saw her 'took an interest in her'. She was a very capable, good servant, seldom went out, and for several years afterwards always called in to see them when she was in London.

What Mrs Matthews did clearly remember was that after the row in the morning, Mary packed her bags of her own accord and left. Mary told Gutch she went to stay with her friend Mrs Baynes, the shopkeeper with the baby, who made decorative plumes and feathers and who sold straw bonnets to Mrs Matthews.

It may have been there, sleeping in Mrs Baynes' workshop in Kennington, that Mary first dreamed of the peacock feather headdresses of Javasu.

After three years in the stifling evangelical atmosphere of Clapham Road Place, Mary meant to go abroad. She packed up all her clothes, sent them home to Witheridge, and persuaded Mrs Baynes to write another of her letters. This one was to her father, and said that Mary had given up her job, had everything she wanted, and 'had left England with a travelling family'.

This idea of travelling abroad, usually to France, is another recurrent theme in Mary's story, and the same 'travelling family' appeared again when Mary told Mortimer about her time in Bombay. Gutch and others who met her and knew her suspected there was some lover, probably French, who inspired these fantasies. Gutch, who talked to almost all those who employed her between 1811 and 1817, was convinced she never had time to go abroad.

What she actually did was to seek admission to the Magdalen Hospital. This, it is possible to date from their records, was the beginning of February 1813.

It was a story that had obviously been a great success with her more broad-minded listeners, like the Earl of Cork and Lord Salisbury, and she repeated it to Gutch.

She told him she had often seen girls walking in the gardens of the Magdalen in Blackfriars Road, had liked their old-fashioned costumes – long brown dresses, white caps and wide-brimmed straw hats – and had thought they were nuns. It was, in fact, a Home for Penitent Prostitutes. Founded in the middle of the eighteenth century, it accommodated about two hundred girls. It was famous for its Sunday services, in a circular chapel at the centre of a complex of buildings in the classical style. The girls sat in the galleries, and some of the hymns were written specially so that they could be sung antiphonally, with a phrase echoed from one gallery to the next.

The chapel was open to the public, tickets being available from any member of the Committee, and lascivious visitors were said to ogle the inmates as they sang their penitential hymns. The girls were under strict instruction not to ogle back. 'The bold and dauntless stare', they were told in their book of advice, would not suggest that they were on the road to reform. Instead they should cultivate a 'humble, meek and downcast look more suitable to those in a state of repentance'.

> Why should you let your wand'ring eyes
> Entice your souls to shameful sin
> Scandal and ruin are the prize
> You take such fatal pains to win
>
> Flee, sinners, flee th' unlawful bed
> Lest vengeance send you down to dwell
> In the dark regions of the dead
> To feed the fiercest fires of hell . . .

Some of the girls were as young as fourteen, and they faced a tough regime of moral drying-out. They were organized, on the Methodist pattern, into strictly segregated classes or groups, each one with its own Superior, and locked in their wards every night. They were employed mostly in sewing shirts and shifts, in knitting stockings and in darning clothes.

They had to be up by six in summer and seven in winter, worked all day long except for half an hour for breakfast at nine, an hour for dinner at one, and were allowed three hours to themselves in the evenings before lights out, at ten in the summer and nine in winter. They said prayers night and morning, grace before and after meals, and read the Bible. They were encouraged to think every night as they lay down to sleep that they would soon 'lie down in death, to awaken no more to this world', and were reminded every day of how close they had come to burning for all eternity in Hell. When they were ill they were taught to think of their illness as 'God's medicine to cure our spiritual diseases'.

The girls were never allowed out, except with a note signed by the Treasurer and two members of the Committee, and there was no communication with the outside world except for visits from members of their own family. Even these could only take place under the eye of the Matron.

The Magdalen claimed roughly a 50 per cent success rate. Of those 'placed in service with respectable families' only about one in five earned the guinea reward for staying in the job for a year. The failures included 5 per cent who died of syphilis, about the same number who were certified insane, 20 per cent who were dismissed, usually for fighting, and 20 per cent who left of their own accord because they were 'uneasy under restraint'.

The regime was easier and better supervised than the workhouse, but it was nevertheless an odd place for Mary to have chosen. It was not, as she pretended to believe, a nunnery, but it might just as well have been. She said herself that she went there because she liked the dresses. It is a move that suggests she felt the need to be protected, the need for some kind of asylum.

The Magdalen Hospital was at the southern end of Blackfriars Bridge, and girls could only apply for admission on the first Thursday in every month at five o'clock in the evening. They knocked at the door of the building on the right of the front gates, filled in a form, and were given a number. When their number was called they went into one of two small interview rooms, where they were questioned by three members of the Committee.

If they were successful they were given a full medical examination – girls with some venereal diseases were rejected – surrendered their clothes, and were issued with the uniform dress, and wide-brimmed hat.

Mary told Gutch and her aristocratic visitors at Bridge Street that she remembered the girls being made to take their caps and bonnets off, and one of the governors asking her how long she had been 'on the town'. She was so innocent she thought he meant 'in the town', and said two years. This was probably an old joke that Mary thought would appeal to visitors like Lord Cork and Lord Salisbury.

In fact, no misunderstanding of that kind would have been possible. On the form she was given when she arrived, which would have been read aloud to her if she had any difficulty understanding it, she admitted that she had been guilty of prostitution, and was 'truly sensible of her offence'.

Gutch was able to examine the Magdalen records only after the *Robert and Ann* sailed for Philadelphia, and Mary had gone a great deal further than a mere admission of her offence. She imagined the plot of an entire novel of betrayed love. As usual it probably contained strands of truth.

She told the Magdalen Committee that she was an orphan, and that her father was a shoemaker who died when she was only a month old. Her mother had died more recently. On her deathbed, her mother commended her to the care of a clergyman called Luxham, Rector of Reckingford – Rackenford was a village to the north of Witheridge, just beyond Bradford where she worked for the Moons, though the Rector was not called Luxham – who took her to work in his house as a maid.

It was while working for the Luxhams, she told them, that she was seduced by a gentleman staying in the house. He took her back with him to London, and lived with her for a month. When he deserted her she was taken to hospital. After leaving the hospital she 'went on the town' – she used the phrase herself – and led a loose life.

The Committee believed her story. Even in Mary's version as she told it in Bridge Street, they 'talked very seriously to her' and made her cry. What the Committee was after was repentance, and with Mary they certainly got it. In the Committee's notes she is described as being 'repentant almost to despondence'. Again, there may have been an element of real depression as well as theatrical expertise.

According to Mary the Committee said that she was very young – this, it is clear from the records, was unlikely to be true, given the age of some of the girls there, but it may have appealed to Lord Cork and Lord Salisbury – and that they would take her in if she was truly penitent. She said she was crying so much she couldn't answer, and she remembered one of them saying, 'Poor thing, she is very much affected, we will admit her.' That part of the story, at least, was true.

Mary was admitted at the beginning of February,

taking advantage of a rule at the Magdalen allowing girls to conceal their real names. She used the name of Ann Burgess.

She was handed a piece of paper, she said, with *Admitted* written on it, and was given a bath. All her clothes and other possessions were taken from her, and she was issued with the Magdalen uniform. She worked there, she thought, for about six months, 'as a sort of housemaid'. This was also true.

She said she was confirmed there by the Bishop – all the girls were under pressure to take Holy Communion, and she needed to be confirmed to take the Sacrament – and learned all the Magdalen hymns. It was only after she was there some time, she told Gutch and her aristocratic listeners, that it began to dawn on her what the other girls had been up to.

One of them was telling a story about her former life, and Mary said she didn't believe her. According to Mary the other girl said, 'You are as bad as we are, otherwise you would not be in this house.' Mary said she had answered back, and that the other girls had reported her to the chaplain, Mr Prince.

Prince questioned her, she told him that she had never been a prostitute, that she had worked for Mrs Matthews, and had taken refuge at the Magdalen as soon as she left. The next day, she said, she was called before the board and expelled. She was given her clothes back, and a pound note that she had had in her pocket when she was admitted.

The truth, according to the records, was very different. After a few weeks, she changed her story and admitted she had been lying. She said there was no such person as Mr Luxham, that since she had been in London she had been in service, first in the Clapham Road Place, and later, presumably to cover her tracks, 'in Edgware', that her name was not Burgess, that she had previously used other assumed names, including Willcocks and – this is the second reference to the name – Baker. She had also been married.

The only part of her original story that was true, she promised them, was that her father had died when she was a baby.

Pressed as to whether she had any living relations she became desperate, threatening that if they ever told her family where she was she would hang herself. The closest relationship she would admit to was a friend, a girl who lived in Exeter, who had no idea what she had been doing in London.

Gutch also found notes in the records about her behaviour in the Magdalen: she was given to depression, and was 'very eccentric', she showed no inclination to sexual misbehaviour, but was always restless.

The story she had told in Bridge Street about being expelled was also untrue: housemaids at the Magdalen were generally recruited from outside, and she was obviously treated, as usual, as a special case. Far from being dismissed, she was very much appreciated. It was she who wanted to leave. She began begging them to let her go at the end of June, they tried to persuade her against it, and only finally agreed that she could leave in the last week of July.

Gutch also found a note in the record that the day after she was discharged she came back wearing very much better quality clothes than those she had been wearing when she left. She told them she had a box of clothes 'at a friend's'.

This is the first glimpse we have of Mary Baker outside the polite, bluestocking world of Knole. It must have been a shock to Gutch to find her displaying such open awareness of sex.

Given her habit of reassembling her fiction from fact, it is even possible that there really was a gentleman at Rackenford vicarage whom she met while she was working for the Moons, and that he was the cause of her coming to London. If there was, the whole story of her walking to London may have been an invention.

With Mary nothing is on very solid ground.

CHAPTER 13

THE WOMAN WITH EIGHT BREASTS

FROM THE END of July 1813 there is a gap of over two years without any written records to corroborate Mary's story, but Gutch was satisfied that he could account fairly accurately for her movements.

She had now worked, either at the instigation of her family or of Mr Pattenden, for two years as a nursemaid in Devon, for a short time as a general servant in Exeter, and for three years – with a short period of running away – in a respectable middle-class Christian household in Kennington. Given her first opportunity to choose what she did, she had spent five months in a home for penitent prostitutes.

Mary now began to drift. Except for the few names and places she was able to remember, which were in some cases confirmed by her parents and other witnesses, her story becomes more luridly inventive. Her fantasies become fact.

She said that her first thought on leaving the Magdalen was to go home to see her father and mother in Witheridge. That hardly tallies with her return to the Blackfriars Road next morning in a new dress, but according to Mary she began immediately to plan her walk home.

She decided that the first stretch of the Great West Road, across Hounslow Heath, was too dangerous 'on account of the robberies and murders then prevalent'. She would dress up as a man. Gutch asked her how she got hold of a man's clothes, and she said she went to a pawn-broker's and exchanged her own dress for trousers and a coat.

Gutch by this time, after several days watching her giggling on the sofa at Bridge Street, looking sidelong out of the window and then suddenly remembering something she had meant to tell him, seems to have been eating out of her hand. His cross-questioning falters and then stops altogether.

Mary said she cut her hair short, powdered it and brushed it forward, and took out her earrings. Then, to see if the disguise worked, she knocked on the front door of the first house she came to and asked if they would employ her. They were entirely taken in, she said. They laughed at her for being so short, and called her 'little man'.

She was shown into a parlour. Gutch asked who was there, and she remembered there being three gentlemen and four ladies. They asked her how old she was, and why she was so short. They liked her, but refused to give her a job 'because she looked so very wicked'.

There is the same shape to this as the story of her finding work in Exeter. She is alone, vulnerable, people like the look of her, but recognize her way-ward streak. There is also an element of sexual provocation. She was telling the story on a hot day in June to a fascinated audience, her eyes gleaming as they do in the Branwhite portrait, presenting herself to the imagination dressed as a boy.

It is the episode that Harry Bonner of the *Bristol Mirror* spends most time on, and Mary was encouraged to develop the idea, giving it the same blood and thunder momentum as the story of Princess Caraboo and the pirates.

With the dangers of Hounslow Heath far behind her, she crossed Salisbury Plain, still dressed as a boy, and was held up by two highwaymen. They asked her if she had any money. She said she hadn't. 'She was going to ask them to give her some.'

The two horsemen liked her, still thinking she was a young man, and offered her a job looking after their horses. They said they worked at night, and Mary asked them what they did. They promised her that if they found her loyal and faithful, they would tell her. Mary was 'determined to find out their business' and swore eternal loyalty.

Gutch, lover of the Robin Hood stories, wrote it all down word for word, unquestioning.

After many miles they came to the highwaymen's house in the middle of the forest. They gave Mary food and drink, and then, 'after about half an hour', four more men came in. They too took her for a young man, and asked if she could fire a pistol. She said no. She'd never been taught how to fire.

They all gathered round and started to teach her. They put the pistol in her hand and showed her how to squeeze the trigger. Mary said she was terrified, and they called her a chicken-heart. She would be of no use to them unless she 'plucked up a bold heart and courage'.

Mary told Gutch she 'fired off the pistol more dead than alive, and screamed out that she was murdered'. Then all the highwaymen knew that she was really a woman wearing men's clothes, and decided she must be a spy sent by the police to find their lair. They said they were going to kill her.

Lord Cork and Lord Salisbury must have loved it. Mary, her beautiful mouth wide, describing how she threw herself on her knees, a pretty girl dressed in men's clothes, now in disarray, alone in a hut in the middle of the forest with six terrifying brigands. She implored them to spare her life.

Then the brigand captain drew his sword, made her take it in her hands, and swear by the sword and all the powers above that she would never betray them. She swore the oath, they gave her 'a guinea and five shillings', and let her go free.

Where this came from, whether from a cheap novel of the period, a children's story, or from a romanticized memory of some real encounter, it is impossible to say.

Some time in the autumn of 1813 she arrived in Exeter by the main road and walked back to Witheridge. Gutch asked her whether she was still disguised as a man, and Mary said she was by now again in women's clothes. Her parents were surprised to see her. The last news they had had was Mrs Baynes' letter to say she had gone abroad with the travelling family.

Even in the middle of a story she pretended was true Mary seemed to think there was nothing odd about admitting she was a compulsive liar. She told Gutch and her other listeners in Bridge Street that she had fobbed her parents off with some tale about leaving the travelling family and losing all her luggage on a coach, and said her father let her have all her old clothes back.

Her parents thought she ought to work in the West Country. She agreed, her mother took her to Crediton, and they found a job for her with a leather-worker and tanner called Pring, again looking after children. She stayed with him for three months, and left because she did not think it was part of her job to be asked to work in the yard 'heaving the hides out of the cart'.

She went first to a village called Lapford nearer home, about seven miles south-west of Witheridge, and then two miles further on to Spring. There she found a job for another three months.

The winter of 1813 was very severe, the house was isolated, and cut off for many weeks by deep snow. It was impossible to get to the butcher's or to the market for fresh food, and the family killed most of their poultry to stay alive. Then one night, according to Mary, they sent her out to see if she could get through.

It was one of her tomboy adventures, and it is possible she volunteered: she struggled as far as she could, finally collapsed and 'sank in the snow'. She said she couldn't get up, and lay there all night, thinking she would never be found. In the morning they came searching for her, and took her home to bed.

She was still so delighted by the effect on her listeners of her adventures dressed as a man that in the version she told Harry Bonner she played the Lost In The Snow scene in men's clothes too, with the delicious punchline that 'when her wet clothes were taken off they discovered her sex'.

That adventure, she told Gutch, was what finally decided her against living in the country: she handed in her notice, and left for Exeter. Again, perhaps because he knew something that Mary preferred Gutch and Elizabeth Worrall not to know, she made no mention of where she stayed, which was with her cousin, William Burgess the carpenter. Instead, she told Gutch she 'inquired for work', and was employed as a cook during February and March 1814 by a lawyer in Goldsmith Street called Sandford.

By the time she left Sandford, claiming that the kitchen was too hot to work in, it was spring again, she felt the need to move, and she headed back towards London, having made enough money to pay for lodgings while she looked for work.

In her first years in London she had stayed south of the river, in Kennington and Newington, never going nearer to central London than the Blackfriars Road. This time she moved north of the river, working for a fishmonger called Hillier, in Dark House Lane, Billingsgate. Hillier's certainly existed, and is listed in the Post Office Directory in 1820 as having premises at 118 Lower Thames Street, on the north bank of the river, in Billingsgate Market.

It was at this stage, in the spring of 1814, that Mary claimed the love affair began that ended nearly two years later with the birth of a child.

She told Gutch that it was while she was working for Mrs Hillier that she went to a stationer's to get some books, and saw a 'gentlemanly-looking man'. After she had gone he asked who she was and where she lived, and they told him. If the story is true Mary must have been a regular customer at the bookshop.

The man's name, according to Mary, was Baker, though when pressed she sometimes said that he was a foreigner and was really called Bakerstehndt or Beckerstein.

That night he wrote to her, and called frequently to see her at Dark House Lane when Mrs Hillier was out. After she had known him for about two months, he persuaded her to leave her job, and they were married by a 'Romish priest'.

They lived together for a short time in London in the autumn of 1814, then moved south of the river to lodgings in Kingston. After that they travelled about southern England, and stayed for several weeks at a place Mary thought was called Battledore, which Gutch interpreted as Battle, near Hastings. There, she said, her husband gave her money to return to London, saying that he was sailing from Dover to Calais and would send for her to join him in France. She never heard from him again.

One element of this story, of a gentleman who lived with her for a month in London and then abandoned her, she had told before, when she was trying to get into the Magdalen, and she subsequently abandoned the whole tale in favour of others, but it is possible, again, that there is a core of truth to some of it.

The Magdalen records have a note of her calling in to see them in October 1814. If the story of the 'gentlemanly-looking man' in the bookshop was true this would have been about the time they were first living together in London. The Matron at the Magdalen said she was well dressed, and told them, which was probably true, that she had walked back to London from Exeter.

She also said she had found the lady she had worked for before, a Mrs Partridge, who had a town-house in Brunswick Square. Mrs Partridge was very pleased she had spent time in the Magdalen, and 'hoped that she would never forget the good advice she received there'. She was about to go to France as a cook.

At this point the thread gets into a complete tangle. Mary spoke at other times of working for a woman near Brunswick Square called Cole. She did, it turned out later, have an employer at 24 Wilmot Street, just off Brunswick Square, but she was called Elizabeth Flower. Partridge and Cole were two more of Mary's family names from Devon, like Burgess and Baker.

Gutch, who was nearly two hundred years closer to the story and spent a lot of time knocking on doors and writing letters, was convinced that the story of Mary's wanderings through southern England with her 'husband' was all invention, and that during that time she was actually working for Elizabeth Flower at 24 Wilmot Street. It is quite possible that the child was conceived when she was on holiday from the job, visiting her cousin in Exeter.

In this mysterious mixture of truth and lies, real life and fiction, one date is certain, and that is 11 February 1816 when Mary had a child. She called him John Edward Francis Baker.

'John Baker' was the name she clung to most determinedly when she was talking about the father of her child, 'Edward Francis' was the name she had invented on the spur of the moment when Mrs Matthews had asked her about the christening she never attended.

Trying to fill in the dates that led up to the child's birth even Gutch, with most of the witnesses still alive, found frustrating.

Mary told Gutch that when her husband abandoned her she returned to London, heavily pregnant, some time in January 1816. According to the woman he spoke to at 24 Wilmot Street – he thought she was called Cole but her real name was Flower – Mary had discovered she was pregnant there, and was sacked.

The atmosphere at the Crab Tree, a well-known pub on the corner of Tottenham Court Road and Percy Street, was more tolerant, and Mrs Clark who ran it allowed Mary to spend the time of her pregnancy there, working behind the bar. She said that she was 'one of the most cleanly, regularly, good servants they had ever had'.

She called herself Hannah, but she had a Bible which she used to read on Sundays, and the name written inside it was Mary Baker. Like Mrs Matthews, Mrs Clark said that Mary very rarely went out, that they all liked her, but that she told 'such odd unaccountable stories, that she became proverbial among them for the marvellous'. But they were stories that never did any harm to anybody, but 'seemed to arise from the love of telling something extraordinary'.

When Mary's baby was due Mrs Clark called a cab to take her to a hospital in the City Road. Long after Mary had sailed for America, Gutch managed to interview the driver. Like many cab-drivers, he had a remarkable story to tell. Even when she was about to have her baby, Mary insisted on laying false trails.

As soon as they had left the Crab Tree, Mary asked him to turn round and go in the opposite direction, not east to the City Road but west along Oxford Street. She told him to put her down in the Bayswater Road, and walked away alone. He said he followed her for a little way out of curiosity to see where she was going, but she managed to give him the slip.

Anyone trying to discover the truth about Mary Baker knows what he felt like.

Where the child was born remains a mystery. Mary herself said sometimes that it was born 'on the road to London', sometimes that it was born in Westminster Hospital, but the cab-driver's story has the ring of truth. It seems likely she was on the way to find the father of the child.

The child was real, but no real father came forward to help her, and Mary was now an unmarried mother in London with no money and no means of support. Mrs Clark told Gutch that Mary came back to the Crab Tree when the baby was about three weeks old, and that she urged her to take it to the Foundling Hospital.

It seems more likely that Mrs Clark simply turned them both out into the street.

Mary was admitted to St Martin's in the Fields on 20 March, when her son was four weeks old, and the child was christened John Wilcox a few days later. They were removed 'by order of Mr Taylor' to St Mary's Workhouse, Lambeth, on 19 April where Mary had stayed for a week four years before when she had run away from Mrs Matthews. It was there that she was persuaded to surrender her child, and they stayed at the workhouse together, according to the records, until 17 June.

Mary's story resurfaces in the books of the Foundling Hospital in Guildford Street, still preserved at the Greater London Records Office, which Gutch never had the chance to examine.

It was officially called the Hospital for the Reception of Exposed and Deserted Children, and had a strange coat of arms, designed by Hogarth. In the centre is a shield, surmounted by a lamb with an olive branch in its mouth. At the top of the shield are two stars and a crescent, in the centre a naked baby, and underneath the motto 'Help'. To the right of the shield stands the figure of Britannia, to the left a naked woman with eight breasts, apparently standing in a wooden tub. She symbolizes surrogate motherhood.

To give her baby to the Foundling Hospital, Mary had to walk across the river into central London on three successive Wednesday mornings to see the officers in a low building at the end of a long elegant yard. Each time she had to answer questions, provide addresses, and explain that she could not afford to support the child she was carrying in her arms. Then she had to walk down St Martin's Lane and Whitehall, past the old Houses of Parliament and back across the bridge to Lambeth.

Her petition for her child to be accepted at the orphanage is numbered 19184. The first page is printed, and explains the rules of the institution.

The mother of the child, if alive, must be the Petitioner, unless a satisfactory reason can be shown to the Committee for dispensing with it.

Petitioners must set forth the true state of the Mother's case, for if any deception is used, the Petition will be rejected, and the child not received into the Hospital.

No application can be received previous to the Birth of the Child, or if the Child is twelve months old.

No person need apply, unless the Mother shall have borne previously a good Character for Virtue, Sobriety and Honesty.

Persons who present petitions to the Committee must attend themselves on Wednesday morning, at half past Ten o'Clock, with their petitions, all of which will be taken into consideration, by Rotation, whilst the Petitioners remain in attendance.

There is then a questionnaire on a separate sheet, filled in as Mary sat with her baby on Wednesday 15 May 1816.

1. Name of Petitioner:
Mary Willcocks of

2. Her Place of Residence:
Lambeth in the County of Surrey (in the workhouse)

3. Married or Unmarried:
Unmarried

4. Petitioner's Age:
Aged 25, was delivered on

5. & 6. Day on which child was born:
11th February of a

7. Boy or Girl:
Male child, which is wholly dependent on your Petitioner for its support, being deserted by the father,

8. Father's Name:
John Baker

9. His Trade:
bricklayer at

10. Place of Residence when first acquainted with the Petitioner:
Exeter in Devonshire.

11. & 12. When the Mother last saw him:
Your petitioner last saw him the—day of March . . .

13. What has become of him:
She knows not.

Signed X The mark of Mary Willcocks.

This did not necessarily mean that she was unable to write her name: an X was all that was required. Underneath is written 'Referred for inquiry by Jam: C; Cox May 15th 1816 and ordered by Jam: C; Cox May 29th 1816.' Then at the foot of the page, 'Child admitted 1st July 1816.'

Mrs Matthews remembered a gentleman from the Foundling Hospital making enquiries at that time, and said that on her last visit to Clapham Road Place six months later Mary had told her, as she told the Hospital, that the child's father was a bricklayer in Exeter.

There is also in the Foundling Hospital records a third page of barely legible handwriting, which seems to be a fuller account taken down during an interview with Mary later in May. It may be that Mary had slightly regained her self-control, it may be that she was getting used to the brutal question-and-answer format of the interviews. In any case, she manages to shift her ground a little to mislead anyone who might have begun investigations in

Exeter, where she had admitted to meeting the father of her child.

It is also interesting that she uses the name Cole, or Coles, for her imaginary employer in Teignmouth. She had, it was true, cousins there called Cole, but it is unlikely she ever worked there. She also admits, which she never did to Gutch, the existence of her cousin William Burgess, who perhaps knew the father of her child. What follows is a direct transcript of her answers to questions.

She was living with Mrs Coles of Teignmouth, Devonshire. Baker, the father, a bricklayer, lived at Exeter, but went to Mrs Coles to set some grates, and from which time an acquaintance commenced.

He corresponded with her and promised her marriage. She has three of the letters in her possession. She left Mrs Coles in a month and then went to Mr Burges [the next three words are difficult to read, except for Orchard] Fore Street Exeter, a carpenter. Baker visited her there and courted her.

Mr Burges objected to the match, but Baker persuaded her to accompany him to his House to see his sister and that he would marry her next morning – he seduced her that night and put her off with promises next morning – she lived with him nine months and then they set off to London. She was delivered on the Road – they proceeded partly riding and partly walking and when they reached Hyde Park Corner he deserted her.

She had lived with Mrs Matthews, No. 1 Clapham Road Place, and intended going there, but she was taken ill on the Road and was taken to Lambeth Workhouse where she remains.

N.B. Baker's sister at St Sidwell, Exeter.

Again, fantasy and memory are interwoven with the collapse at Hyde Park Corner coming back like a recurring nightmare: it is probably the nearest Mary ever came, under the stress of having to part with her little boy, to telling the truth, but how close she came we shall never know.

There is another sheet attached, apparently a statement taken from Mrs Matthews. It is dated 20 May 1816, and is headed 'Mary Willcocks'.

Mrs Matthews of Clapham Road Place was in want of a servant about three, or four, years ago, when Mrs Matthews applied to the Lambeth Workhouse for some person to supply the place till they could obtain a proper servant, and they sent the Petitioner, who staid there near two years. She was sober, honest and industrious, but appeared sometimes to be deranged in her understanding. She left her situation about two years ago abruptly, and Mrs Matthews heard nothing of her, till she called there the other day. She referred me to the Rev.d Mr Pattenden of Clerkenwell.

About four or five years ago, Mr Pattenden, having some business to transact at St Giles' Workhouse, the Petitioner, then in a very weak condition, was introduced by the Matron to him as a distressed but a deserving object. Mr Pattenden became her friend, and recommended her to some humane

ladies, who clothed her, and Mr P. proposed her to
Mrs Matthews. He had not heard of her, since she
left Mrs Matthews, until the other day.

I understand the child is by her Master, who is a
Married Man. I have wrote to Exeter but have no
answer.

(Signed) R. A.

There is also part of another letter, of which the
bottom half is missing. This is dated 22 May 1816,
Exeter, and is almost certainly from her cousin,
William Burgess, the carpenter.

Sir,

In answer to the letter you sent me about Mary
Wilcocks I have made all the Inquiery in my power
and find that she always bore a very sober honest
character. I sent to her Parents to let them know I
had heard from you. Her father came here yesterday
and he tells me that they had heard nothing from
her for eighteen months and they are very sorry to
here that she been so let fall, but the Circumstances
they are in will not inable them to do anything for
her and shall be . . .

The last page is a brief handwritten note, dated 28
May 1816, and is also headed *Mary Willcocks*.

I wrote to Exeter on the 17th, not receiving an
answer, I wrote again on the 23rd, and the 24th
received an answer to my first, which is attached to
this paper.

I have waited a second time on Mr Pattenden, to
inquire more particularly respecting the sanity of the

Petitioner's intellect. Mr P. will not say she is insane, but in some instances she has talked and acted in a wild, incoherent manner. His wife, and daughters have taken pains to assist, and save her, and he hopes, that if the child is received, it may still be effected, and she may be recommended to a situation. (Signed) R. A.

Mary left the Lambeth workhouse on 17 June, and moved in with a staymaker in Kennington Lane, Mrs Forbes. On 1 July she left her child, John Edward Francis Baker, at the Foundling Hospital, who put him in the care of a woman called Mary Denyer of Mereworth, in Kent.

The same day Mary wrote another letter to her parents.

CHAPTER 14

THE WILMOT
STREET MYSTERY

A CCORDING TO GUTCH, who was shown the
letter by her mother, the handwriting 'had
more the appearance of a male than a female
character'.

London, July 1st 1816

My dear Father and Mother,
What apology to make I know not for may undutiful
conduct, for which I beg your forgiveness. I have been
travelling abroad with a family this long time back, and
have lately returned from the Continent. You have, I
believe, heard that I was married, and have got a young
child about four months since, which we have called John
Edward Francis. I am going to Norwich with my hus-
band, who is a native of that place; but I am not sure
whether we shall remain there or not, but I will write to
you every three months, and let you know every particular
of our situation. Give my love to my brother Thomas,
and sister Susan: let me know what trade you intend to
bind him to. I send you – as a small mark of my love and
duty, and I shall send you in future, please God, half-a-
crown a week; but it will answer as well to send it
quarterly.

I beg you will write to me directly, for fear I should happen to leave London before I receive your answer.

I conclude with my love to brothers and sister, and kind compliments to all friends.

Your ever dutiful daughter,

Mary Wilcocks.

P.S. *Direct for me to Mr Paddington, No. 29, Coppice Row, Clerkenwell, London.*

My husband (Baker), whose christian name is the same as the child, sends his love and duty to you.

The letter does not sound as though it was written by Pattenden. Whoever wrote it for her, the style of writing is certainly not that of a bricklayer, or of a foreigner.

Pattenden now found her another job working for two ladies, Mrs Field and Mrs Ferret, at 32 Thornaugh Street, off Tottenham Court Road. They liked her, said she stayed with them for six months, during which time she was entirely open about her baby and went to the Foundling Hospital every Monday, as permitted in the regulations, to ask after his health.

It seems unlikely that she would have been allowed to attend the child's second christening, which took place on 6 July 1816 at the Foundling Hospital. The Reverend Samuel Colman MA, Rector of Bushmere, Suffolk, baptized John Edward Francis Baker as Edward King. The name, if she ever knew it, must have come back to Mary as she sat in state at Knole as a princess.

Some time towards the end of October Mary

found a new job, working for a family called Starling in Norfolk Street, since renamed Melville Street, a row of houses off Essex Road in Islington. She continued to walk down to the Foundling Hospital every Monday, but at the end of October she called for the last time. The final entry is in the Foundling Hospital's Nursery Book.

19184 Edward King died 27th October 1816.

Mrs Starling remembered Mary going into mourning, and described her suddenly appearing in black, 'so quick that they were surprised when she put it on'. She told them the child had died at her mother's house. Mary never told them the father's name, but said he was a Frenchman and that they had been married by a Catholic priest. Like Patten-den, Mrs Starling said 'she could not recollect a quarter of her vagaries', but she remembered some very interesting things. She said, for instance, that Mary used to go somewhere regularly once a month to get money, but she could never discover where.

This is the first time that Mary ever had any money to spare or save, and taken together with what Gutch called the 'masculine hand' and educated style of the letter written after the birth of her baby, it amounts to strong evidence that she had some kind of protector at 24 Wilmot Street. It could have been the person that Mary called alternatively Mrs Burgess or Mrs Cole, and who signed herself Eliza-beth Flower, or someone else who lived there.

But if the father of her child, as seems most likely, was a bricklayer in Exeter, her new protector was educated and could well have been the person with whom she devised her imaginary language.

Mrs Starling also said that Mary told the children stories about 'travelling people' that frightened them, that Mary once came into the parlour dressed up as a gypsy, and that the children did not recognize her.

Mary also told the children she had been to the East Indies, and that her baby had been born in Philadelphia, by the side of a river, and that a lady and gentleman going by in a carriage had stopped and taken her and her baby with them.

Allowance has to be made for the fact that the Caraboo story had now been in all the papers, and that Mrs Starling's husband claimed he had been afraid of writing to Elizabeth Worrall when he first read about it for fear that Mary might return to London and waylay him as he walked home through the fields to Islington.

Whether or not Mrs Starling, too, was embroidering on the truth, she was very fond of Mary. She said she was the best servant they had ever had in the house, but that she was 'so odd and eccentric that she frequently thought she must be out of her mind'.

After the death of the baby she had more cause to think it: in November, Mary began setting fire to the beds.

Mrs Starling said Mary probably did not intend to let the fire get out of hand, and called it 'playing tricks'. Mary was at first hysterical, then calmed down and said she did it to incriminate another servant she did not like and whom she wanted sacked. Whatever her imaginary motive, she had started two fires in one week, and was sacked herself.

Where Mary went in November 1816, four months before her first appearance in Almondsbury, is another mystery. At the end of January, Thomas Willcocks in Witheridge got a letter from 24 Wilmot Street, where Mary had worked until she became pregnant. It was written, according to Gutch, in the same masculine handwriting as the letter written in July about going to Norwich. It is signed Elizabeth Flower.

Dear Sir,
Being a friend and acquaintance of your daughter's, Mrs Baker, who went to France before Christmas to her husband, she left me a pound note in charge for you, which I now enclose. I would have sent it before according to her orders, but waited in hopes of receiving a letter from her, that I might be able to acquaint you of her safe arrival in France: but as I have not heard of her since, I judged it not right to delay sending you this letter and its inclosure any longer.

I hope you have heard of her before now. I have a box of clothes belonging to her, as also a check on the bank for £25 which she desired me to send you in case of anything happening to her. She sent by Betsy Dinner two gowns for her sister before she went to France. I almost forgot to mention that her child died about a fortnight before she left London.

*You will please to answer this by return of post, as I
mean to write to her shortly.*

I am, Sir, with respect, your very humble servant,
ELIZABETH FLOWER

*Please to direct to me at No. 24, Wilmot Street,
Brunswick Square, London.*

If Mary ever went to France it was then, at
Christmas 1814. Some time in February she returned
to the West Country, on this occasion by coach. She
told her parents about the death of her child, and
said she did not see her husband any more, that she
had left him at Dover, and that she had come to say
goodbye before she went to the Indies.

Gutch's reporter asked them whether she had said
the West Indies or the East Indies, but they couldn't
remember.

The one thing they did remember clearly was that
Mary seemed 'very learned', and used to sit in bed
in the morning for two or three hours with her sister
Susan, now fifteen, prattling away in French. Gutch
asked how he knew it was French, and Thomas
Willcocks said that folks in the village had told him
so.

She stayed ten days, left them some money, and
went with her mother to Exeter. There she sent a
trunk of clothes ahead on a coach to Bristol, where
she meant to sail for the Indies.

At this point in her story there is something very
odd going on. She has enough money to travel to
Devon by coach, she may even have been to France

at Christmas, she sends her sister a present of two gowns, gives money to her parents, has a box of clothes at Wilmot Street and £25 in the bank, and behaves like a rich woman, sending her trunk ahead to Bristol. She should logically have followed in a carriage.

Instead, according to her own account at least, she takes to the road, begging, on foot, and heading in the opposite direction. If what she told Gutch is true, she must have been seriously deranged, and that was when she began to turn into Caraboo.

It was a bitterly cold month, and she claimed to have followed a strange zig-zag course that took her not towards Bristol but Plymouth. If she meant to sail from there, why send her trunk to Bristol?

It is possible that she thought of going abroad in a ship from Plymouth, but if she did she changed her mind. On the way there, she said, she met some gypsies. She was hungry, she asked them for food, and they gave her tea. She stayed with them for three days. The gypsies wanted her to stay longer, and promised they would make her rich, but they asked her to do things she did not want to do, and she left them.

She then described turning off the Plymouth road, south towards the coast at Teignmouth, then north again through Exeter and east to Honiton and back across country to the main road to London. At some stage on that aimless journey, she told Gutch, she began begging in what she called her 'lingo', the made-up language her father had heard her talking sitting up in bed with her little sister. She arrived in Bristol in the worst of the cold weather on 10 March.

Mary claimed afterwards that she went to Bristol, as she had told her parents, to find a ship for Philadelphia. She enquired at the shipping office, and was directed to a ship loading on the quay. The captain told her he was already well booked, but that she could travel steerage to America, if she brought or paid for her own food, for five guineas. They were sailing in fifteen days, at the end of March.

She then set off, she said, to raise the fare.

Gutch never pressed her about what had happened to the £25 mentioned in the letter from Wilmot Street, but she still had enough money to pay for lodgings for the night. She went to the Post Office, collected the trunk she had sent ahead from Exeter, and met a woman who took her to Mrs Bennet's lodging house off Lewin's Mead. That house was full, but one of their ex-lodgers was a Jewish girl called Eleanor.

Mary, telling Gutch the story three months later, could not or would not remember Eleanor's surname. Gutch made enquiries, and discovered that it was Joseph.

Eleanor Joseph told Mary that she was out working during the day, and that she could share her room in Lewin's Mead for a shilling a night in the lodging house belonging to Mrs Neale and run by her two daughters.

Mary and Eleanor Joseph gave them reason to

remember them, two high-spirited girls up to mischief. Gutch never discovered what Eleanor Joseph's 'work' actually was, but it allowed her time to go out begging with Mary. Again, there is an odd conflict: staying in a respectable lodging house at night, and begging in the streets by day.

It is almost as though Mary had been both distracted and strengthened by the death of her son. She was capable now of saving money, giving presents to her family and travelling by coach, but instead she chose to relive her old life as a beggar on the road, this time as a kind of mad game, a theatrical performance.

At first, nobody gave them any money. Then Eleanor Joseph persuaded her 'for a frolic' to make her black shawl into a turban. It never occurred to Gutch to ask how they thought of it, but Mary told Harry Bonner they had got the idea from seeing 'two or three French lace-makers from Normandy', who wore high lace headdresses.

'She watched their movements, and perceived that everybody stared at them. She fixed her eyes on the French Girls' peculiar headdress.' As a foreigner, she would be more intriguing. Encouraged by Eleanor, she 'outlandished' her appearance and began talking her lingo.

Gutch did not cross-question her about this, but as she left Bristol at about the time the ship would have sailed, it seems she did not succeed in raising the fare during the two weeks available and that she left Bristol hoping to do better out in the country. On the other hand, Mary's life was never very

reasonable, and she may have become distracted by
the pure fantasy of the character she was playing.

The most likely explanation is provided by a piece
of paper she was carrying when she was questioned
a few days later, before she got to Almondsbury.
Written on it were the words 'Charles Harvey Esq.
Queen Square, French Consul.'

Playing a French girl, she approached a gentleman: like many gentlemen before and after he was
keen to help her, and sent her to the French Consul.
He, Mary knew, would speak real French. Life
became too complicated, and she simply ran away
up the hill towards Gloucester and London.

She left Bristol on April Fool's Day. If she
thought that life playing the part of a mysterious
foreigner was going to be less complicated in the
country, she was wrong.

From the beginning of her journey, her performance was all too successful. At the top of the hill,
where the road skirted the grounds of the country
home of Lord de Clifford, she begged from estate
workers who listened to her 'lingo', took pity on
her as a poor foreigner, and asked her into the house.
Fearing trouble, she walked on, and was invited in
by a farmer and his family to share their midday
meal. Gutch asked her what they had to eat and she
told him roast veal, greens and potatoes.

Afterwards the farmer sent his daughter to take
Mary back to the big house to see Lord de Clifford's
cook. The cook was more alarming even than
Charles Harvey: he not only spoke French, he was a
Frenchman. Mary said she did her best to get away,

but she was surrounded by estate workers and servants, and she had to go in.

The French cook offered her a drink, and she refused it. She spoke her lingo, the cook couldn't understand it, and asked her if she was Spanish, *espagnol*.

Mary said *Si*.

This in itself lends some support to her story that she had been to France, or at least had some idea of French and Spanish. It also illustrates how quick she was, given the circumstances, to improvise. But one avenue of escape from reality was now closed: she could no longer pretend to be French. She was Spanish. If she was proved not to be Spanish she would be in trouble.

One of the servants immediately offered to take her into Bristol to meet some Spanish friends, and Mary bolted. She told Gutch that she 'ran to get her bonnet' and escaped across the fields. This did not convince Gutch: he thought she was wearing a turban, that was part of her French impersonation that had got her into trouble in the first place. Mary said no, she was wearing a bonnet then, she only wore the turban the next morning.

It is possible, as with all Mary's stories, that she imagined the whole episode, or based it on what she thought might have happened if she had been compelled to meet Charles Harvey. What was unquestionably true was that she was now determined to go on playing the part of a girl who spoke only gobbledegook. She was locking herself into a fantasy from which she would find it hard to escape.

Gutch managed at least to find a witness to her next adventure. She told him that she had begged a bed for the night, still talking her lingo, in a farm-labourer's cottage a little further away from Bristol. The labourer was called Yates, and Gutch visited him at his cottage 'in the Lanes by the Cherry Orchards'. He confirmed the truth of her story with some embarrassment.

Mary said she could hear him through the mud and wattle wall at night talking to his wife in the next room. Perhaps she was a rogue, or a man in disguise, or someone come to murder them.

Mary said she 'couldn't sleep all night for laughing', and Gutch took the trouble to write down her exact words as she told the story: 'I thought I'd have died with laughing before the morning! The woman was nearly in fits through fear that I was a disguised robber!'

Like the sound of her Devon accent in her letter from Mrs Matthews' or the gleam in her dark eyes in the Branwhite portrait, it gives a hint of how charming she must have been in conversation, giggling on the sofa as she remembered the whole amazing lark.

But Gutch was now struggling hard to resist her charm. Realizing that he was close to the moment of transformation from poor beggar girl to princess, he returned to his cross-questioning, obsessively collecting facts and details, trying to convince himself, as he wrote at the end of the book, that Mary 'was in her usual manners and common appearance by no means elegant or striking'.

He asked her exactly what she had had for break-fast the next morning, and she told him one cup of tea.

It was now 2 April, and she headed west, 'across the Marsh, and into the Passage Road'. This was almost certainly the road towards what is now the Clifton Suspension Bridge, where there is a long tunnel-shaped cave called the Passage, used by the BBC during the bombing of Bristol.

Gutch was desperate for more precise details. She told him she was wearing her turban and met a man on the road. This was the wheelwright's son who was later to denounce her at Knole. Gutch asked her what he said. Mary remembered he said it was a fine morning, and that she answered in her lingo. He fell into step beside her.

When they came to the next village he said what a pity it was for her to go on without knowing anyone or anybody understanding what she was saying. She made no response.

According to Mary, it was the wheelwright's son who suggested she should meet another language expert, a French governess – Gutch confirmed that the woman in question existed and worked for a gentleman called Mr Llewellyn – who also con-cluded that she was Spanish. This time she seemed to have less trouble in getting away, and walked on alone towards the Passage.

It was by now very hot, Mary said, and she sat down on a stone bench outside a public house to rest. The landlady came out, heard that she spoke in a strange language, and asked her in for a drink. By this time the wheelwright's son had caught up with her, and came to sit beside her. He told the company he had been given money by Mr Llewellyn's French governess to look after her.

Everyone in the pub gathered round and offered her different things to eat and drink, but she refused them all. Then the wheelwright's son told them she was Spanish, and they decided she would like brandy. They thought a lot of brandy was distilled in Spain, and the landlady brought her a decanter of it. She waved it away. Then they brought her a decanter of gin and a decanter of rum. She sniffed both, and finally accepted a little rum, and filled the glass up with cold water. She also ate some biscuits.

According to her father, Mary genuinely disliked alcohol and never drank, so it is possible that she accepted it out of desperation as the only way of getting a cold drink. But as she sat, the centre of attention, in the country pub she was learning a great many things that would help her in the weeks ahead: how fascinating a foreigner could be, a strange creature in captivity; how people would imitate the sounds she made, trying to understand them; and above all how they would offer any theory about her that would allow them to show off their own knowledge.

She managed to get away, staying on the road towards Clifton, the wheelwright's son still with her, and met two men coming in the other direction, one of them a soldier. Asked if he spoke Spanish the second man said he had lived there for years, spoke it like a native, and wished he was there now. Mary gibbered in her lingo, he gibbered something back, and Mary gibbered on for quite a long time.

The wheelwright's son and the soldier looked at the linguist, and asked him what he thought. He said she was definitely Spanish, and came from Madrid Hill.

They asked him what she was talking about, and he told them: she had a father and mother who were following her along the road.

Mary, trying not to laugh, wandered away to a gate to stroke the horn of a cow, and the linguist rushed after her to stop her. He made wild signs: cows were very dangerous. He explained to the others that Spanish cows were not like English cows, and that in Spain women rode on their backs. Mary must have been grateful to him: he gave her valuable practice in how to deal with Dr Charles Hummings Wilkinson and, more immediately, how to use the Portuguese traveller Manuel Eynesso.

She escaped again, but the wheelwright's son insisted on coming with her. She turned round, producing her piece of paper with 'Charles Harvey Esq. Queen Square, French Consul' written on it. She showed it to the wheelwright's son, making signs that she wanted to go back to Bristol. He was daunted, as she intended him to be, by the name of a gentleman living in the most elegant square in Bristol, but insisted on first taking her back to Mr Llewellyn's French governess.

On the way there she let him buy her a steak and a cup of tea at the public house, and then allowed herself to be taken to another meeting at Llewellyns'. This time the governess was able to show off her new protégée to a lady and gentleman who had travelled in Spain. They could not speak Spanish, but told the governess everything they knew about the country and its customs. The wheelwright's son told them about the man on the road, and they were quite happy to accept his judgement. The gentleman then gave the wheelwright's son more money, and told him he was to take her to a Spanish family living in Clifton.

This is the only detailed account we have, extracted by Gutch at a time when Mary's memory of events was still relatively fresh, of her life on the road, and it is valuable evidence of how she managed the problem of men.

She was by now very bored with the wheelwright's son, and determined to ditch him. She stayed with him until they were in Bristol, took him to Queen Square, again showed him her paper with Charles Harvey Esq. written on it, and persuaded him to ask someone to explain exactly where he lived. While he was asking them she gave him the slip, and hid behind a barrel on the quay until he gave up looking for her and went away.

It was now getting dark and she was tired. She abandoned her character to ask in English where she could find lodgings for the night.

This is another odd inconsistency in her story. She was in the middle of Bristol, within half a mile of Lewin's Mead. She always said that her luggage was at Mrs Neale's in Lewin's Mead, and that when she ran away from Knole she went back to Bristol to find it. Had she had a row with Eleanor Joseph, or with Mrs Neale? Was she covering up some episode she preferred Gutch not to know?

Wherever she spent the night, she set out again the next morning on the road to Gloucester. Gutch asked her again what she was wearing: she said she started out wearing a bonnet, and regained her courage enough on the road to make her scarf into a turban again. Gutch never asked her what she did with the bonnet before she reached Knole. In Patchway, she stopped at a public house and was given a glass of beer.

Then she walked on up the hill and turned off the main road to take the winding lane down through the cherry orchards into Almondsbury.

CHAPTER 15

AN IMPENETRABLE
HEART

HAVING HEARD HER story, Gutch was more than ever amazed by what she had done. Following Coleridge's German doctor, he set out simply to record what he called the 'Detail of Facts', allowing his readers to draw their own conclusions, but he could not conceal his own bafflement at how she had got away with it.

Like everybody else, he was half angry with her. Flashing her eyes at other men she had convinced them she was the Princess Caraboo; flashing her eyes at Gutch she had convinced him she was a dazzling confidence trickster, worthy to take her place with all his favourite fraudsters. When he began his interviews with her in June in Bridge Street, and splashed her Javasu characters across three columns of his newspaper, he described, like Dr Wilkinson, the beauty of her eyes, the regularity of her white teeth, her gestures and 'animation of countenance which it is impossible to describe'.

Now, writing up his notes in July after she had gone to America, the dream had begun to fade and he could only ask questions.

How could 'an illiterate, uneducated girl unaided

by education, with no apparent object but an ambition to excel in deceit, have so conducted herself both in the language she made use of and in her general demeanour, as to have induced hundreds to believe she was no less a personage than an unfortunate, unprotected, wandering Princess from a distant Eastern Island, cast upon the shores of Britain by cruel and relentless Pirates?'

She had been flattered, tricked, shouted at, constantly surrounded for ten weeks, as Gutch put it, 'by persons of superior talent and education as well as by those of her own rank of life, who were always on the watch to mark any inconsistency, or to catch any occurrence that could lead to detection'.

Comparable frauds had been perpetrated before, and the gullibility of the public could never be underestimated. At fairs, and even in theatres, such things were commonplace. Sixty years before, an audience had filled the Haymarket to see 'Signor Capitello Jumpedo, a surprising dwarf, no larger than a tobacco pipe, who can jump down his own throat', and had wrecked the theatre when they discovered such a person did not exist.

But the same longing to be amazed existed outside the theatre: Mary Tofts, the wife of a clothworker in Godalming, 'of a very stupid and sullen temper, unable to read or write', had given birth to rabbits: everyone immediately stopped eating rabbits, and the King himself sent doctors to watch them being born who came away entirely convinced. It was only when another doctor threatened to operate that

Mrs Tofts confessed she had been concealing baby rabbits inside her vagina.

George Psalmanazar, no more oriental than Mary Baker, had passed himself off for years as a native of Formosa, and had even published a book about his 'homeland'.

A century later, in 1920, there was the story of the girl who claimed to be the Princess Anastasia. She was pulled out of the Landwehr Canal in Berlin in February of that year, wearing by an odd coincidence very similar clothes to those Mary was wearing when she arrived in Almondsbury. She bore little resemblance to photographs of the murdered daughter of the Tsar, and spoke no Russian.

'Anastasia' sustained the character for sixty-one years, surviving to a ripe old age in Charlottesville, Virginia, where she died in 1981. Plays and films were written about her, and she fired the imagination of millions.

She was subjected to every kind of test, and gruesome analysis of the bones of those murdered at Ekaterinburg have since finally proved the case against her, but the reactions of people who met her, even in some cases members of the Russian Royal Family, are an interesting pointer to how Mary Baker carried off her more modest hoax in Almondsbury.

She first began to suggest that she was the lost Princess Anastasia in the lunatic asylum she was taken to in Berlin. The nurses subsequently noticed that she was hiding under her mattress newspapers with illustrated stories about the Russian Royal Family. She was collecting information for the role she had, consciously or unconsciously, chosen to play, and this enabled her to answer enough questions about her imaginary past to give her story some credence.

Later, as she was brought into contact with people who had known the Romanovs from a distance, all of them keen to boast of their royal connections, she was able to gather more facts to sustain her impersonation.

Mary Baker at Knole was able to follow exactly the same pattern. Her one great advantage, spotted by Gutch as the key to the hoax, was that from the outset everyone believed she was incapable of speaking or understanding English, let alone of reading it.

Once she had chosen to strike out, not as a Frenchwoman or as a Spaniard but as a more exotic foreigner, by identifying the picture of the pineapple at the Bowl, she was able to learn a great deal about her chosen 'homeland' from the books shown to her by George Hunt.

Initially she seemed to have been dreaming of China. Having pointed to a picture of a Chinaman and claimed her father was Chinese she could not then go back: he remained Chinese. But as she listened to Elizabeth Worrall and her friends talking about her un-Chinese appearance and realized it was weakening her story, she brought in her Malay mother and moved the scene of her 'homeland' to Sumatra or Javasu.

After that, like Anastasia, she was able to gather

more colourful and convincing details from those who came to ask her questions.

But what was central to the success of the deception in both cases was the desire of the victims to be deceived, and Gutch incorporates a Latin tag to that effect on the title page of his account.

The Grand Duchess Xenia, the Tsar's sister, who met Anastasia at Oyster Bay in 1928, was convinced the girl was her lost niece. Later, she described their conversations. 'I deliberately chose not to ask her any questions about the past. I wanted to give her every chance to reveal her true personality to me, without my influencing her with memories of her childhood or with questions.'

What finally won the Grand Duchess over, in theatrical terms, was the consistency of her performance. 'I confined myself to a constant observation. And it was above all through this observation that I was able to convince myself finally that her behaviour did not consist of studied posturings or words she had learned, but rather that she was herself.'

This, of course, raises the question asked in both the case of Princess Caraboo and of Princess Anastasia, which is whether they had convinced themselves, whether they both really believed that they were of royal blood. Anastasia, in her last years in Virginia, was known locally as 'Apple Annie', and in the course of Gutch's enquiries Mary Baker's sanity was frequently called into question.

But in both instances a great many people desperately wanted them to be authentic. In Anastasia's case this was for a variety of reasons, from guilty relatives who spent sleepless nights knowing they could have rescued the family from Ekaterinburg, to romantics who dreamed that, despite the horror, a girl had survived the bayonets in the cellar, to people like the man who finally married her, John E. Manahan, who was accused by one journalist of treating her like a 'totem', a collectable blue-blooded royal.

In the case of Princess Caraboo, Samuel Worrall may have felt the same, particularly as the blue-blooded royal was shoring up the prestige of the Tolzey Bank. But most of those who wanted her to be a princess seem to have been moved more by a Romantic yearning for another world: Wilkinson's first letter to the *Bath Chronicle* is printed quite by chance alongside a review of Thomas Moore's poem *Lalla Rookh* or 'Tulip Cheek', the story of an Indian princess from Delhi wooed by a young poet, who turns out to be the man she is travelling to marry in Kashmir. It is all about the magic of the East, a vague world of Shalimar, the Valley of the Roses, of lutes and harems and veiled Arab maidens, and Caraboo was the perfect embodiment of that dream.

But she was also the perfect excuse for anyone who saw her to show off their knowledge and retell their travellers' tales, put forward their learned theories and demonstrate their *salaams*.

Able to understand every word they said, Mary had more instruction and more material on which to base the role she was playing than any actress would have dared to ask for.

She was also able to provide the consistency that

impressed the Grand Duchess Xenia in Anastasia's performance at Oyster Bay. She was not only very clever at catching the tone of a person's voice, she also had a remarkable memory. Mrs Neale, talking to another journalist, remembered the time they had gone to church together in Bristol. When they came back afterwards, Mary had impersonated the clergyman, and repeated whole passages of the sermon word for word.

Gutch noticed too, when he met her, her knack of completely 'changing her face' when she was being Caraboo, which may account for the dreamy expression in the portrait by Edward Bird.

It was the same with her handwriting and drawing of oriental characters: anything that was put in front of her she was able to copy, and Gutch wrote rather sanctimoniously in *Felix Farley* of how sad it was that her 'knack at imitation' in that field could not be put to some more useful purpose, like painting china or designing fabrics.

But it was Harry Bonner who noticed the most interesting thing about her calligraphy. Even her signature was a copy. Someone else, possibly Bonner himself – Gutch's handwriting is small and neat and the signature is large and flamboyant – wrote her name on a piece of paper and she copied it. It was as if she had no character of her own: she had learned to write, but did not appear to have any recognizable handwriting. She simply imitated whatever was put in front of her.

This is perhaps the central clue to her performance. Compared with Coleridge's German girl who talked Greek and Hebrew in a fever, Mary was a conscious fraud. But the two girls still had a great deal in common. The character of Caraboo was a dream-self of Mary's, but she would never have developed or performed it without a great deal of outside pressure over which she had no control. Elizabeth Worrall, loving her as she seems to have loved her, gave her another childhood, the indulged freedom to improvise.

Gutch and many others believed that a lot of the 'lingo' Mary started with had been learned from a foreigner, and that she already knew something about the Far East before she reached Knole. Certainly there were words she used for coins, like *Tanner* and *Bob*, and *Maglish* that meant a woman, which were Romany. But a lot she learned at Knole.

Quite what her sources were it is impossible to establish, because Gutch suppressed so much. He was a friend of Elizabeth Worrall, and unwilling to hold Bristol intellectuals up to public ridicule any more than was absolutely necessary. He talks only about 'the learned travellers, the philosophers, the cogniscenti, the blue-stocking ladies and the numerous dupes of various denominations who were so completely juggled and outwitted'.

Having seen Caraboo, we are not now surprised at the facility with which her spectators fell into the snare. We will, therefore spare both names and characters, at Bristol and Bath, believing we should ourselves have been duped also.

Apart from the occasional dignified appearance of Captain Palmer, the only recognizable clown is Dr Charles Hummings Wilkinson.

But when it comes to books the task is a great deal easier. Neither of the two source books Gutch talks about, Hager's *Elementary Chinese* or Fry's *Pantographia*, is as daunting as they sound. They were practically coffee-table books, easy reading on a wet afternoon for any Bristol lady or gentleman interested in learning enough about the Mysterious East or the Wonder of Language to provide them with something to talk about at supper that evening.

Joseph Hager's *An Explanation of the Elementary Characters of the CHINESE with an Analysis of their ancient Symbols and Hieroglyphics* shows with simple illustrations how the first Chinese characters were derived from two parallel horizontal lines, the top one complete, the one below cut into two. There is then a bit about Ying and Yang, the perfect and the imperfect, heaven and earth, the male and the female, Isis and Osiris.

Dr Hager then goes on to explain about the knotted cords used for counting in China before the invention of the abacus, or *suon puon*, and shows how they can be seen to form the basis of some Chinese ideograms.

Comparing Hager's bold illustrations of Chinese characters with Mary's own efforts, it is easy enough to see how Hager helped her to amaze the gentlemen who leaned over her shoulder, watching her black eyelashes flicker as she drew the lines on a sheet of white paper.

But it is the second book, Fry's *Pantographia*, that contains the most direct proof of her technique. Turning the pages two hundred years later in the London Library, I felt closer to events at Knole than I had ever felt before.

There are samples of script, very like the characters that Mary drew, in Abyssinian, Armenian, Atooi – 'one of the Sandwich Islands in the South Seas' – Bungalee, Chinese, Georgian, Greek, and Japanese. All over the world, scholars had questioned people to find out what they called things: some Englishman in the remotest part of northern Australia had pointed to a canoe ('maragan'), a man ('batuma'), a woman ('mootjel'), and written down the sound of what they said, in English script.

On the page for Mindanao, the word for God is 'alatallah'. One is 'isa'. Mary's word for one was 'eze'. I felt I might be getting close. Malayan, a few pages further on, has all the 'Arabic' flourishes that Mary used in her letter of thanks to Mortimer, and may have inspired her choice of a Malay for a mother. Underneath there is a note, written in English like everything else, that High Malay is spoken along the Malabar Coast and in Batavia.

Almost on the last page is Sumatran. A man is 'tapo'. Then, on page 320, are the two dialects 'spoken in Sumatra', Lampoon and Rejang, that Mary identified as her own language. There is a short vocabulary in Lampoon, beginning with God ('Alla-talla'), and then a few words in Rejang.

Among those few words are all that Mary needed to convince the experts that her father chewed betel-nut: when she told them her father had black teeth, she had only to read from the list at the foot of page 320.

Father: bappa
Black: meloo
Teeth: aypen

Mary's motives and conscious decisions are more difficult to disentangle. To trace her behaviour from the time she walked down into the village, her turning in at the shoemaker's was very natural. Her own father was a shoemaker, there was something familiar and comforting about the smell of the leather, the sound of the hammer tapping in nails. She was still playing her lingo game, and she was rewarded with the bread and butter and a glass of milk.

Then there was the first encounter with Hill, and her visit to the vicarage. She tried to sleep there, and was turned away by Mrs Hunt. Hill offered her sixpence, and she refused it. This was odd, as she had been begging all day, and had only got a few halfpennies and a sixpence she probably knew was a dud. It is possible that she was genuinely very tired and preferred the idea of somewhere to sleep to the sixpence to look for lodgings.

She was now taken down through the village and up the hill to Knole. Gutch asked why she resisted, and she told him she was 'fearful of being found out'. The same thing had happened before at Lord de Clifford's and Mr Llewellyn's house. Her instincts were right: she said the Worralls' Greek servant asked her 'continually' what language she spoke. She did not like him.

Gutch wondered why she always tried to persuade him to go boating on the lake with her. Mary laughed, and said she wanted to get him out into the middle of the lake and push him in.

The first real hint of growing confidence was when she pointed to the picture of the pineapple in the Bowl. Then she played the game upstairs of pretending not to know what a bed was for. It may have been no more than a whim of the moment, to amuse herself and the landlord's daughter at the inn.

There is no reason to think that she intended to stay. Elizabeth Worrall came down unexpectedly early next morning to the Bowl and found her in a mood of dejection 'with strong traces of sorrow and distress on her countenance', and she may have been thinking about another day on the road, with only her lingo and her French turban to look forward to. Then she saw Elizabeth Worrall, and 'expressed much joy'.

This is, perhaps, the closest we shall ever come to the birth of Princess Caraboo. She recognized real love in Elizabeth Worrall.

Elizabeth Worrall had two sons, but no daughter. By the time her granddaughter, Georgiana Lucy Worrall, was born, she was in her mid-sixties, but she loved the child passionately. Georgiana died when she was nearly five. Her grandmother was heartbroken, and spent a great deal more than she could afford on a memorial on the south wall of the

chancel of Bristol Cathedral: it is by far the most
opulent of the Lechmere monuments, with Georgiana Lucy carved in marble on her deathbed, and a
long poem, probably by Elizabeth Worrall herself.

> Here sweetly sleep awhile blest child, thy sun
> Hath early set, thy state of suffering done
> But not in vain thy birth! Thou hast not sown
> Yet life's immortal harvest is thine own . . .

Underneath is carved, 'This tablet is erected to the
memory of a beloved child by her bereaved and
afflicted Grandmother ELIZABETH WORRALL.' There is
no mention of the child's father or mother, and
Elizabeth Worrall's own memorial stone is next to
Georgiana's in the floor of the chancel.

Elizabeth Worrall seems to have felt something of
the same love for Mary.

Once Hunt arrived with his books and suggested
the possibility that she came from somewhere far-
off with a strange-sounding name, from romantic
islands in the South Seas she had dreamed of, Mary
began the more elaborate charade. But it was Elizabeth Worrall, again in theatrical terms, who was the
director giving her the confidence to play the role.

Gutch, as a friend of Elizabeth Worrall, seems to
have been aware of this: he not only makes Elizabeth
Worrall the innocent heroine-victim of his account –
A Singular Imposition on a Lady of Quality – but
allows her space to justify herself again and again.

By far the most implausible moment in his
account is when Elizabeth Worrall, having brought
Mary back to Knole, makes a long formal speech to

her. The rest of the book is written in a very rough narrative style, and Gutch even apologizes in a note on the flyleaf for the fact that it was taken down during several interviews, and contains 'many ungrammatical and vulgar expressions'. Elizabeth Worrall's speech is the only direct quotation in the book, and it sticks out like a sore thumb.

> My good young woman, I very much fear that you are imposing on me, and that you understand and can answer me in my own language; if so, and distress has driven you to this expedient, make a friend of me; I am a female as yourself, and can feel for you, and will give you money and clothes, and will put you on your journey, without disclosing your conduct to anyone; but it must be on condition that you speak the truth. If you deceive me, I think it right to inform you that Mr W. is a magistrate, and has the power of sending you to prison, committing you to hard labour, and passing you as a vagrant to your own parish.

Elizabeth Worrall may have wished she had said this, and by the time she was talking to Gutch in June or July she had probably convinced herself that she *had* said it, but the evidence is that, like all the gentlemen, she adored the girl and wanted nothing more than that she should be Princess Caraboo.

Mary does not seem to have been capable of any sustained love in return. One of the clergymen Elizabeth Worrall sent to talk to her in Bridge Street told Gutch that nothing he could say 'made any impression on her impenetrable heart'.

No attempt was ever made to compile what would be called today a psychological assessment of Mary, but there is a 'craniological report' made at the time by one of the visitors to Bridge Street.

Craniology, Dr Spurzheim's 'science' of reading character from the shape of the skull, was treated by the *Bristol Mirror* and other papers with considerable scepticism. There was a story a month before describing the excitement of one phrenologist at seeing a 'bump' on the back of the head of a lady in Clifton which turned out to be a hairpin. But the report is interesting as a record of the impression she made on someone at the time, who was familiar with all the contemporary gossip and came into close physical contact with her on a hot June day in the Mortimers' house in Bridge Street.

The examination, according to the *Bristol Mirror*, showed that she was 'constitutionally cold, and indifferent to physical love – or, to speak more intelligibly, not amorous'. She was, on the other hand, socially ambitious, which explained her desire to be accepted as a princess. She showed no sign of combativeness, or destructiveness, or, more important, of any covetousness: 'that is, she is perfectly indifferent to the acquirement or keeping of money or property'.

The head-feeler also found that she possessed circumspection or caution 'to a *monstrous* degree'. She was wary, and she was also vain. She was lacking in benevolence, but had a great sense of respect. He commented on her capacity to remember people and things, and on her ability to imitate. He may even have been right when he said she was lacking in imagination.

Whether from conversation with Gutch or from a very sensitive observation of Mary, the phrenologist said she was unlikely to produce anything *original*, but would always be able to borrow from things she had observed, to provide an exact copy: 'her imitation would be the thing itself'.

The shape of her skull suggested too that she was of a roving disposition, and that she would always prefer her freedom to a comfortable life and a collar, 'even although it were of gold'. In the phrenologist's judgement her 'knowing faculties' were far stronger than her 'animal propensities', and she was ruled more by her intellect than her emotions.

At Knole her intellect may have been in charge when she was learning about the customs of the East, at other times she simply played like a child.

Once she had discovered about native worship and 'Alla Tallah' she started to play to her sun-worshipping game, but to begin with she was very calculatingly after Christian sympathy, trying the church door on the way back to Knole, laying the cross from the hot cross bun against her breast in the servants' hall.

It may have been a trick she picked up from the gypsies. The first gypsies to arrive in Europe in the fifteenth century got round the vagrancy laws by pretending to be Christian pilgrims, and in 1817 apparent piety still brought its rewards in the form of money and food dished out to gypsies by Christian missionaries keen they should settle down and lead god-fearing lives.

Mary's running away from Knole the first time was characteristic, as we have seen, however comfortable the surroundings, but hard to justify on reasonable grounds. She told Gutch she went back to Bristol to try to catch another ship to America, walking across country all the way, seven miles there and seven miles back. She told another journalist she had gone to pay Mrs Neale and send her trunk back to Witheridge.

Neither story makes much sense. If she was tempted to take the ornaments and trinkets she had been given as Caraboo, she resisted the temptation, and it is hard to believe that she left the house calmly, without a penny, yet intending to buy a ticket to Philadelphia. Nor is there any evidence that she saw Mrs Neale, or any reason why she should have sent her trunk back to Devon, when she had sent it to Bristol in the first place in order to sail for America.

She certainly collected clothes from somewhere in Bristol – Gutch's only criticism of Elizabeth Worrall is that she did not question her more closely as to where they came from – but it seems unlikely that she ran away with any conscious motive.

Her second escape, first to Bristol and then on to Bath and her stay at the Pack Horse, is even more irrational. Most people at the time, including Gutch, assumed Mary knew about Wilkinson's letters to the press and decided that the game was up. But to hitch a ride on a cart, still talking her lingo, to spend a morning, as Wilkinson reported, strolling with the fashionable crowds in the Circus, to be as happy as she was entertaining a new audience in the ladies' drawing room in Russell Street, all suggest that she had become very deeply involved in the invented character, and that Princess Caraboo, as the Grand Duchess Xenia would have said, 'was herself'.

After the confession in Bridge Street, Elizabeth Worrall was wounded, but she retained her dignity. Mary remained steadfastly unrepentant, enjoying her sittings with Thomas Lawrence and Branwhite, her visits from the Earl of Cork and Lord Salisbury, and all the attention she was getting in the newspapers, the general agreement that she was made for the stage.

Then, the day before she sailed for America, she wrote Elizabeth Worrall's name at the top of something she had written. Gutch calls it a 'singular epistle', but it is hard to say whether it is a letter, a bit of another sermon she had half-consciously memorized, or something she had copied out from an uplifting book she found at the Mortimers'. Gutch printed it as he received it, in prose, but it is clear from the rhymes that it was originally written in verse. As in her earlier letters from Mrs Matthews' house in Kennington, Mary is playing a part, assuming a very different voice from her own mischievous broad Devon.

It was Elizabeth Worrall's last glimpse of her before she left for Philadelphia, unable to say a word of gratitude or apology or love, heartlessly mimicking a fashionable literary lady of the day:

friendship thou charmer of the mind
Thou sweet deluding ill
The brightest moments mortals find
And sharpest pains can feel
Fate has divided all our shares
Of pleasure and of pain
In love the friendship and the cares
Are mixed and joined again

The same ingenious author in another place says 'tis dangerous to let loose our love between the eternal fair for pride that busy sin spoils all that we perform . . .

There the words ran out. And so, it seemed, did the story of Princess Caraboo.

PART THREE

CHAPTER 16

FLYING WOMBATS

I MET MICHAEL Austin when we were both working on the film *Greystoke*, the 'true' story of
Tarzan. When he originally began telling me the
story of Princess Caraboo over lunch at the Quai St
Pierre in Kensington in the summer of 1984, I
responded like all Mary's other admirers.

I was immediately hooked by the idea of her
speaking no known language, and when she recognized the pineapple I was as quick to show off my
knowledge of French and German as Dr Palmer had
been to show off his knowledge of betel-nut chewing in the Far East.

As soon as it became clear it was all a hoax I
changed my tune, thinking what a wonderful joke it
had been at the expense of the pseudo-intellectuals.

We then set about the problem of telling the story
on film: if the audience knew she was Mary Baker
from the very beginning, they would be rooting for
her all the way. On the other hand, to begin with
the mystery was irresistible.

We also needed to know a great deal more about
her. Michael had come across the story in a book by
Edith Sitwell called *English Eccentrics*, first published
in 1933. Edith Sitwell's picture appears on the cover
of the Penguin edition, with her birdlike face, her

hair twisted into a mock-mediaeval knot, her hands laden with rings, an English Eccentric herself. Like Caraboo a hundred years earlier, she had no trouble in creating a highly implausible character and persuading the public to accept it. But Edith Sitwell had the advantage of birth, money and education.

Sitwell's account is extremely brief. She has lifted the story from a book called *Sober Truth* by her brother Sir Osbert Sitwell and a Miss M. Barton, published three years before. She sets Caraboo in her chapter on travellers, between Henry Blaine, a Bible-thumping eighteenth-century parson who made his trip down the Thames to Ramsgate sound like a cross between *The Pilgrim's Progress* and a voyage round the world, and Louis de Rougement, who had visited Bristol in the late nineteenth century to address the Society for the Advancement of Scientific Knowledge.

De Rougement told them he had been King of the Cannibals in Australia. He had won the Cannibals' admiration as a 'great and powerful personage' by killing a giant alligator with his tomahawk. He had married a Cannibal wife called Yamba, who often walked a hundred miles to gather his favourite herbs. When he was ill – he was eventually cured by sewing himself inside the carcase of a freshly killed bull – Yamba had realized that she could not nurse both him and their child, and had eaten the child.

De Rougement's story was confidently reported in several issues of the *Wide World Magazine*, and he aroused only mild scientific curiosity when he described his memories of watching thousands of wombats – the small warthog-like denizens of the Australian bush – 'rising in clouds every evening at sunset'.

Louis de Rougement eventually turned out to be a former footman of Fanny Kemble, called Mr Grün or Grin. He had been to Australia, not as King of the Cannibals, but as butler to Lady Robinson.

Edith Sitwell, with icy snobbishness, dismisses Mary Baker as 'a servant-girl from Devonshire with a far from unblemished reputation', and spells Javasu throughout, perhaps from some quirk of upper-class pronunciation, as '*Jevasu*'. Her only real stroke of originality, having been brought up herself in a great country house, is to imagine Elizabeth Worrall's relief, when Mary disappears for the first time, at the departure of a guest who had overstayed her welcome. She describes her feelings of 'irrepressible joy, mingled with a decorous and dutiful despair'.

The tale of Caraboo meeting Napoleon on St Helena she appears to accept without question.

The story of Princess Caraboo had cropped up again and again, it seemed, with all the main details recurring, in newspapers and magazines, from the middle of the last century until the present day.

In February 1945 a version appeared in a magazine called *Britannia and Eve*, written and illustrated by Fortunino Matania. Matania's pictures are by far the most sensational part of the story. They have the moody reality of soft porn photographs, and show Caraboo as a permed forties pin-up. In the main picture – 'Assisted by the landlady of the inn, she undressed, donned night attire, and then knelt down in the middle of the room to say her prayers' – she is stepping naked out of her clothes, with her back to us, one shy nipple exposed, while the landlady of the Bowl kneels in front of her, staring in sultry fascination at a spot seven or eight inches below the girl's navel.

Matania, like the Bristol journalists in 1817, liked the theatricality of the story. 'The details could not be more amusing, nor the unexpected ending' – her meeting with Napoleon – 'more effective as a final "curtain"'.

He takes occasional liberties – Samuel Worrall rather than Elizabeth is 'renowned for his wisdom and kindness towards the village folk', Caraboo's leather shoes rather than her turban have 'an Oriental appearance', and 'Javasu', perhaps under the influence of Edith Sitwell, becomes '*Jer*vasu'. Caraboo is seen in one picture practising archery indoors, and hides up the tree not out of terror of the servants but for fear of some mysterious stranger.

But Matania too accepts the Napoleon story as true, and the last illustration shows her rapturously submitting to a Charles Boyer-like Bonaparte in full uniform, watched by a cross Hudson Lowe.

All the versions, however, can be traced directly back to Gutch's book. It is sixty-eight pages long, and bound in plain boards. There is also a broadsheet published at about the same time, from Harry Bonner's account in the *Mirror*.

Going back to these main sources, and the Bristol newspapers of the day, it was possible to dig through independent records, some of which Gutch did not have the time or the opportunity to consult.

Michael Austin and I drove down to Almondsbury, off the main road from Bristol to Gloucester, a mile past the Rolls-Royce works where the engines for Concorde were made, and had lunch at the Bowl. It is still there, though extensively restored. We also visited the church, cleaned of its white render now, but still with the same herring-bone patterned lead spire.

The Poor Books kept by Mr Hill were in the vestry but the book for 1817 was missing. It was the beginning of a very long search, assembling lost pieces of a puzzle that is still far from complete.

We walked up to Knole Park. Only a part of the old tower remains, the rest having been pulled down in the early nineteen-sixties to make way for a housing development.

In Bristol Cathedral we saw Elizabeth Worrall's poem on the monument to her granddaughter. We also visited the Bristol City archives, and discovered a certain amount about Samuel Worrall and the Tolzey Bank, John Haythorne and the Bristol Corporation.

In London I also managed to get hold of the records of the Foundling Hospital, still in roughly the same place – with Hogarth's portrait of its founder, Thomas Coram and glass cases full of the little tags, rings and bracelets that were left with babies by mothers like Mary Baker – and still finding foster parents for unwanted children.

We met Mr Masters, the secretary, and I mentioned that Mary Baker, before leaving her baby with them, had spent a short time at the Magdalen, a home for reformed prostitutes. He was quite clearly shaken. 'I don't know where you got that information from.' They would never have accepted a child with that kind of background. Mary Baker's submission came to light, however, as did the letters to her relatives in Devon.

The Magdalen records still existed, as did some papers relating to admissions to the St Giles' Workhouse Hospital. Other evidence had been lost or destroyed in the bombing of Bristol.

There were, as with any detective story, a lot of red herrings and dead-ends. I spent some days reading the anatomical lectures of Dr C. H. Wilkinson before I realized it was the wrong Dr C. H. Wilkinson, though their dates were almost identical.

Concentrating on the main part of the story that Michael had told me in the Quai St Pierre, we completed the script, simplifying certain elements, concentrating on the time at Knole and giving Mary a less complicated past. We made Gutch a younger unmarried man, and as it turned out when we came to cast it, a younger unmarried Irishman. We turned his short infatuation with her into a serious romantic passion, but the more I read about Gutch, the more I thought it was justified.

We also expanded the tea party with the two ladies in Bath into a ball for the Prince Regent.

As often happens with film scripts, I heard nothing more. Michael didn't seem able to raise the money and went back to New York, and I got on with other work in London. But I often thought about the story, and felt very flat when I heard some time in the spring of 1991 that a television series about Princess Caraboo was in preparation, and possibly a book.

Then, in early 1993, Michael Austin, unaware that any other production had been planned, rang me to say he had not only raised the money, he also had a strong international cast with Kevin Kline, Wendy Hughes, Phoebe Cates and Stephen Rea, and was going to direct it himself.

We re-wrote the script, the film went into pre-production, and as the art department set about recreating the world of 1817 odd things began to turn up, including a copy of the Magdalen Hymn-book with an engraving of the uniform that Mary wore in the spring of 1813.

I went back to Bristol, mainly to reassure myself that we had got the main points of the story right, but aware that there were questions to which it seemed we would never find the answer.

Who was Manuel Eynesso? Was he, as some later versions of the story suggested, an accomplice or even a lover, or simply, as I finally decided, another garrulous traveller – like the man on the road to Clifton – keen to prove his knowledge of languages, and possessed of a romantic imagination?

Who was John Edward Francis Baker, the father of her child? Was he really a Frenchman, or the 'educated gentleman' she had met in the bookshop, or the bricklayer in Exeter, or the man from Norwich, or was there someone else who gave her a monthly allowance when she was working at the Starlings' in Islington and who took her to France for Christmas 1814?

Like many other men who in some way or another have fallen in love with Mary Baker, I became obsessed with the question of who she had been to bed with. Was it even possible, despite the phrenologist's sense that she wasn't interested in sex, and her understandable shrinking away from Wilkinson, that in her crazier moods she slept with a great many men and didn't know who the father was?

There was also the question that had puzzled Gutch of why Mary had wanted to go to Philadelphia, and what happened to her after she got there. She was then in her mid-twenties, with most of her life in front of her. Tracing a working-class girl who emigrated to America in 1817, according to a librarian I spoke to at the Philadelphia Historical Society, would be 'like looking for a grain of sand on the seashore'. But she had been famous, and Gutch's book went all over the world.

It was then that I came across a footnote to the Princess Caraboo story in a collection of early nineteenth-century frauds. There was a reference to a book published in the same year as Gutch's *Singular Imposition*, 1817. It was called *Companion for Caraboo* and was the story of a man called Henry Frederick Moon, of Brighton, 'now under sentence of imprisonment in Connecticut'.

I was convinced I was finally on the way to

solving the mystery. Mary worked for the Moons at Bradford Barton, she claimed she was in Sussex in the months before her baby was born, and now her 'companion', Henry Frederick Moon, had turned up in Connecticut the year she arrived. I knew that 'Baker' was one of her assumed names. The rest seemed perfectly simple.

She fell in love, not with the gentleman at Rackenford Rectory as she had told the Magdalen, but with one of the farmer's sons at Bradford Barton. They had quarrelled when she walked over to the farm to show him her white dress, but she had never forgotten him. He had moved to Brighton, met her again in London, made her pregnant, and abandoned her. She had taken the name Baker, left the child at the Foundling Hospital, and then he wrote to her, from America, asking her to join him.

I ran the book to earth in the New York City Library, though I discovered afterwards I could have found it more easily in the British Library.

It is now very rare, the New York copy bound in leather and dog-eared. Its full title is *Companion for Caraboo – A Narrative of the Conduct and Adventures of HENRY FREDERICK MOON alias Henry Frederic More Smith, alias William Newman, A Native of Brighthelmstone in Sussex, and now under sentence of imprisonment in Connecticut, in North America; containing an account of his unparalleled Artifices, Impostures, Mechanical Ingenuity & etc & etc displayed during and subsequent to his Confinement in one of His Majesty's Gaols in the Province of New Brunswick, by WALTER BATES ESQ., High Sheriff of King's County, New*

Brunswick, with an Introductory Description of New Brunswick, and a Postscript containing some account of Caraboo, the Late Female Impostor, at Bristol.

The preface has a moralizing tone entirely absent in Gutch's account, foreshadowing the pall of Victorian respectability that was soon to fall over the bright world of Princess Caraboo.

It could be argued that Moon had behaved a great deal more badly than she had. The purpose of publishing Moon's story was to warn others against a life of crime, but there was also, as with Gutch, a note of almost grudging amazement at what the man had achieved. The story showed that 'a man knows not what he can do till he tries'.

I still had high hopes, but the last paragraph of the introduction was not encouraging. 'The impostures practiced by Henry Frederick Moon will irresistably remind the reader of those of Caraboo, the late female adventurer at Bristol.' The stories were, it went on, very different but also rather similar. 'The two names have therefore been connected on the title page, and some brief documents concerning Caraboo have been added as a postscript.'

Moon, in other words, had never been Caraboo's 'companion'. The title was a catch, like the gratuitous commercial plug for New Brunswick that followed, with its rivers teeming with fish and unlimited opportunities for new settlers as farmers or lumberjacks.

Any hope of finding Caraboo's lover, the boy she had fallen in love with when she was sixteen, had lived with in Brighton, had even perhaps been the father of her child, and whom she had followed to America, now faded. Moon, it seemed, had never met Caraboo, though they had been within a few miles of each other in New England in the autumn of 1817.

But Moon's story is a very remarkable one, and it does throw a kind of reflected light on Princess Caraboo.

A neat, wiry, gentlemanly young man of fastidious habits, formerly a Methodist preacher, Moon was pursued for nearly three hundred miles by a Canadian gentleman called Knox who claimed Moon had stolen his horse. Moon produced apparently valid proof that he had bought the horse from someone else, but Knox pressed charges and Moon was kept in prison.

During his confinement, he appeared to be dying. He said Knox had kicked him. He showed them a bad bruise under the ribs, brought up a great deal of blood, alternately shivering with cold and sweating with fever, and after a fortnight was so frail that a charitable family living near the prison sent round a feather mattress for him to die on. He called out in the night for a hot brick to warm himself with. The gaoler's son went to fetch it, left the door unlocked for a moment, and he had gone.

He was eventually recaptured, and was fitted with a neck-iron, handcuffs and leg-irons by the local blacksmith, all shackled together and fixed to an iron ring in the wall, making it impossible for him to move. Late one night his gaoler heard a suspicious sound and searched his cell. At first everything seemed to be in order. Then he discovered that the bars of Moon's cell were almost sawn through. He raised the alarm, searched Moon, and found that he had somehow freed himself from all his chains.

He was fitted with heavier irons, but next morning was free again, asking his gaoler how anyone could be expected to wear them. He was repeatedly searched, and eventually a tiny saw was discovered that he had managed to make from cutting tiny serrations in a steel watchspring.

What followed was a great deal more mysterious: he appeared in court, seemed to have gone mad, singing and whistling when he was charged, and was condemned to death. He was returned to his cell. There he refused to speak or to take food, ranted and screamed, tore off any clothes he was given, and was found one night, despite new bars in the window and stronger locks on the door, with a woman kneeling beside his bed. It was a remarkably lifelike effigy of his wife. He had made it in pitch darkness from straw and scraps of torn cloth.

Then, left alone, handcuffed in the dark, with no tools of any kind, using straw and scraps of cloth with charred wood and his own blood for colouring, he made a whole cast of life-size puppets. It is described by the High Sheriff who had condemned him to death.

The exhibition consists of ten characters, men, women and children. The uppermost is a man whom he calls the tambourine-player or sometimes Dr Blunt, standing with all the pride and appearance of a master musician, his left hand akimbo, his right hand on his tambourine. Next to him, below, is a lady – genteelly dressed, gracefully sitting in a handsome swing; at her left hand stands a man, neatly dressed, in the character of a servant, holding the side of the swing with his right, his left hand on his hip, in an easy posture, waiting the lady's motion. On her right hand stands a man, genteelly dressed, in the character of a *gallant*, in a graceful posture for dancing.

Beneath these three figures sits a young man and a young girl, (apparently about fourteen), in a posture for *tilting* [playing see-saw] at each end of a board, decently dressed. Directly under these stands one whom he calls Buonaparte, or sometimes the father of his *family*; he stands erect, his features are prominent, his cheeks red, his teeth white, set in order, his gums and lips red, his nose shaded black, representing the nostrils. His dress is that of the harlequin. In one hand he holds an infant, with the other he plays or beats music.

Before him stand two children, apparently three or four years old, holding each other by the hand, in the act of playing or dancing, with a man, dressed in fashion, who appears in the character of a steward, sometimes in one situation, and sometimes in another.

Then commences the performance. The first operation is from the tambourine-player, or master, who gives three strokes on his tambourine, that he may be heard in any part of the house, without moving his body. He then dances gracefully a few steps, without touching the tambourine, the lady is then swung two or three times by the steward, then the gallant takes a few steps. Then the two below tilt a few times, in the most easy, pleasant manner, then the two children dance a little, holding each other by the hand, and everyone dances to the tune, with motion, ease and exactness not to be described.

People came from as far away as Boston to see Moon and his puppets, all expressing amazement, and some believing he was in league with the Devil, an idea Moon if anything encouraged by saying, 'The Devil has no chain about *his* neck!'

Charmed by his ingenuity the authorities gave him a free pardon. He waved the pardon about, apparently unable to understand what it was, but left the gaol, and was re-arrested some months later under the name of Newman in the United States for burglary, having stolen an earring from beside a young lady as she lay asleep.

At the time the book went to press in the autumn of 1817 he was serving a three-year sentence in a far more terrible prison, held underground in a disused copper mine in Connecticut, excused forced labour and allowed to work as a tailor because of his 'violent epileptic fits'.

Wilkinson's letters about Caraboo are appended at the end.

Moon was not her lost lover, but his story contains three elements of great relevance to hers. The first is the figure of Napoleon dressed as a harlequin, the 'father' of Moon's family of puppets, and the dream lover imagined for Caraboo by John Matthew Gutch. Even chained on his rock in the middle of the South Atlantic, he continued to dominate the Romantic imagination of the age. He was the man who had destroyed the old order, who had opened the gates of the social prison-house, who had shown that dreams could become reality, and that a great deal of so-called reality of the old order was no more than a dream.

Moon and Mary Baker were also both escapologists: Moon, more violently and dramatically, throwing off his leg-irons and shackles, but Mary too in managing against all the odds to escape from the limitations imposed on girls of her class. Most important of all is the fact that her name was considered worth printing on the title page. Moon's story was remarkable enough to sell, but Mary's fame on both sides of the Atlantic was considered great enough to help the book.

Then, just as Henry Frederick Moon proved to be another red herring, one of the researchers in the art department, checking through the files with me in Bristol Library, came across a more recent press cutting that was to lead me closer to Mary Baker than I had ever thought possible.

In 1985, it appeared, within a few months of my first visit to Almondsbury with Michael Austin, the television writer Roger Stennett had had the same idea: he had written a play about Princess Caraboo which had been performed by the Orchard Theatre and which toured the West Country.

I rang him. He had heard the news that we were

making the film, but was extremely magnanimous and agreed to meet for lunch. We met, and I realized how close we had come to losing the race: he had begun work a few months after we had, with the idea of writing the story for television. The BBC had initially shown great enthusiasm, but had then havered for months over the script.

They accepted it in principle but worried, as Michael and I had done, about when to reveal the hoax. In the end Roger got tired of waiting and wrote it as a stage play.

As we talked I realized that we had both been obsessed with her. At the end of lunch he said it was as if we'd been talking about a girl we had both been in love with.

He gave me his play to read. It approaches the story more poetically than we did: Wilkinson is slightly more sinister, and there is a highly erotic scene where he drugs Caraboo and slides his hands up under her skirts, but the core of the story is Mary's relationship with Elizabeth Worrall.

Perhaps the best scene in the play, and one I wished we had written, is where Elizabeth Worrall, believing that Caraboo cannot understand what she is saying, confesses her loveless marriage to Worrall. She is all the more shattered at the end of the play when she realizes that Mary has understood every word and has doubly betrayed her trust.

I met someone else. The Orchard Theatre tour of Roger Stennett's play had received a lot of advance publicity in Devon and Cornwall, and on the first morning of rehearsals, according to the press cuttings, a woman had walked in. She had read about the play in the local paper. She thought she might be able to help them.

She was directly descended from Thomas Willcocks, and was the great-great-granddaughter of Mary's younger brother. Her name was Mrs Medley and she lived in Brixham.

I rang Directory Enquiries. There was only one Medley in the Brixham telephone book. I telephoned her, and within days we met in London. She was now a grandmother, but as she appeared on the doorstep of my studio I found myself looking into the face of Mary Baker.

She was almost exactly the same height as Mary, and had the same mischievous eyes. They were blue, rather than brown, and when we talked about it she said she thought Mary might have had Spanish blood: survivors of the Armada had landed on the north coast of Devon and settled there, and she knew other members of the family who had Mary's dark colouring and brown eyes. Perhaps, after all, the man on the road to Clifton who said she came from Madrid Hill had been right.

Christine Medley arrived in London late: her train had been delayed by a tree across the line, brought down by gales in the West Country the day before. Walking through Kensington, her attention was immediately caught by the bough of a holm oak that had fallen across the pavement and was being sawn up: she stopped to show me the reddish scales of the bark, and said how pretty it was. It seemed to me that Mary would have looked at things in the same way, that she would have talked to people who walked along the road to London with her about the same things.

Driving through London that evening, she was obviously thrilled by the big shops all lit up for Christmas, and I realized again the excitement that Mary must have felt on the road at the very idea of London. It was easy to forget that she was a country girl, and that London meant freedom. When we talked about Mary's white dress I wished she had been in Witheridge in 1817: Christine Medley didn't believe for a moment it had been 'dishonestly come by'. Think of the drab clothes she had to wear every day on the farm: any village girl would have bought a pretty dress given the chance, why shouldn't she?

Christine also brought with her the Willcocks family tree. Mary's grandfather and great-grand-father are listed as blacksmiths, and the date of her father's christening, which gave me the clue to Caraboo's celebration of Jessee Mandu's birthday at Knole. Then the date of her parents' marriage, when Thomas Willcocks was twenty-four and her mother twenty. From the register of baptisms it seemed likely that he had married her when she was already pregnant with the first son, Henry. Then the names and dates of birth of all Mary's dead brothers and sisters.

There, on the same page, too, were all the names she had resorted to when being Mary Willcocks was too hard to bear: Burgess, Cole, Partridge and Baker, all inter-married. It struck me that Mary's inventions were very innocent and simple-minded.

Christine Medley also brought with her photographs of old Witheridge: solid little stone-built houses in the main street with the moors beyond, horses and carts on market day, the big church with the spire. It was a village more than a town, avoided by the railway in the eighteen-thirties so that the nearest station was seven miles away, a place that has been losing inhabitants steadily since Mary's time.

She showed me on the map where Mary's father had lived, in Stretchdown or Stretchtown, in a cottage that had now been demolished, and told me the old village story about Nelson and his mistress, the foreign princess. She knew that because there was still a Willcocks cousin farming the land in Witheridge: his name was Thomas Gibson. I asked her where she had found the family tree, and she told me that it had been drawn up by another Willcocks/Burgess cousin, Bernard Spaughton. It was to be some months before I met Thomas Gibson, but Bernard Spaughton lived in Cheam, and I was to meet him within the next few days.

CHAPTER 17

COUSIN BERNARD

Lunch with Bernard Spaughton followed a week or so later, and once again I found myself looking into Mary's eyes: blue, like Christine's, but with Mary's sense of mischief and a deep, thoughtful intelligence. A chartered accountant who worked for most of his life with Bowater's, he had been all over the world on financial investigations, and he had applied his detective skills to the story of Princess Caraboo. He was even more obsessed with her than I was.

For the last twenty-five years he had dreamed of writing a book about her: now he had come to the conclusion he probably never would, and with a generosity I have never before encountered in thirty years of writing, he handed over all his research.

He even had the lading list for the *Robert and Ann*. He had gone over every detail of Gutch's narrative, making a year-plan almost identical to the one I had made myself, showing where Mary was, from her admission to St Giles' Workhouse Hospital until her arrival at Knole. In some cases he had followed false trails I had already discounted, like a workhouse belonging to the other St Giles' in Seven Dials: in others he had made identical mistakes, like finding the wrong Dr C. H. Wilkinson, the anatomist. But

I was amazed by his dogged attention to detail, the precise filing of every fact that could lead to a solution of the mystery.

Bernard Spaughton had photocopies of all the Bristol newspaper stories I had painstakingly copied out by hand at Bristol City Library, photocopying of their bound volumes not being allowed there. He had traced every mention of Princess Caraboo since 1817, collecting photocopies of obscure periodicals I had never heard of, comparing every one of them to Gutch's original account, and noting any variations in the story.

In 1981, for instance, there was a programme on BBC2, in which the Princess Caraboo story had been retold and in which Manuel Eynesso had been portrayed as Mary's paid accomplice. Bernard Spaughton had written in to ask where this information had come from, and Clive Doig, the producer, had written back, quoting 'more modern accounts', without specifying what they were.

He had searched, as I had, for more information about Edward Bird and Nathan Branwhite, and had had less luck than I had, my own break coming when I made a last trawl through the Bristol City Library and found a catalogue, printed by John Matthew Gutch, of an exhibition of Bird's pictures shortly after his death to raise money for his widow, with a biographical note on the back.

As I had hoped, Mary's notoriety in England had aroused the interest of newspapermen in America, and Bernard Spaughton had succeeded, in the course of business trips to America, in finding several references to Caraboo's arrival in Philadelphia.

He had also made another fascinating discovery. It had never really occurred to me to wonder why Mary should have called herself 'Caraboo'. If I'd thought about it at all, I assumed it was an odd, outlandish sound that had come to her on the spur of the moment, remembered perhaps from stories of Canada, and of caribou.

Talking to cousins like Thomas Gibson who still lived in the West Country, Bernard Spaughton had heard of a legendary 'King of the Gypsies' who died twenty years before Mary was born. Unlike de Rougement, he was a genuine King of the Gypsies, elected in the eighteenth century as successor to the previous king or chieftain, who was called Clause Patch. He was a gentleman by birth, who had run away from school after angering local farmers by damaging crops when he and three other schoolboys were hunting a deer, and had joined a gypsy encampment.

He was notorious for his tricks, and was eventually transported as a convict to Maryland. Like Henry Frederick Moon, he was put in irons, escaped, and was fitted with a heavy iron collar. He escaped again, and joined a tribe of friendly Indians who released him from the neck-iron.

He then made his way to Philadelphia, posing as a Quaker. Returning to England by way of New York, he avoided re-arrest by pricking his hands and face with the point of a dagger and rubbing them in salt and gunpowder to convince those who tried to arrest him that he was suffering from smallpox.

Back home, he was reunited with his wife and daughter, travelled to Scotland, and came south with Bonnie Prince Charlie: later a member of his family offered him money if he would abandon his gypsy ways and settle down. He refused, but eventually did so, according to the story, after winning a big prize in a lottery.

He was born in Tiverton, less than twenty miles from Witheridge, he was a local hero, and every detail of his story would have been known to Mary from her earliest childhood. His name was originally Bampfylde Moore Carew, and he was known throughout the West Country as 'King Caroo'.

'Philadelphia', like Brecht's 'Surabaya' or 'Bilbao', has a sweet poetic sound to it, and it is at least possible that Mary's yearning to go there began as a child in Witheridge, like her choice of a magical gypsy name for herself, listening to the story of King Caroo.

But the search on which Bernard Spaughton had spent the most time, money and patience was for more solid documentary evidence, contained in a very rare copy of Gutch's book which had come up at auction in the nineteen-twenties. It was advertised in the sale catalogue at the time as 'including three autograph letters from America'. Bernard Spaughton had pursued it relentlessly, finding the original private library from which it had been sold, the dealers, and even the publishers of the sale catalogue:

he had been after it for over twenty years, and had drawn a blank.

It was at that stage, quite by chance, that I asked the art department if I could borrow a photostat of their copy of Gutch's book to save myself the trouble of taking it out of the London Library. Clipped to page sixty-eight of the photocopy were what looked like four handwritten pages. They were letters from America.

The original book from which the photocopy had been taken was in the Bristol Museum. The curator, Francis Greenacre, had bought it only a few months before, in 1993, from a bookshop in the town called Ambra Books, and they were unable to tell me much more about it. Written on the flyleaf of the book, I now saw, was the name H. L. Worrall. This was Elizabeth Worrall's younger son, Henry Lechmere Worrall, who was still at Westminster when Mary arrived at Knole. It was almost certainly Henry, home for the holidays, who called her a fraud. Soon after that, I discovered, he joined the Indian Army, married in India in 1822, and was stationed at Cawnpore.

Francis Greenacre showed me the original, with the copies of three letters at the end: he had examined the watermark, and found that the paper they were written on was made in 1836. This coincided with Henry's first leave from India, when his mother was seventy-three. Elizabeth Worrall, it seemed, still had the original letters, but refused to part with them. Henry made copies, which he bound in at the end of Gutch's book.

Henry Worrall eventually became a general, and his first wife died in Clifton in 1866. His second wife, Ellen, survived him by nearly fifty years, dying in 1929, which explained why the book had come up for sale at that time.

I immediately typed the letters out and sent them to Bernard Spaughton. With his research from Philadelphia I now had enough material to reconstruct at least the first few weeks of Mary's adventures after she left England.

The first is headed 'Copy of a letter to Mrs Worrall from Miss Lamb, one of the Moravian Sisters, by the return of the Robert and Ann Cap.n Robertson from Philadelphia Sept. 10th 1817' and is written at Elizabeth Worrall's request to have 'the earliest information relating to the unfortunate young woman in whose welfare you took such a lively interest'. The second and third are written, or at least signed, by Mary Baker herself, one dated 17 September, from Philadelphia, the other 'New York America', 3 November 1817.

The first two letters from Philadelphia give sharply different accounts of Caraboo's arrival. The last, written at the beginning of November from New York, contains Mary's own reactions to America, and the most vivid account of her reception during the first eight weeks she spent there.

Ann Lamb's letter does not begin very reassuringly for Elizabeth Worrall. She says she has 'the painful task to tell her that interest she took in Mary was misplaced, and has been repaid by the basest ingratitude'.

Mary behaved very well on the voyage out.

> Mary's conduct was unexceptionable, and from our conversations with her I flattered myself that the deceptions she had practiced would now be forgotten, and that she would once more endeavour to become a respectable member of society, notwithstanding it could plainly be perceived that she gloried in the part she had acted, and was pleased whenever she could get anyone in the ship to listen to her story.

Mary's version was, characteristically, more colourful. She begins her letter 'My dear friend and Benefactress', and goes on in a style that, like the letters from Wilmot Street 'written in a masculine hand', sounds a little too self-assured.

> With heartfelt pleasure and gratitude I sit down to write you and give you a small account of our voyage and my reception here . . . The voyage was very long and tedious, our water very bad and offensive which obliged us all to make use of more spirits than was agreeable.

Whether under the influence of spirits she was not accustomed to, or simply because of the familiar effect she had on 'gentlemen', she also suffered the embarrassment of a one-sided shipboard romance.

> The Cap.n was very kind to me as also most of the ship's crew, but the Mate because I would not

consent to marry him has behaved with the greatest
unkindness and indecency towards me.

Whether the Moravian sisters were aware of what
was going on with the Mate, they did their best to
make Mary feel ashamed of the Caraboo hoax. Ann
Lamb tells Elizabeth Worrall that they 'endeavoured
to impress her mind with the idea that if she should
be known, the Americans would treat her with the
utmost contempt.'

'You may guess our surprise,' Ann Lamb goes
on, 'when on our sailing up the Delaware the ship's
boat was sent on shore for provisions. On its return
the people brought us intelligence that the English
newspapers had arrived before us with the account
that she was on board this vessel and that public
curiosity was as much awakened *here* concerning her
as it had been in England. From this time our
arguments had less weight and we could plainly
perceive that Mary's vanity was highly gratified.'

It certainly was. 'The English papers were out
here before ourselves,' Mary writes to Elizabeth
Worrall, 'everybody was acquainted with my whole
history – the ship had scarce let go her anchor before
the wharves were covered with people to see me.'

One newspaper correspondent, from the *Philadelphia Gazette*, seems to have made his way through
the crowd and talked to Mary in the company of the
three Moravian ladies, writing down what
amounted to a True-Life Confession that Mary had
'made herself notorious in England' and that she
now intended 'to escape the odium which she had

incurred by her preposterous impositions and to seek in America honest employment and obscurity'.

Events then moved very quickly, and another visitor elbowed his way on board, an immediately recognizable figure from the world of early nine-teenth-century show business called Sanders.

'Our first anxiety on our arrival,' Ann Lamb writes, 'was to get her private lodgings, fearing that the ship would be too public a situation for her.

> Our own immediate connexions being out of town, we applied on her behalf to a gentleman of the name of Sanders who had introduced himself on board the vessel as an Englishman. He mentioned the circum-stance to his landlady, also a native of England, who kindly offered her an asylum in her house free of any expense till she could procure a suitable situation.
>
> Thither she accordingly went while we in the mean time took the opportunity to mention her to several of the most respectable families in the city, who kindly offered to take her on our recommen-dation, when to our great surprise she refused to accept of either. The lady with whom we were staying kindly went with us in her carriage to entreat her to accept an asylum with her till she could obtain such a situation as she could wish, but all in vain.

Sanders, they discovered, had a reputation.

> 'Mrs Longstreete, the lady alluded to is the wife of a very considerable merchant who would I believe have done anything to save her from accompanying

him. A Mr Myers, a reputable sugarbroker, offered her 100 dollars a year to enter his family as cook, but', Ann Lamb repeats, 'all in vain.'

It was then that they discovered what Sanders was up to. He was going to put her on the stage. He was offering her the early nineteenth-century equivalent of a big Hollywood contract.

'We learned upon enquiry', Ann Lamb puts it, 'that Mr Sanders had taken pains to induce her to exhibit herself and offered to advance money on her behalf assuring her that she would make a fortune.'

The Moravian ladies struggled to hold her back. Even Captain Robertson was enrolled in a desperate attempt to save her.

As a last trial, when we learned her intention, Captain Robertson went to her himself and affectionately entreated her to consider what she was doing, and to accept Mrs L's kind offer, when she plainly told him that she had met with kinder friends in America than she had in England, and that tho' she felt obliged to us for the interest we took in her welfare, she thought she was quite old enough to think and act for herself.

Mary had already said she wanted to play Caraboo. Now she had the break into show business that every newspaper in Bristol and many of her visitors at Bridge Street said she deserved. It would have been impossible for her to refuse. Her version of the story is inevitably rather different from that of Ann Lamb.

An English gentleman took me on shore . . . and he has kindly placed me under the protection of several ladies, his friends. Many offers were made me immediately for service, but some gentlemen who have found themselves here [apparently the producers of some kind of touring company] have determined other ways for me and they have engaged Washington State Rooms for the purpose of a concert for my benefit which they say will be most beneficial to me since the public singers are engaged and the time is fixed for Tuesday and Thursday next.

'So you see my ever dearest friend', Mary writes, 'that I am to be public in spite of my endeavour to the contrary.'

'The Gentleman under whose immediate protection I am', she admits, 'is a married man.' He also seems to be already finding Mary quite a handful. 'He has', she says, 'very much persuaded me after the concert is over to return to England to the bosoms of my friends, which I intend to do.'

'Lest I may not return' – Mary herself, whatever Sanders says, is obviously still in two minds – 'I hope my dear Madam to be favored with a letter from you which if directed to Mrs Baker, Post Office, Philadelphia will reach me.'

Ann Lamb's letter ends on a note of pious resignation.

Here then we must leave her, and I have no doubt the intelligence will give pain to her kind patrons in

England as well as to us, but you have this heart-consoling reflection that you have done your best, and that if she is unfortunate she is willingly so. I must say for my part I cannot help thinking, even now, that the strenuous efforts and prayers of so many of God's dear children on her behalf will not be in vain. Grace can reclaim even the heart of Caraboo. Should I ever have more welcome news of her it will give me great pleasure to communicate it. In the mean time I remain, Madam, Yours most respectfully, Ann H. Lamb.

Mary herself, whoever's guidance she was writing under, seems entirely unaware that she has upset anyone, or that the news of her taking to the stage will in any way distress Elizabeth Worrall, and her first letter ends on a note of thoughtful affection and gratitude.

My kindest love and duty to Mrs Mortimer and the rest of my kind friends both ladies and gentlemen, most particularly [this is rather surprising, and may explain Henry Worrall's interest in preserving copies of the letters as a memento of her visit to Knole] to Mr Worrall and sons. Rest assured, my dear Madam, that I will continue to do all I can to deserve your further countenance and friendship. God bless you, my dear friend, and accept my grateful thanks for your past kindnesses, and I remain your ever dutiful and grateful servant, Mary Baker. P.S. I will write to you after the concert and let you know how I succeed.

It is clear from the first reaction of the press that she was in for a rough ride. In her letter from New York, Mary gives a glimpse of the hysteria that was stirred up by her arrival: it might be fanciful to credit Mary Baker with the introduction of the turban as the highest fashion for English ladies in the eighteen-twenties, but there is no doubt that the 'Carraboo' craze – she gained an extra 'r' in America – hit the East Coast like a tornado.

'My likeness was taken at Philadelphia', she tells Elizabeth Worrall, 'and seen both there and here at all the shops.' According to the *New York Gazette* this was 'a clumsy likeness carved upon a large block of box-wood', which the paper refused to print. Their rates, they wrote, with heavy irony, were 'double for any species of quackery'.

Other papers, however, reproduced it, and she was recognized in the street. The showmen may also have persuaded her to dress the part to be more easily identified.

'The House I live in here', she writes from New York at the beginning of November 1817,

has, ever since my being in it was known, filled with visitors, their curiosity and impertinence was so great that I have been scarcely able to walk out, and could never eat my dinner without people staring in at the windows. Several ladies have been taken for me at the theatre and in the streets and were followed by crowds to their great discomposure.

She was a star, and a controversial figure. Some of the earliest coverage is sympathetic, possibly orchestrated by Sanders as part of the publicity build up to her first stage appearance, like the story in the *New York Gazette*, printed in the middle of September.

A gentleman who left Philadelphia on Tuesday morning called on the editors yesterday and communicated the following particulars concerning Miss Mary Baker, alias Miss Carraboo.

He informs us that he is recently from Witheridge in Devonshire where Miss Carraboo was brought up and says he knows her connections. He states that Miss Baker is a most beautiful woman, now about twenty years of age, rather tall but elegantly formed; her hair, eyes and eyebrows are very black; she writes the Carraboo language with great facility having made several private exhibitions of her capacity in this respect in Philadelphia.

Our informant adds that a number of gentlemen in Philadelphia have taken a warm interest in her behalf, having satisfied themselves as to the purity of her character and views. Under the charge and direction of these gentlemen this beautiful and fascinating young lady will in a few days exhibit herself at the Philadelphia Washington Hall in the same dress she wore in England when hoaxing the people of Bristol.

As soon as the curiosity of the Philadelphians is satisfied, Miss Carraboo intends to visit this city. In the meantime, we expect a further and more minute sketch of this singular stranger.

The dress was a new one, and nobody who had seen her could have called her 'rather tall', but it all helped to sell tickets.

Some of the newspapers treated her simply as a joke. Her name was associated with any kind of trick or deception, as it was on the title page of the book about Frederick Moon. A few weeks later there is a story from Augusta, Georgia, using 'a Miss Carraboo' as a figure of speech to personify some stock-market ramp to raise the price of cotton.

A week before her show opened in Philadelphia, the *Patterson Express* in New Jersey carried a story about her that may have been concocted as part of the promotion for her concert, or by local joke-smiths keen to cash in on the Caraboo craze, but which was certainly a good yarn.

What inflamed the imaginations of gentlemen in New Jersey, as it had inflamed imaginations in England, was the idea of her swimming naked in the lake at Knole. According to the *Patterson Express* she not only swam down a waterfall, she swam up it again.

Miss C. visited on 20th September [that would have been the Saturday before she opened in Philadelphia] with a few confidential friends, the Passaick Falls. She precipitated herself in their presence from the highest rock into the basin, performed some won-drous exploits in the swimming way, and then to the great astonishment of spectators, swam up the falls to the summit of the rock, where she was received with repeated cheers by her companions.

Just in case anyone believed the story, an obviously bogus authentication is added underneath. 'In witness whereof she, with her friends, have signed this with their names in the Carraboo language,' followed by a few squiggles imitated from the facsimiles in the Bristol papers.

But the general response was hostile. There was a certain amount of ridicule of the English for being 'imposed on by such impostors and then to be laughed at by the rest of the world'. 'Such things do take place,' the *Daily Advertiser* recorded smugly, 'and in no spot of the globe more frequently than in England . . . But it would be very extraordinary indeed if our citizens should be drawn into so ridiculous a predicament as to countenance the detected hoax.'

Mary herself, in her letter from New York, says that she has been 'much disappointed in America', and has found Americans, particularly in Philadelphia, 'very reserved and much prejudiced against the English'.

You have no idea how prejudiced the people are against old England, it is hardly possible to sit in their company without being obliged to listen to the greatest illiberality, and I am frequently under the necessity of expressing my opinions pretty freely not only on the difference between the two countrys, but also to explain to them that such kind of conversation is seldom heard in England. Here they call the English foreigners, which is not done by the English when speaking of America.

Americans were still smarting from the hostilities following the War of Independence, and more recently from the burning of the Capitol by a British raiding party in 1812. Some local people, it was clear, were furious at the mere idea of a British confidence trickster appearing in a hall named after George Washington, opened with great patriotic pomp and ceremony only a year earlier. In one letter to the *Philadelphia Gazette*, written even before her first show at the Washington State Rooms was officially announced, there is a long attack on Mary for having 'made herself notorious in England' and for 'insulting the public sense of decency by exhibiting herself as a show for money'.

There was a strong sense of moral outrage, of the terrible respectability that would soon settle on Victorian England, in which Princess Caraboo and even Mary Baker herself were soon to disappear.

If Mary expected theatrical success that would enable her to rise above this kind of abuse, Sanders was no great help to her. The first and only advertisement for her concert appeared in the *United States Gazette* on Monday 22 September, twenty-four hours before the show opened. 'Miss Carraboo has the honour of informing the inhabitants of Philadelphia that a Grand Concert of Vocal and Instrumental Music will be performed for her benefit at Washington Hall on Tuesday Evening 23rd. Instant.'

Tickets could be bought at various places in the

town, including 'Mr Hope's Lottery Office and Captain Shaw's near the Swedish Church', or at the door. The concert would begin at seven-thirty in the evening, and copies of Gutch's book, or a pirated edition of it, would be on sale during the interval.

The evening began with Martine's *Overture to Henry IV*. Then there were various romantic songs, sung by Mr Gillingham, the conductor of the orchestra, a 'German Amateur' and various ladies – 'Wild Roses', 'Jessie the flower of Dunblane', and 'Softly waft ye southern breezes'. There was a 'recitation' by Mr Betterton, – presumably a descendent of the great Thomas Betterton – a minuet by Haydn, and Schmitt's Grand March. Mary appeared midway through the first half, after an orchestral introduction by Gyrowetz, and with a Mrs Hewson singing 'I'll never to so any more' after she went off.

Mary was led on to the stage 'by two gentlemen', and her entrance, according to the *United States Gazette* the next morning, 'was received with a general burst of applause'. She was then given a large sheet of paper, and 'wrote a letter in that language which puzzled Oxford and Cambridge'.

Cambridge had never seen a specimen of her writing, and Oxford had dismissed it as 'humbug', but that was part of the story that Sanders had told to promote the concert and it was another good joke at the expense of Old England.

Faced with a large paying audience, and as an amateur surrounded by professional performers, Mary seems to have been inhibited in a way she had never been at Knole. There is no mention of her dancing or performing her sword-fight, and Sanders must have invented her farewell. 'Her taking leave of her audience, in the language of the Moon, was much applauded.'

The review of the concert is, sadly, the only account that has so far come to light of Caraboo in America written by someone who actually met her or saw her, and it suggests that if others had had the chance she might have had a far warmer welcome.

'Her appearance and manner', the eye-witness writes, 'silenced those insinuations which have been so industriously circulated to injure an innocent and unoffending female.'

At Knole, in private, she had charmed her most cynical critics into believing in her. In America, as a public figure, she rarely had the opportunity of converting her enemies.

According to the *United States Gazette*, the concert was 'numerously and respectfully attended'. 'The Hall was splendidly illuminated, the music good and the vocal performers acquitted themselves in a manner which gave general satisfaction.'

But in the same paper Miss Carraboo's conventional notice of thanks to 'those Ladies and Gentlemen who did her the honour of attending the concert last night' ends with the announcement that her second concert, planned for the following day, has been postponed.

The *Baltimore Federal Republican* claimed that the concert was 'poorly attended', and 'the money produced from the sale of tickets of admission was not sufficient to defray the expenses'.

Other local newspapers, as in England, reprinted the story, and the hostility increased.

> The astonishing prowess of this lady in practical jokes is eulogised in the newspapers of Philadelphia as a most admirable thing. We take these exhibitions to be only preliminary to others of the same character. After this poor worn out English joke will cease to gull the Philadelphians out of their money, we presume it is the intention of this lady to visit other seaports on this continent. Whether New York or Baltimore will be the first favoured with a visit remains to be seen.

It seems that the first seaport to be favoured was neither New York or Baltimore, but Norfolk, Virginia, probably at the end of September. Mary makes no mention of it in her letter to Elizabeth Worrall from New York, but on 1 October 1817 the *Norfolk and Portsmouth Herald* printed a letter signed 'No Joker'.

> Gentlemen, having seen it mentioned in a late New York paper that the famous Miss Carraboo, whose arrival in Philadelphia you noticed in your paper some time past, was about to pay a visit to N.Y., I beg leave through the medium of your paper to undeceive the public upon that highly important subject.
>
> Miss Carraboo, allow me to say, has recently

arrived in this borough and rented the brick house No. 1 near the head of Talbot Street, where she had established herself with a numerous retinue and may be seen at all hours of the day. It is a subject of much regret with the respectable inhabitants of that neighbourhood, for decency's sake, that the police of the neighbourhood have not, ere this, waited on her ladyship and conducted her and her maids of honour to more suitable lodgings.

The letter, like the account of Caraboo bouncing up the Falls, could well be a hoax, but there is something about it that rings true. Norfolk, Virginia, would have been a natural move for any showman intending to work the cities of the East Coast. If Sanders and his travelling company moved into a respectable district of the town it is likely they would have been met with that kind of moral disapproval – the implication that 'her ladyship' and her 'maids of honour' were prostitutes was typical of the generally held view of actresses current at the time among respectable god-fearing citizens – and 'Miss Carraboo' would have been singled out for attack as the star.

In the same week there is a warning in the *New York Gazette*. 'Should it be the intention of this impostor to visit N.Y., she is informed that we have a statute called the Vagrants' Act, and a place called Bridewell' – the old English word for a prison – 'ready to receive them. It is hoped she takes notice.'

Some papers were more sympathetic, like the *National Advocate*, which announced her arrival in

New York on 18 October. 'The reports which have been circulated to her prejudice, we learn from good authority, are wholly unfounded, and that her conduct since her arrival in this country has been very exemplary.'

All this stress and excitement brought on another recurrence of Mary's rheumatic fever. 'I have been for the last fortnight very ill,' she writes to Elizabeth Worrall on 3 November, 'and think you would scarcely know me. I assure you I wish myself back again in England. The only amusement I have had in America has been reading, the ladies and gentlemen at Philadelphia supplied me with books and there are plenty of them in the house at New York.'

She seems disappointed and homesick, and complains about the American countryside being 'by no means to be compared to England in appearance'.

Wherever Sanders may have taken her, he was unable to book her any more dates. 'After the concert given for my benefit in Philadelphia I was advised to visit New York and . . . give one there, but for many reasons my friends did not think it would be beneficial.'

She says that she has written a letter to Mrs Mortimer 'which I make no doubt she showed to you, giving a description of the concert, including my dress', but Elizabeth Worrall has made a note in the margin that this 'was never received'.

Mary is afraid that her first letter to Elizabeth Worrall has gone astray too, having had no answer. She says she gave it to Captain Robertson to bring back to England, and thinks that as he was sailing by way of St Andrews in Scotland the letter might have got lost or delayed, and is sending this second letter 'by British Mail'.

Captain Robertson, it seems, forgave her very quickly for going off with Sanders: Elizabeth Worrall did not, or at least had failed to answer her letter. But Mary still seems to have no idea that she can possibly have upset anyone. She asks to be remembered kindly 'to Mr Worrall and your two sons, your master Vaughan, Mrs Russell, Miss Lucy and Miss Hester, Miss Ludman, Mr and Mrs Mortimer, likewise to Ca – – – t' – this name is illegible, but it could just be the Worralls' Greek manservant – 'and Cross.'

She tacitly admits her unpopularity in America, asking her friends 'who treated me so kindly in England' to write to her 'as it will show the people here that I am not considered by them in an unfavourable light'. This may, of course, be the hand of Sanders, fishing for the equivalent of celebrity endorsements from England to help him with future promotions.

> I hope I shall never forget the favors I have received from you, and hope that I shall prove to have deserved them. Please to direct to Mary Baker, Post Office, Philadelphia as I am known here to everyone as Mrs Baker. I remain my dear benefactress your obliged and affectionate Mary Baker.

In the same letter, where she talks about the anti-British prejudice in America and her excited horror of being mobbed as a celebrity, she admits that she prefers New York to Philadelphia. 'From what little I have seen of New York I like it best.' But she cannot bear being stared at. 'I have been so much annoyed that I return tomorrow to Philadelphia.'

The next day was Sunday 4 November 1817. It is the last sighting of Caraboo in America, and the last time we ever hear her voice.

CHAPTER 18

FANNY'S PALACE

O N 18 JANUARY 1818, the *American Beacon* carried a story headed 'Another Carraboo' about an 'interesting female' of nineteen found asleep on a heath in New England who spoke no known language. Mary was still famous, but the craze was fading, and after that she seems to disappear entirely from the American newspapers.

The only record in the Philadelphia census that might fit her is a Miss Mary Baker who lived at 140 Brown Street in 1818 and 1819, but as Mary herself wrote to Elizabeth Worrall saying that everyone knew her as 'Mrs Baker' it is by no means a certainty.

Mary now vanishes in America for nearly six years. Somewhere there may be playbills advertising another concert, or diaries recording her presence in a private house as a servant, wandering, as Michael Austin liked to imagine, among the Indians, even restored to the Moravian fold in Bethlehem, but they have not yet come to light. It is probably pointless to speculate, and we can only hope that one day more missing pieces of the jigsaw will be found.

She reappears again, very briefly, in William Tegg's *Every Day Book* of 1827, which claims that

she remained in Philadelphia until 1824, when she
came back to England and exhibited herself as Princess Caraboo in New Bond Street at a shilling a
time. From the London street directory for that
year, turned up by Bernard Spaughton, it was most
probably at number 23, which had 'public rooms',
and where two midgets, some Java sparrows and
canaries were shown off that same year, also at a
shilling a time.

This is the only evidence to suggest that Mary
had stayed in show business during the intervening
years, but it could equally well have been at the
suggestion of a fellow-passenger on the voyage
home who thought, like Sanders, that he could make
some money out of her. If there was such a person
he was disappointed. 'The exhibition did not attract
any great attention', and as in Philadelphia the
takings failed to cover the rent of the public room.

According to hearsay – a visitor to Bristol several
years later – Mary then travelled abroad for the
remainder of the eighteen-twenties, in France and
Northern Spain. There the trail seemed to run out.

Then, at a party in London, I was talking about
Caraboo to an old academic friend who thought he
remembered coming across her name in *Notes and
Queries*, a kind of literary-historical *Exchange and
Mart* popular with bookish folk, founded in the
nineteenth century. Subscribers wrote in with
unusual stories, requests for information, or questions that puzzled them, and other readers wrote
back, supplying the answers.

The magazine did not exist at the time of the

original hoax at Knole, but Gutch in his later years was one of its regular contributors, supplying *Notes and Queries* with the 'authentic' record of the inquest on the death of Chatterton which was later proved by another contributor to be a fake. The tale of Princess Caraboo was exactly the kind of story that appealed to its readers, and I looked through the index in search of some later reference to 'Caraboo'. There were several of them, and they occurred in a little cluster in the spring of 1865.

The correspondence was started by a brief obituary in *The Times* on 13 January of that year, under the heading 'Death of the Princess Caraboo'.

Such of our readers as are interested in the history of imposters will remember that many years since a person who styled herself the 'Princess Caraboo' created a sensation in the literary and fashionable circles of Bath and other places which lasted till it was discovered that the whole affair was a romance cleverly sustained and acted out by a young and prepossessing girl. On being deposed from the honours which had been accorded to her, the 'Princess' accepted the situation, retired into comparatively humble life and married.

The article compares her to the 'native of Formosa', George Psalmanazar, mentions, apparently without having read it, the publication of *Companion for Caraboo* in 1817, her return from America in 1824, and the show in New Bond Street.

'There was', *The Times* goes on, 'a kind of grim humour in the occupation which she subsequently followed – that of an importer of leeches; but she conducted her operations with much judgement and ability and carried on her trade with credit to herself and satisfaction to her customers . . . The quondam "Princess" died recently at Bristol leaving a daughter, who, like her mother, is said to be possessed of considerable personal attractions.'

No one, it seems, got on the train to Bristol to interview her daughter, or if they did the record of their conversations remains still to be discovered: but the article did stir a few memories, not all of them entirely accurate.

In April 1865 a correspondent who signs himself F. C. H. writes to say that his father visited Knole at the time Mary was there. He remembered him both talking about her going up on the roof to worship the sun and claiming to have been 'mainly instrumental in her detection'.

As a linguist, he had been invited to pay her a visit with a view to ascertaining what language she spoke. When he entered the room some gentlemen had placed before her an Oriental manuscript, making signs that she should read it. She at once began to read it with great apparent facility, and aloud. My father observed quietly to a gentleman near him, but loud enough to be heard by 'Caraboo', that the language of that manuscript was read, like Hebrew, from right to left.

Mary, he claimed, had been pretending to read from left to right, and shortly afterwards changed, beginning at the right margin. 'This opened the eyes of those in the room to her imposture, and she was very soon forced to own it.'

The remaining entries in *Notes and Queries* are mainly cuttings from newspapers of 1817, including the St Helena story sent in by Bristol City Library, and one unusually pompous denial of it by 'F. C. H.', not on historical grounds but on the track record of the British Civil Servant. 'I cannot think that the smallest credit is due to the tale of Caraboo at St Helena. It is *prima facie* too romantic and improbable. Who could believe that any amanuensis of the State Paper Office would so far commit himself as to forward a letter from Sir Hudson Lowe to a newspaper?'

But there were also three more interesting letters. One is from a correspondent in Oxford who remembers being at the university when Mary's language was sent for analysis, and identifying the dons who dismissed it as 'humbug'.

The second letter is from a writer in Bristol who has been trying to find out more about Mary's death. A woman who was famous in two continents forty years before, has already disappeared almost completely: even a few weeks after she died, in a relatively small place like Bristol, he has had trouble finding out any precise details. The best he can say is that she appears to have died 'about the close of the year 1864'. He does not know where she is buried.

The third letter is obviously written by someone very interested indeed in Mary's story, also a Bristolian. He has taken the trouble of verifying her baptism in the parish register at Witheridge and he has examined the records of the Magdalen Hospital. He has also spent time trying, without success, to identify the father of the child she left at the Foundling Hospital. But what makes the writer of this letter different from anyone else is that he has actually met her since her return from America.

He saw her and spoke to her, he says, in Bristol in December 1849, when she was fifty-seven. He says she was very reluctant to talk about her life, but gathered from her that she spent the late eighteen-twenties travelling 'in the South of France and in Northern Spain'.

'She then lived under Pyle Hill, Bedminster, and earned a living for herself and her daughter by selling leeches to our Infirmary Hospital, and to many other druggists.'

I realized that this single sentence was the key to Mary's last years in Bristol.

The letter ended sadly. 'She avoided as much as possible any conversation with regard to her former career, of which she was much ashamed: and nothing annoyed her more than when a neighbour's child ventured to call after her "Caraboo"!'

The idea of Princess Caraboo ending her life selling leeches seemed at first sight terrible. The writer of her obituary in *The Times* found 'a kind of grim humour' in it, presumably at the thought of someone he considered to have been a parasite dealing in parasites. But the truth turned out to be a great deal less unpleasant.

Leeches, clinging to Humphrey Bogart's legs in

The African Queen and having to be burned off with a lighted cigarette, are thought of as creatures of horror. In the Middle East, very small leeches can attach themselves to the inside of the throat or the nostrils and drive animals and men mad, even causing death. But it may come as a surprise that medicinal leeches can still be bought from John Bell and Croydon in London, and are still in use in the late twentieth century for cleaning small and inaccessible wounds.

In Mary's time they were used exclusively for blood-letting. In the Bristol Infirmary's two leeching rooms, the patient's skin was dabbed with a little milk or fresh blood, and the medicinal leeches were applied. They made three tiny incisions with their sharp, serrated teeth, and their powerful muscles began to expand and contract, sucking out blood, at the same time releasing an anti-coagulant that kept the blood flowing, even after, as happened in some cases, the leech was cut in half to make it easier to extract it from the wound.

But blood-letting, even as it was practised on Mary herself at St Giles' Workhouse Hospital, was not thought of as in any way antiquated or barbaric, and there was no more shame associated with dealing in leeches than there would be today with supplying aspirin or herbal remedies or any other kind of medical supplies. Mary was a dealer, not a gatherer. Standing in ponds until the creatures fixed themselves to your legs and then prising them off was not a pleasant occupation, and it was rapidly dying out in the British Isles. Experts blamed it on improvements in agriculture and the draining of waste land. Leech gatherers survived, and one of them was interviewed a few years earlier by the poet Wordsworth. The poem he wrote about him, *The Leech Gatherer*, inspired one of Lewis Carroll's best parodies about the Aged Aged Man, who roamed the moors in search of haddocks' eyes, and turned hill-water into Rowland's Macassar Oil.

> 'I'll tell thee everything I can:
>   There's little to relate.
> I saw an aged, aged man,
>   A-sitting on a gate.
> "Who are you, aged man?" I said
>   "And how is it you live?"
> His answer trickled through my head
>   Like water through a sieve . . .'

Wordsworth's Leech Gatherer may have been equally boring but even he admits it is a dying trade.

> He said that, gathering leeches, far and wide
> He travelled; stirring thus about his feet
> The waters of the pools where they abide.
> 'Once I could meet with them on every side;
> But they have dwindled long by slow decay;
> Yet still I persevere, and find them where I may.

Experiments in growing leeches commercially had failed in England. Ponds were vulnerable to predators, and one account described twenty thousand leeches in Norfolk being gobbled up in twenty-four hours by a sudden invasion of ducks. Leeches by the eighteen-thirties were largely imported from abroad. Visitors brought back descriptions of beautifully laid-out leech-farms, with a central farmhouse shaded with trees surrounded by a vast geometrical grid of small, shallow oblong ponds. There were tales of cruel farmers driving horses or cattle into the ponds to feed the leeches, but the more practical and efficient alternative was to suspend in each pond linen bags filled with the blood of a recently slaughtered animal.

Almost all these farms were in the South of France and Northern Spain, which seems to support Mary's story that she had been there. She may even have become involved in the trade abroad, and continued to deal with people she had met during her visit. It is even possible that written records of her dealings there survive.

The leeches were sometimes packed in mud, either in baskets or linen bags, having to be regularly soaked with water during transit. More often they were transported in casks filled with a mixture of clay and water, or in clear water in glass jars. To be sold they were tipped out, drained and weighed, and dishonest dealers were said to over-feed their leeches before selling them.

The French suppliers offered them in five categories: '*filets*' or young leeches, from one to five years old, small medium leeches, from five to eight, large medium leeches, from eight to twelve, mother or large leeches, which were fully grown, and 'cow leeches', described as being of 'enormous size'.

Mary also entered the business, commercially

speaking, at the best possible moment. Imports from France had increased to something like fifty million a year, with the Infirmary in Bristol using 50,000 of them, and prices were the highest they had ever been, having risen more than ten times over between 1805 and 1820. The trade was also extremely profitable, with a profit of about fivepence on every sixpenny leech sold to the hospital.

If it was unlikely that traces of Mary's business activities would ever turn up in France or Spain, it seemed possible that records survived in the hospital records in Bristol.

The Infirmary Hospital changed its name in 1850, with the approval of Queen Victoria, to Bristol Royal Infirmary, but it is still there, at the top of the hill above Lewin's Mead, with some of the old buildings still standing that were there in Mary's time. It was founded, like St Peter's Hospital for the Poor, by the more public-minded members of the Bristol Corporation to care for 'our poor neighbours', with the motto 'Charity Universal'.

When Mary worked there it was still barbaric by modern standards. In 1833 there was a scandal about feeding used poultices to pigs that were later eaten by the patients, and in the absence of any regular source of corpses, other than condemned criminals, for dissection classes, two of the Infirmary doctors were arrested and fined £6 each for digging up a newly buried body from a local churchyard. But as the shadow of Victorian respectability began to fall the Infirmary too became more sedate. The Board

Room, where corpses were traditionally dissected, had a pulpit installed and was used for religious services.

It was already a big hospital, with nearly three hundred beds, treating over a thousand cases a year, including sixty major operations. All these were carried out without anaesthetic, and with patients strapped to the operating table. Sometimes opium or brandy was used to dull the pain, and one of the surgeons, needing to have a tumour removed himself, made do with a cigar.

Anaesthetics had, ironically enough, been available in Bristol since the turn of the century, when Thomas Beddoes's assistant, Humphrey Davey, inventor of the miner's lamp, had experimented with laughing gas or nitrous oxide. It was a huge success with intellectuals like Coleridge and Southey, but for amusement only, 'to inebriate in the most delightful manner'. But surgeons remained cautious. Ether was eventually used in America in 1846, chloroform in England in 1848, but neither was used at the Infirmary before 1850.

Out-patients waited in a room where the atmosphere was described as 'tainted and poisonous', with the victims of street accidents, pregnant women, drunks and those suffering from serious illnesses weeping, brawling and shouting, with a policeman employed to keep order, and an orderly to decide whether they needed to see a surgeon or a doctor.

They were then sent through to one of two rooms, where either the surgeons or the doctors carried out a more thorough examination: men and women were stripped and examined together in public, but in 1848 there was official criticism of 'the great indelicacy of this arrangement'.

It cannot have been a place that Mary much enjoyed visiting, with its memories of St Giles' Workhouse Hospital. But she was no longer a patient, she was working on equal terms with a great many intelligent and entertaining doctors, and she was part of a widely respected institution, with a reputation for excellence. Collections were taken for the Bristol Infirmary in pubs and churches throughout the West Country and even into Wales, and anyone would have been proud to be working for it.

The Infirmary's archives are preserved in the Bristol Public Record Office, now lodged in one of the huge square brick-red tobacco warehouses that dominate the south bank of the river by the New Cut, pictured on old Wills' cigarette packets. It was there that I began the search.

The minutes of the quarterly committee meetings are kept in a collection of big ledgers, bound in old powdery leather. The bulk of the business recorded is to do with the mending of windows, the provision of new pipes to clear blocked water closets, or the misbehaviour of hospital porters. But there are also regular accounts of income and expenditure.

Most of the Infirmary's regular suppliers are listed as 'Yearly and Quarterly Tradesmen', firms appointed under contract at the beginning of each year. They include Elizabeth Tripp, who may or may not have been related to the Mr Tripp on the

Board of Governors, who provides several hundred pounds' worth of meat every year, and a long list of carpenters, grocers, glaziers, dealers in wine and brandy, mops and brushes, vinegar, chemicals, lard, milk, black and green bottles, splints and coffins.

No leech dealer appears on this list, and I thought at first that I had drawn a blank. I then noticed that a lot of other firms appeared in the accounts, sometimes among the Yearly and Quarterly Tradesmen, sometimes at the foot of the page with the nurses' and porters' salaries. In September 1833 I finally found a large order – £79.6.6 – for leeches. The supplier was Zaccheus Hunter.

Using the winter of 1849 as the date at which I knew from *Notes and Queries* that Mary was said to have been working for the Infirmary, I took down the minutes of the finance committee for the eighteen-forties, and opened them quite by chance at the entry for April Fool's Day 1844. At the foot of the page, after all the usual supplies, was what appeared to be a late entry. 'Richard Davis, Salary, £25.0.0., Robert Johnson, Salary, £30.0.0., Mary Wheeler, Salary, £15.0.0., Mrs Tripp, Meat, £212.18.00, Mrs Baker, Leeches, £20.15.0.'

I don't usually thump the table in a library, but I did then. It was the first direct evidence of Mary working in Victorian England, and as far as I know the entry had never been examined in nearly a hundred and fifty years.

The minutes of the finance committee, however, turned out to be incomplete. There were no accounts for 1845. But in June 1846, where she appears as

Mary Baker rather than Mrs Baker, she earns
£60.12.0, in September 1846 £33.4.0, and in November the same year £32.0.0. Even presuming these
records are complete and that she had no other
customers, it means that in one year she was earning
£125.16.0. At the current profit margins this would
have given her an income of nearly £100 a year.
Senior nurses in other parts of England were earning
annual salaries of as much as £50, but at the Infirmary
their most recent pay rise had taken them to £16.

After that the finance committee accounts are even
less complete, but her earnings seem to drop. In
December 1848 she is paid £21.4.0, in March 1849
£19.5.0.

In April 1849, William Higgs gets £13.5.0 for
cheese, and Elizabeth Tripp £263.6.0 for meat, but
there is no record of Mary Baker. At that point, too,
all the detailed accounts of the finance committee
stop. There is one annual figure of overall expenditure, and after a few pages even that peters out. The
rest of the book is blank.

I now took out the minutes of the Infirmary
'House Committee'. This proved to be more complete, and offered at least the possibility of discovering when Mary started to work for the Infirmary
and when she left.

Like so many things about Caraboo, her first
appearance at the hospital is extremely mysterious.
In December 1839 there is an almost illegible entry
noting a payment of £14.14.6 for leeches to something that looks like Mary 'Berighasse', which, as
Bernard Spaughton pointed out, sounds suspiciously

like a phonetic transcription of the name Burgess spoken with a broad North Devon accent, but in July 1840 the Infirmary is buying leeches from Pedle and Quire.

Then, in September 1840, there is a payment for leeches to what looks like 'L. Baker' and the same name occurs at the end of the year. In the spring of 1841 the 'L' looks more like an 'R', and in June of the same year the entry is expanded to 'Rich Baker'.

In the course of 1841 Rich Baker earns a total of £60.12.00. Rich Baker continues to appear in the quarterly records of 1842, earning altogether £90.12.00. Then, in December 1842, the name becomes Mary Baker.

There seemed to be two possible explanations. One was that the clerk was deaf, had never met her and was unfamiliar with her name, and misheard 'Mrs' for 'Richard'. The other and more likely one was that she was using a man to deliver the leeches, and that he used the name of Richard Baker. It was to be some time before I discovered the truth.

After that she appears almost always as Mary Baker, and occasionally as Mrs Baker. Some of the House Committee accounts are missing for several months at a time, but it is safe to say that Mary was sole supplier to the hospital for twenty-five years. Her income of £125.16.0 for 1846 was higher than average, but throughout the eighteen-forties she continued to earn a reasonable living of about £80 a year.

This gradually declined from 1850 onwards – Mary herself would now have been in her early

sixties – and between 1857 and 1859 there is no
record of any leeches being bought at all. After that
her income dwindles to a few pounds a quarter,
though she may still have been earning money from
supplying other customers.

Following the information in *Notes and Queries*,
that Mary died 'about the close of the year 1864', I
followed the entries to that winter, picturing her
becoming older and feebler as she hobbled up the
hill to the Infirmary, less and less able to support
herself. Sure enough, her name disappeared from the
records in 1864, and that winter the ledgers are full
of troubles to do with a typhoid epidemic.

I turned the page to 1865, and found another entry
that seemed absolutely typical of Caraboo. 'January
24th 1865' – a fortnight after her obituary appeared
in *The Times* – 'to Mary Baker, Leeches, £3.2.0.'
Then another: 'February 27th 1866, Mary Baker,
Leeches, £2.5.0.' That was the final mention of her,
but it left me with what seemed to be two insoluble
mysteries.

Why, when she first turned up in the Infirmary
records, should she have been called Richard rather
than Mary, and how was it, more than twelve
months after her obituary was published in *The
Times*, that she was still apparently alive and well
and working for the Infirmary?

I left the Bristol Public Record Office and caught
a bus to an outlying suburb of Bristol to visit Anton
Bantock. His name had been given to me by another
Bristolian, Peter King, supervising make-up artist
on the film of *Princess Caraboo*: if I needed to know

anything about the history of Bristol, he said, Anton would know the answer, or at least where the answer could be found.

I arrived at what Anton Bantock described in his directions on the telephone as an 'orange bungalow'. It was partially hidden by straggling privet hedges, there was a large billboard on the wall saying 'University of Withywood' and the sign on the garden gate said 'Fanny's Palace'. I rang the bell and a lean grey man in his sixties opened the door.

It was early November, the bungalow was unheated, and stacked with books, old newspapers, geographical charts, drawings and posters, and one of the photographs on the wall was of General Ojukwu, the Biafran leader in the Nigerian civil war. He was a retired schoolmaster, famous throughout Bristol for his remarkable journeys all over the world, made during the school summer holidays at minimal cost, which he was now in the process of writing up with his own illustrations as Xeroxed pamphlets.

He was also historical advisor to the Malago Society, named after a river running through Bedminster, which concerns itself with local history. Within minutes he had unrolled a huge chart showing details of the building of the New Cut, and plans of mediaeval Bristol where the course of the river had been changed before to enlarge the walled city.

He had heard of Princess Caraboo, and remembered meeting an old man in Bedminster some time in the nineteen-forties who had heard rumours as a boy about where she was buried.

When I showed him the reference in *Notes and Queries* to Mary living 'under Pyle Hill' he produced a map of the town in the early nineteenth century, and showed me a little grid of streets at the foot of a hill just behind what is now Temple Meads railway station. There was Bedminster Parade, facing the New Cut, Queen's Street and Prince's Street. He warned me that a lot of the area had been pulled down and given over to light industry, but he suggested I might be able to find more information in the records of the national census.

With the Victorians' growing interest in statistics, a census of every household in the country was taken in 1841, and it seemed possible that I might find Mary in that. Two more were taken in which she might appear, the first in 1851 and the second three years before her death, in 1861.

The census returns in the Bristol Public Library are preserved on microfilm, and I joined the row of researchers at the pale grey screens. The parish of Bedminster was a big one, and the census books cover three long rolls of film. I took the first spool out of its container, untied the string, removed the cardboard cover, and fed the microfilm into the winding machinery.

It was obviously not going to be an easy job. The lamp on the machine was dim, and the pages were closely written. Finally, after finding two other Mary Bakers, I came on to a little lane listed next to Prince's Street, called Holy Brook Place, and the following entry:

Richard Baker aged 60 Leech Dealer born in County
Mary Baker   50   not born in County
Mary Baker   12   born in County

Her daughter's birth in the County in 1829 at least set a date for Mary's return from France and Spain. And both the questions raised by the Infirmary archives were now answered. The 'Richard Baker' listed as providing leeches for the hospital in the autumn of the previous year was not a mistaken hearing of Mrs Baker, nor even a boy she sent up with the leeches. It was her husband.

He died, probably in 1842, and certainly before the second census in 1851, when Mary is listed as head of the household and she and her daughter have moved to 11 Prince's Street, paying £8 a year rent to a landlord called Cameron.

Mary's name continued to appear in the accounts after her death because her work was carried on, for two years at least, by her daughter, Mary Ann Baker Junior.

But the question that came back with renewed force was the same question that had obsessed all Mary's admirers in the summer of 1817. Whom did she go to bed with? The father of her first child was called John Baker, the father of her second child was called Richard Baker. Could they possibly have been brothers, or could they even have been the same man?

CHAPTER 19

A FREE WOMAN

A FEW MONTHS later I was sitting in a pub in Witheridge with another of Mary's distant cousins, Thomas Gibson. He was a small, wiry, weatherbeaten, hard-working yeoman farmer in his seventies, half in love with farming and half in love with books. One of his sons followed him into farming, one became an academic, a Cambridge graduate with a first-class honours degree in Modern Languages from Peterhouse.

Thomas Gibson, too, was interested in languages, and he had just explained to me how you spelt 'fish' G. H. O. T. I. 'GH' as in 'enough', 'O' as in 'women', and 'TI' as in 'initial'. But he also had a remarkable instinctive gift. The first time he met Bernard Spaughton, he told me, he'd been worried for days afterwards by something about Bernard's smile he knew was familiar. Then he remembered a member of the Burgess family he knew in Exeter, and through that he had eventually traced the family connection to Mary's cousin, the carpenter.

We had spent all the morning talking about Mary, and now we returned to the question of her lover. Or lovers.

Was it simply a coincidence that the fathers of both her children should have been called Baker?

There was an interval, it seemed, of just under fourteen years between the birth of the first in 1816 and the second in 1829, and I was wondering out loud whether the report that appeared in the Exeter paper just before she went to America about her having been tried at Exeter Assizes in 1815 was true after all.

According to that story her lover had been transported for fourteen years, roughly the same gap as there was between the conception of the two children. Could a man called Baker have suffered all those years of privation and the lash in New South Wales for encouraging Mary to steal cloth, and then have come back to share the end of his life with her in Bedminster? It was, like the thought of her following Henry Frederick Moon from Bradford Barton all the way to America, a highly romantic idea.

Thomas Gibson shook his head. Cousin Bernard had been through the archives. The 'sweetheart' who was transported was called William Blackmore: there was the evidence of all the Bakers at the trial, and he was fairly convinced that Mary had never called herself 'Baker' in the West Country.

Bernard Spaughton, it turned out, had ransacked the archives for Richard Baker.

According to the census, Richard Baker, like his daughter, had been born in the county. I remembered that he had found one Richard Baker in the same Moravian church in Bristol as the three ladies who had sailed with Mary on the *Robert and Ann*, whose age matched that of the Richard Baker in the census, and who might have gone to Philadelphia.

Both he and I followed this up with the Moravians who still work in Nazareth outside Philadelphia. They had records of all three Moravian ladies who travelled on the *Robert and Ann*, with details of whom they later married, but there was no trace of a Richard Baker, or of Mary.

When I gave Bernard the material I had found in the Infirmary archives, pinpointing the date of Richard Baker's death, he began a systematic search for anyone of that name who had died in Bristol in the early eighteen-forties and discovered no one whose age or occupation matched Mary's husband, the leech dealer.

I was building up to a conclusion. Mary was the feminist heroine, making her lovers take her own name of Baker. Other women happily adopt the name of the man they live with to legitimize their children. Why shouldn't Mary, I thought, who had above all else been independent, the tomboy, her own woman, have persuaded her 'husband' Richard to take hers?

Then, just before this book finally went to press, Bernard Spaughton managed, if not to capsize my theory, at least to set it wallowing pretty dangerously in the water. Through his interest in local family histories, he turned up a certificate in the Bristol City Archives. On September 4th, 1828, in St John's Church, Bedminster, a Richard Baker had married a Mary Burgess. The witnesses were Jane Phillips and Benjamin John Room.

Richard Baker is described as a widower, Mary Burgess as a widow, and against her signature –

May Burges – there is a note that 'This is the Mark of Mary Burgess who attempted to write her own name.'

I imagined Mary immediately, sunburned from her time in France and Spain, heavily pregnant, too distressed at the wedding to write straight.

But there was still the mystery. Was Richard Baker perhaps the brother of John Edward Francis Baker, or was he the same man, the father of both her children? Was he the father of neither, merely a convenient member of the family who agreed to marry her to legitimize another mysteriously fathered child?

Was he, as I had originally suspected, not called Baker at all? Mary had been using that surname publicly for the best part of ten years, and, if it really was her marriage certificate, was perjuring herself by signing the name Burgess. What proof did we have that she was not making Richard do the same thing?

Maybe my theory was right all the time. It was, after all, Mary who ran the leech-dealing business for twenty-five years after her husband's death. She was the heroine. If she had lovers it was in a way logical that they should have taken her name.

That morning, Thomas Gibson and I had driven along the windy ridge, with the wide moors stretching away to the long horizon on either side. In the hollow lane at Stretchdown he pointed out the old well he discovered on a visit with Christine Medley, where the family would have gone to fetch their water. We walked into the church, now overloaded with a massive Victorian tower, where Mary was baptized. Then we parked by the old mill at the other end of the village, and Thomas Gibson quoted a German poem by Eichendorff, about a millwheel turning.

> In einem kühlen Grunde
> Da geht ein Mühlenrad
> Mein' Liebste ist verschwunden
> Die dort gewohnet hat . . .

We talked about how Mary must have felt when the Bristol intellectuals began to take her 'lingo' seriously, and he told me how just after the Second World War he himself had spoken German to German prisoners of war. To his surprise, perhaps because he was wearing an old dyed army jacket, they assumed he was German, and he'd let them go on thinking it.

'Like Mary, I wasn't really deceiving them: I just let them imagine what they wanted.'

He showed me the stretch of water, once covered with waterlilies, where Mary learned to swim, and I saw the farm at Bradford Barton where Mary worked for the Moons: the cobbled yard where she carried sacks of apples still there, the old orchards all round.

On the same journey I walked through Exeter, climbing the hill from the bridge, up Fore Street where she had worked after she left Bradford Barton, past the ancient churches and the few old streets that survived the German bombs, in any one of which she might have bought her white dress, and out on to the green in front of the cathedral where she may have walked when she was eighteen with her lover the bricklayer.

I returned to Bristol, watching from the train window as the hump-backed hills of Devon broadened out into the rolling green valleys of Somerset, wondering at the energy and determination that had kept her going, mile after mile, tired and often soaked to the skin, with no idea where she was going to sleep or where her next meal was coming from, to a bigger world where she dreamed of being a princess, and riding, as she told Gutch, in her own carriage and four horses.

I drove out to Almondsbury, and walked down the same hill she walked down when the blossom was on the trees, saw again the herring-bone spire of Almondsbury church, and had lunch at the Bowl, looking at the old fireplace where she sat and cried the morning Elizabeth Worrall called to take her back to Knole. John Alley, the present landlord, even took me upstairs and showed me one of the rooms where she may have spent her first night. Then I walked across to the church, and looked at George Hunt's memorial, and Samuel Worrall's, buried alone in 1822.

I walked on through the village, and up the hill to Knole. Dr Wilton, who lives a mile or two away now, pulled the old house down in the early nineteen-sixties. It had been bought by Middlesex County Council as a school for delinquent children. He showed me photographs of it before the demolition: a gaunt, vandalized wreck, with broken windows, damp spreading through the walls, the garden where Caraboo played overgrown. The only part of the house that was spared was the tower, the rest of the stone re-used to build half-a-dozen houses in the park.

When I went there with Michael Austin ten years earlier we found no one at home in the little modern house built on the site: this time I met the present owner, whose name, by a strange coincidence, was Baker. He showed me more pictures of the inside of the old house: the vast hall with the wide oak staircase that Mary saw when she first arrived, the dark panelled drawing room with an elaborately decorated plaster ceiling where Princess Caraboo was presented to the experts, the old Jacobean staircase down to the cellars, still there today, the arches carved with the initials of Thomas Chester who built it, now filled with rubble.

Then Peter Baker found a key and unlocked the little door to the tower: inside the winding oak stairs were still there, just as they were when Mary climbed up to say her prayers. The height of the tower was reduced by about fifteen feet at the time of the demolition, but from the top even now it is possible to see the view she saw, westwards across the Bristol Channel to the blue hills of Wales. Beyond what used to be the garden is a low-lying stretch of land, now occupied by a brickworks, which seems the likely site of the lake where Mary tried so often to take the Greek manservant boating so that she could push him in.

Some of the outbuildings are still standing, and

what may have been a dairy to the north has been converted into another house. On the way down the hill I passed one of the little cottages built out of the rubble of Knole, and saw a stone in the wall above a doorway, cut with symbols oddly like Mary's Javasu script.

I stayed the night in Bristol, and went next morning to find the place where Mary had lived for most of her years in Bedminster, 11 Prince's Street. Anton Bantock had sent me copies of articles written about Bedminster in the second half of the nineteenth century, describing the squalor and poverty there, with damp, unheated houses, high unemployment and terrible overcrowding.

It was, by the early nineteenth century, a rough industrial suburb of Bristol, with coal-mines, factories, forges and tanneries, which speculative builders had gradually built over to provide cheap accommodation for the workers.

Prince's Street was older and more respectable than the worst slums, and despite the smell from a vast tannery on the other side of the road, it was clear from the census returns that Mary and her daughter were living in comparative affluence. Almost every other house in the street had eight or twelve people living in it: tailors, stay-makers, dress-makers, labourers, and paupers. Only Mary and her immediate neighbours had more room. On one side was George Champion, a painter and glazier with four children, who may have been the ones who ran after Mary in the street calling 'Caraboo', and on the

other Richard Naish, Superintendent of the Customs
Office at Chichester Harbour.

No children play in the street today. Only the
roadway itself remains: all the houses have been
pulled down and replaced with warehouses and low
office buildings set back behind a wire security fence,
but it still has a kind of bleak poetry. Its name
changed soon after Mary's death, and perhaps even
in memory of Mary, from Prince's Street to Princess
Street. Part of it is a park for lorries belonging to
Gulliver's Truck Hire, with a silhouette on each
lorry of Swift's imaginary explorer holding a tiny
Lilliputian in the palm of his hand, and there is a
red-brick complex of offices called Princess Business
Units.

I could only imagine the old house: shabby perhaps outside, with a front door in need of paint, but
furnished inside in a style that Mary remembered
from her days in service, with what Elizabeth Gaskell called Elegant Economy: a threadbare
respectability.

I like to think she imported leeches in glass jars.

Leeches are rather interesting creatures to keep as
pets: they are hermaphrodites, and reproduce by
absorbing each other's sperm through their skin.
Their average lifespan is fifteen years. 'Their colora-
tion', one leech-lover wrote, 'could not be improved
upon: it is a delicious harmony of reddish-browns
and greens and blacks and yellows, a beautiful soft
symphony of velvety orange and olive and black,
the markings being repeated on each segment. So

beautiful are they that the fastidious ladies who adorned the *salons* at the height of the leech mania during the beginning of the eighteenth century used to deck their dresses with embroidered leeches.'

They are also beautiful to watch in the water, 'moving like looper-caterpillars, stretching out their anterior sucker, attaching it to some object, and then releasing the posterior sucker and drawing the body up towards the mouth'. They can, if they choose, float free, 'assuming the shape of a piece of red tape and, by a series of the most seductive undulations, swim through the water'.

The poet Cowper kept leeches and swore that their sliding above and below the water-line of their tank was a better guide to the weather than any barometer. When they moved about it was a sure sign that it was going to be windy or rainy, and when they became particularly agitated it usually meant a thunder storm.

Lord Erskine, the Lord Chancellor, who was treated with two leeches during an illness at Portsmouth, was convinced they had saved his life, took them home with him and christened them Home and Cline after two well-known surgeons. After dinner he put them on the table in their glass jar and used them as an oracle to settle judicial decisions. If they crawled up the inside of the jar the answer was 'no', if they swam free in the water the answer was 'yes'.

I set out, as Mary did, from Bedminster, to walk to the Infirmary. I thought when I first looked at the map that it must have been a sort of Via Dolorosa through the gloom of Victorian England, with its black bonnets and respectability, its smoking factories and ragged poor, the raw earth of the new railway cuttings and the massive chains heaped beside the steamships on the quay. I imagined her as an older woman, forced to remember the happier days of sunshine and muslin dresses when she was Princess Caraboo.

As I walked along the southern side of the New Cut and crossed the bridge to climb Redcliff Hill I began to think it was a lap of honour.

At the top of the hill, rising to the north from the New Cut, stands St Mary's, more of a mediaeval cathedral than a parish church. With its loft where Chatterton claimed to find his ancient manuscripts, it is a kind of Guild Church for Frauds. From its churchyard the whole of Bristol is spread out in front of you, and Mary cannot have failed to be amazed, as she walked down into the city, at the extent to which her old enemies had been overthrown.

Dr Wilkinson, for instance, had hardly triumphed. His last appearance in the newspapers, while Mary was still in Philadelphia, was when he was trying to persuade Swansea Pier to buy gas lighting with a display of sixty lamps in the shape of an anchor, and shortly afterwards his own gas-lit Kingston Baths Lecture Theatre caught fire and was burned to the ground.

A correspondent in *Notes and Queries* remembers him being pursued to the end of his days with the nickname 'Doctor Caraboo'.

But a great deal more had gone than the Kingston Baths. While Mary was in America and travelling in Europe, the old order had been almost entirely undermined, and she was back in Bedminster in time to witness its final collapse.

In 1819 Samuel Worrall's Tolzey Bank failed, his banknotes printed with the Bristol High Cross becoming as worthless in the eyes of the world as the Bank of England notes had seemed to Caraboo when she scattered them in the drawing room at Bath. Worrall resigned from his office as Town Clerk, and retired to Knole, where he died in 1822.

Gutch himself turned from being a slavish supporter of the old regime into a full-blooded Romantic revolutionary. Between the autumn of 1822 and the spring of 1823 he launched an attack 'on the most cherished notions of the most powerful interests then in the city'. He received warnings that his life was in danger, and, as he put it himself, 'threats of midnight assassins'.

Restoring *Felix Farley's Bristol Journal* to its old radical past, and adopting the pen-name of 'Cosmo', he wrote a series of public letters to his erstwhile friends on the Docks Company. They were, he said afterwards, 'in good strong English, and put the facts and the arguments with clearness and dignity'.

Few newspaper campaigns have ever been so successful. Before he had printed half the proposed series of letters the Docks Company caved in, a new Chamber of Commerce was elected with Gutch as one of its first vice-presidents. A ship built in Bristol was named *The Cosmo* in his honour, and even his old rivals on the *Gazette* wrote triumphantly that the Cosmo Letters 'spread a halo of glory round the Editorial Brows of a Provincial Newspaper Publisher'.

In the autumn of 1825 he ran an even more damaging campaign attacking 'the Erroneous Mode of Electing the Mayor, Sheriffs and Common Council of Bristol' and Haythorne, who had sat in judgement eight years before on whether Princess Caraboo was a fraud, was himself arraigned before the House of Lords, having no democratic right to the title, for '*claiming* to be Lord Mayor of Bristol'.

But even Gutch's life could not be called an unqualified success. In 1823 he married Mary Lavender, the daughter of a banker in Worcester, and became a partner in his father-in-law's bank. Then, in 1828, encouraged by the reputation he had gained as Cosmo, he started a new national newspaper, *The Morning Journal*. He only just escaped going to prison the following year when the paper alleged that Lord Lyndhurst had taken what amounted to a £30,000 bribe to make a friend Solicitor General.

Gutch, not for the first time, was dismissed as 'a dupe'. He had, according to the judge trying the case, 'been gravely misled regarding the character of his fellow proprietor'. Gutch sold up his share, his fellow proprietor was later sent to prison for libelling the Duke of Wellington, and the paper was suppressed.

Gutch continued to spend a day every week in Bristol, editing *Felix Farley*, but his political judgement became increasingly erratic. Appalled by his own daring, he retreated into his old reactionary position. He condemned the Duke of Wellington for appeasing the liberals in allowing the Catholics to vote, damned the commission investigating other corrupt city councils as 'more inquisitorial than anything since the Star Chamber', and opposed the Great Reform Bill as 'suicidal'.

The Reform Bill tore Bristol apart, and Gutch made the mistake of being on the wrong side. In 1831, with Mary safely installed with her husband Richard and her two-year-old daughter across the river in Bedminster, the whole apparently solid reality of entrenched power, that could hang a man for sedition and transport a woman to Australia for stealing a meat pie, simply went up in smoke.

In 1830 there was a revolution in France, and the Mayor of Bristol, Charles Pinney, a friend of Gutch and Coleridge, took the chair at a meeting to celebrate it. Encouraged by Gutch, the reactionaries came out into the open, including those in favour of retaining the slave trade. Their hero, Sir Charles Wetherell, was due to open the Bristol Assizes, and there was a riot. It began in Bedminster, less than half a mile from where Mary was living.

Wetherell arrived in the outskirts of the city, was booed all the way to Queen Square by a violent crowd, some of whom threw stones at his carriage, and he was forced to flee in disguise. Troops were called in, there were cavalry charges, and one of the demonstrators was shot in the back. The next day, a Sunday, moderate Reformers – many of them respectable property owners like Gutch – stormed the Bridewell prison and the New Gaol, both of which surrendered without a shot being fired.

Less moderate crowds broke into the Mansion House in Queen Square, forced the Mayor to escape over the roof, and drunk all the wine in his cellars.

After that things got out of hand: Bishop Grey, who had collared the living of Almondsbury and had now appointed his son as Rector, had his palace attacked and set on fire: he fled to Knole and hid in the cellars. The Palace and the Cathedral were saved, but the Chapter House was burned to the ground, together with centuries' worth of records. So was the Customs House, the Mansion House and most of Queen Square, where looted pictures, furniture and silver were heaped in the street in the glare of the flames.

It was only after a great deal of pleading from the actors that the mob was persuaded not to burn down the Theatre Royal.

Finally the Mayor called in the cavalry again: they charged repeatedly, using their sabres. In all, twelve people were killed, and ninety-four were taken to the Infirmary. Eighty-one of the rioters were convicted and imprisoned, four ring-leaders were hanged. But Bristol would never be the same again: nothing could now stop the Reform Bill, which broke the power of the old ruling families and made Parliament responsible to a wider electorate. Bristol has never forgotten the role it had played in clearing the way for it.

Gutch had already taken on a partner to run *Felix Farley*, and he now moved away to Worcester, where his bank, too, collapsed, and devoted the rest of his life to the happier world of the imagination, republishing the story of Robin Hood and several collections of old ballads from the safety of his own study in the country. *Felix Farley's Bristol Journal* was eventually bought by a high-church clergyman as a pulpit for his views on the future of the Church of England, and folded soon afterwards.

If the correspondent from *Notes and Queries* found Mary disinclined to talk about her past life and 'much ashamed' of having been Princess Caraboo, I prefer to think he met her in one of her moods of depression. Walking on into Bristol she could have crowed with delight at her success.

Coming down the other side of Redcliff Hill, she could see on her left the quays where she fulfilled her dream of sailing to America. Crossing the river into the old city she could see on her right Mortimer's house in Bridge Street, where painters and aristocrats and many other admirers had come to visit her in the month of June 1817. She would then have climbed Broad Street to the corner of Corn Street and could have looked left to see the Council House and think of Haythorne 'claiming to be the Mayor of Bristol', and of Samuel Worrall, with whom she had shared an apartment in All Saints' Lane beside it. Perhaps she had been fonder of him than I imagined, the proprietor of what had turned out to be an imaginary bank.

She then walked down Small Street, past Gutch's old printing office, through the stone arch flanked with two ancient stone figures, both wearing crowns. I hope they reminded her of all the grand ladies who had curtsied to her when she was a royal princess.

Then she crossed Lewin's Mead where she had stayed with Mrs Neale and Eleanor Joseph and first put on the turban, and up to the great Infirmary by Lower Maudlin Street, whose name could only bring back memories of the hospital for repentant prostitutes in London.

I like to think, too, that she was proud of the Infirmary. With its fine, high, pillared portico, added at the end of the eighteenth century, and its pale stone façade, more reminiscent of Bath than Bristol, it was one of the most impressive buildings in the city, and at night gas-light blazed white behind the high sash windows.

It was also a monument to kindness and humanity, and as she walked in under the great imposing portico with the words 'Charity Universal' carved in stone above it, she must occasionally have felt that she had become a benefactress, like Elizabeth Worrall.

I would also like to think, on the evidence of the letters that Elizabeth Worrall refused to part with in 1836, that the two women somehow remained friends.

POSTSCRIPT

IT WAS, INEVITABLY, Bernard Spaughton who found Mary's death certificate. She died on Christmas Eve, 1864, still walking.

She was going up Mill Street in Bedminster, not far from her home, and died so suddenly that an inquest was ordered. She was seventy-five, and she almost certainly had a heart attack. Her death was attributed, in the medical language of the day, to 'Natural Decay'.

All the cousins – Christine Medley, Bernard Spaughton and Thomas Gibson – believed a story told in the family that someone had been left a hotel in Bristol at the end of the last century. It could only have been left, they thought, by Mary Baker Junior, said in 1849 'to be possessed of considerable personal attractions'. She must have married a rich man.

The truth came to light at the same time as Mary's burial record. Bristol Public Record Office found a letter written in March 1893, saying that young Mary was now living in Queen Street, a few yards round the corner from her mother's old house in what was now Princess Street. She would, by then, have been fifty-four, and was unmarried. She was still carrying on her mother's business, selling 'chemists' sundries etc.', and living 'in a most filthy and unwholesome condition'.

An even less sympathetic account describes her as selling 'quack medicines, such as pills' and says that her house was full of stray cats.

> Sometime about the year 1900 there was a fire at her house, and the neighbour with whom she was friendly burst open the door and found her body partly burnt, but recognizable as Miss Baker, and reported it to the police, who took possession of the premises.
>
> They found money and trinkets and other antiquities strewed all over the place, and as no relatives could be found, eventually a well-known firm of Solicitors in this City took up the matter and wound up the Estate. They advertised all over the world for any next of kin, and eventually two nephews were traced at Ilfracombe who could prove they were legally entitled to the residue of the Estate.

The census of 1891 confirms the address, together with her claim that when she was born her mother and 'Richard Baker' were living in Redland, in the north of Bristol. Redland was by then a fashionable part of the city, and she probably invented it as her birthplace to suggest that she had known better days. A death certificate confirms that she died on 11 February 1900, at 2 Queen Street, Bedminster.

A few days before this book went to press, Bernard Spaughton rang me. He had managed somehow to trace the papers relating to Mary Baker

Junior's estate. The lawyers, it turned out, had not 'advertised all over the world', but there had been a dispute.

She had died without making a will, and everything she had was given to the first claimant, William John Bright Burgess, a bootmaker, of Tiverton, the son of Mary's carpenter cousin from Exeter. This was then successfully contested, not, as the newspaper report suggested, by 'two nephews', but by another cousin, Thomas Willcocks. He did live in Ilfracombe.

The 'money, trinkets and other antiquities' were valued at £21.10.2, reduced to £21.2.6 by the time the claim was settled. But her property was valued at £888.0.0, more like £100,000 in today's money. It seemed, after all, that the family legend was true. If there wasn't a hotel, there was, at least another large house. Mary Baker Junior never married. Was there a rich lover, or was it capital that she and her mother had managed to save?

Before he rang me, Bernard Spaughton had talked to Christine Medley. She recognized the address in Ilfracombe. Thomas Willcocks was her grandfather.

I asked her if there was anything in the house that might have survived. Never having even considered the possibility that she had inherited anything directly from Princess Caraboo, Christine thought about it. Then she remembered.

She said there had always been two heirlooms in the family. One was a painting of a grey horse, valued at several thousand pounds, and signed 'R. B. 1825'. The other was almost too good to be true. It was, she said, a morocco-bound book, with gold-edged pages. It was 'The Continental Annual and Romantic Cabinet of 1832', with illustrations by Samuel Prout, and contained views of Rouen, Prague, Padua and Lake Como. On the flyleaf were the words 'Tom to his sister, December 17th 1832.'

It was a present from Mary's favourite brother, and suggested a great deal: Mary's lifelong fascination with travelling to Europe, a way of life a great deal more elegant than anyone might have expected for a dealer in leeches, and a loving literate family.

It was another piece in the jigsaw puzzle, and more, I am sure, will turn up.

A last mystery remained about where Mary Baker was buried. According to the printed pamphlet about Bristol's Arnos Vale Cemetery, her grave is there, but unmarked. Anton Bantock's old friend in Bedminster after the war told him it was not. He said her grave was in the Hebron Road Burial Ground in Bedminster.

After a great deal more work, the Bristol Public Record Office were able to find the burial record for me. Mary was buried four days after she died, on 4 January 1865, and Anton Bantock's old friend was right. She was buried by the Reverend James Ward, in the Hebron Road Burial Ground. Anton Bantock and I walked over to see it.

The Hebron Road Chapel is now a Spiritualist church, and beginning to fall into disrepair, but when it was built a hundred and fifty years ago it must have been almost as impressive as the Infirmary. It stands at the top of the highest hill in

Bedminster, with a pillared entrance like a Greek temple, towering over the low houses on the other side of the road.

It was built by a sect of primitive Methodists, with the date 1853 on the portico, carved between encircling wings. There are heavy wrought-iron gates, now rusted, and I imagined Mary as an old lady arriving with her daughter and the respectably dressed Victorian congregation on a Sunday morning, walking through the gates when they were new and gleaming black, up the shallow steps and into the Chapel to listen to sermons about the terrors of eternal fire and the beauty of paradise, and the long extempore Methodist prayers.

The Hebron Road Burial Ground to one side was locked. We looked through the high, rusty railings and saw an old motor tyre lying in the deep grass. Everything was overgrown, with only a few gravestones visible under the tangle of grass and bushes, the only one of any distinction being the monument to friend of Coleridge and Gutch, Joseph Cottle, another Bristol publisher.

Somewhere under the tangle of long grass and bushes lay the remains of one of the most remarkable women ever to make their home in Bristol, her grave forgotten and unmarked. Perhaps one day there will be a memorial there, and someone will restore the garden, in honour of Princess Caraboo.